DREAM

Book One in the
the Kerr

"A FASCINATING AND LYRICAL STORY,
TOLD WITH GREAT INVENTION . . ."
—PETER STRAUB,
author of SHADOWLAND
and GHOST STORY

CRUISER DREAMS

Book Two in the Three Part Saga of
the Kerrion Empire

"PACKED WITH INTRIGUE, SPICED WITH
ROMANCE . . ."
—*Publishers Weekly*

"FASCINATING . . . RECOMMENDED!"
—*Booklist*

JANET MORRIS

The brilliant young author of the *Silistra*
series, which has catapulted her to fame in the
science fantasy field, Janet Morris lives with
her husband on a peninsula extending into a
vast and legend-heavy sea.

Berkley books by Janet Morris

CRUISER DREAMS
DREAM DANCER

JANET MORRIS

CRUISER DREAMS

BERKLEY BOOKS, NEW YORK

This Berkley book contains the complete
text of the original hardcover edition.
It has been completely reset in a type face
designed for easy reading, and was printed
from new film.

CRUISER DREAMS

A Berkley Book / published by arrangement with
G. P. Putnam's Sons

PRINTING HISTORY
G. P. Putnam's Sons edition / September 1981
Berkley edition / August 1982

ISBN: 0-425-05382-2

A BERKLEY BOOK © TM 757,375
Berkley Books are published by Berkley Publishing Corporation,
200 Madison Avenue, New York, New York 10016
The name "BERKLEY" and the stylized "B" with design
are trademarks belonging to Berkley Publishing Corporation.
PRINTED IN THE UNITED STATES OF AMERICA

CRUISER DREAMS

Chapter One

One full moon in tinderbox autumn, the legend of "Shebat of the Enchanters' Fire" was graven a second time into the consciousness of twenty-third century man.

It happened over the rubble-strewn streets of New York City, as it had happened once before, upstate.

The enchanter who witnessed the event could do nothing about it: his horse screamed and reared and pawed the wind's dark tresses. Like the ignorant natives of Earth, there was no convincing the nervy black stallion that the roar swooping down upon the city, followed by light from a midnight sun, was not supernatural in origin.

When the light blinked out, and the roar turned to a keening whine, when above their heads a softer glow illuminated two figures hanging by a ladder from the belly of Leviathan—*then* trouble, swathed in the hoary robes of religion, began. There was not one enchanter among the lot of those secessionist oppressors who had fled from Orrefors space to make a last stand on ancient, wizened Earth that did not recognize the danger. But there was nothing they could do.

The two figures danced wildly, hanging from their ladder before the moon.

Alley dwellers and scavengers edged out from hiding into the intersection where the miracle had just taken place, heedless of the enchanter in the face of this more astounding magic.

When he had his horse calmed, he rode it full tilt through the midst of them: order must be preserved.

• • •

Her fingers would never hold her.

She would fall back down among the ruins, die upon impact. All that would be left of her would be her bracelet, wailing and blinking green in a puddle of sticky red pulp.

The wind rushed round her ears, her pulse thundered louder than the ship drawing them upward. She craned her neck, squinting in the lemony illumination from the shuttle's bottom. In the middle of the glowing waffle-work was a dark maw. Into that the ladder was being drawn. Around the edges of one of the supergravity pads, St. Elmo's fire danced, a product of the strain on the system.

Shebat hung from the lowest rung.

On the rung just above hers, another pair of hands clung desperately to life.

He called out something: the wind and whine stole away his words.

The ladder swung wildly, half its length swallowed up. If they should be gusted against those bright quiltings, they would never even realize that they were about to die.

The man above shouted again, but she could not understand. He took one hand from the rung, extended it down to her. She saw it, bilious in supergravity's light, reaching out. Every auburn hair tracing his wrist stood apart from one another, preternaturally clear.

She took it in hers. After a moment's hesitation, in which her teeth nearly fused while her stomach somersaulted and her slick grip almost slipped away, she hauled herself up, parallel to him.

The swaying of the ladder eased.

His neck craned, eyes narrowed and streaming tears, Chaeron judged distance and danger. "Just be still!"

She lip-read it, before she closed her eyes against the glare, trusting to fate, which had seen fit to scoop her up from exile and would not have done so for meager purpose.

When she opened them, all was dim and quiet, sheltered from the wind and the shuttle's glow. The bracelet on her wrist gleamed intermittently, sighed low, then ceased to sing altogether.

"Watch your feet!"

She drew them up. The bay doors smacked shut, locking out earthly nightmares.

The red warning-light was on in the little shuttle, she realized; she had thought it had been her vision, the distortion of fear.

Her husband let loose of the ladder and dropped to his knees upon the closed bay doors, wiping his hands on his thighs, while all around the lights went amber.

"You can let go now," he said softly, his hands encircling her waist to prove his words.

She let her grip relax, felt herself in his arms, turned in them, pressed to his chest. His lips brushed her forehead, nuzzled toward her mouth.

She turned her face away.

He turned it back. "This is the first, perhaps only, heroic deed I may ever have to my credit. Am I not deserving of even one kiss?"

Above their heads, the emergency ladder continued to draw itself up into the piped and strutted ceiling of the cargo bay. There was a click, and it was gone.

"Chaeron . . ." She looked straight at him, just before his lips closed upon hers.

The lineaments of his face, sensuous, yet bold enough for the walls of Persepolis, were washed ethereal in the amber safety-lights of the shuttle's cargo bay. Chaeron's beauty was his curse: men disparaged him for it and women distrusted him because of it. In the orb of it, Shebat was filled with doubts. Again she turned to miss his kiss, let it brush against her brow.

". . . *Why*, Chaeron?" Long-unused Consulese came rusty to her tongue. On her barbaric homeworld, she had had no need of it. In the anguish of her self-imposed banishment, she had shut everything about him and his worlds beyond the sky away. Now it came rushing back too fast, raising her hackles as the vibration beneath her feet and the sharp smells of machine oil and insulation and her own fear could never have done on their own. But that was Chaeron's style, was it not?—to make a person's soul kneel down before his sorrel-maned elegance, then offer to cover that nakedness with the cloak of his favor?

"Why?" he repeated, worldly lips drawing back into a trained smile. He unhanded her, settling into a squat dissolved of ardor. His teal eyes flickered, his fist slamming home a toggle where the bay doors met. "Because you are my wife. And because my brother Marada has exceeded his authority. And because—"

Shebat felt the quaking of her orientation as the little powerboat struck for deeper space (or as his gilt-lashed eyes flickered up to her face), so that she too sank down breathless on her haunches, pulling her knees up to provide a barrier between them. Could it be possible? Had she hurt him? No, not the Draconis consul, Chaeron Ptolemy Kerrion, scion of the consular house of Kerrion, inheritor of stars! *What am I doing here?* she wailed without words, clasping her hands tightly so that she might meet his unwavering gaze.

"And *because,*" Chaeron repeated in a serpentine voice, "I got your message, sent by means of your ship, that you needed help." His visage grew severe without changing. "You *did* send it?"

"No, I—" That far into betrayal of her only ally, a tendril of the cruiser *Marada's* thought reached her, a tickle in the back of her brain, barely audible, as if from much farther than the four hundred miles of space remaining between them. "Yes," she rushed in, "I suppose I did. I had to."

The first lies exchanged, each sat back a little. His blue eyes were no more hooded than her gray ones, during that intolerable interlude wherein chests rose and fell slowly and schemes and conjectures roiled fast behind placid masks.

The *Marada,* her cruiser, deep spacefish whose capacity for loyalty surpassed that of the entire Kerrion family into which Chaeron's father had adopted her, tried again to reach her mind. She caught his whispered message, so brief, so cautious, and unclenched her hands, raising one wrist before her face, glad of something to do in the awkward sandpaper silence. "I am still wearing your betrothal gift, husband," she teased, not yet willing to accuse him in this tiny powerboat made for raiding by pirates long ago in their shared past.

The bracelet so displayed on her wrist was still shining softly, the green stones on it raised half out of their settings. A short time ago, it had been singing, caroling, then screaming in the moonlit night. "You never said what it was," she pouted, her lips glistening. "I might have run the wrong way, when it began to pulse and howl. How could you be sure I would know enough to run to wherever the sound got loud?"

He sighed a soft laugh down through his nose. "Whatever way you ran, I could have found you. May I?" His long fingers touched the directional beacon, the green stones sank down flush with their bezel and ceased to glow. "There. I just did not want to lose track of you. Can you blame me?"

She let his question go unanswered, seeking for anything else that might clear the dross from her throat. "So you let me crumble under your brother's onslaught, allowed him to tote me off to my isolation like some unclean carrier of a plague, secure in the knowledge that when you were ready you would have no trouble finding me again!"

"I had rather thought," he murmured, "that you two wanted some time together—alone."

"Alone was what I was, with him! You knew full well that once I had married you, I would become a traitor, an enemy in his eyes! You only forgot to tell me."

"Shebat!" Anger, effort, then control labored in the one word. "I have come a long and difficult way, thinking you called me. I am still full of my expectations, and you are not fulfilling any of them. Say thank you."

"Not yet."

"Then not at all! I—"

A squawk cut through whatever he would have said, too soon, and he saw the wariness in her silver gaze take the hard edge of distrust.

"Yes, we are," he answered the pilot's query as to their health. She should have realized, when he did not immediately urge her into the little ship's control room, that there was some other pilot controlling the shuttle as well as the ship that had disgorged it into Earth's atmosphere. But she had not, he saw from her stony face and straight back. When her words finally slid through colorless lips, he had been waiting so long for them that even his infinitely cultivated Kerrion aplomb was shaken.

"You let another . . . person . . . fly my cruiser?" She could not even say "pilot"! "And will you suggest next that I bed this . . . person . . . who is enjoying proscribed interface with my ship?" So that was what was wrong with the *Marada,* whose cautions were so urgent and greetings so abrupt. The cruiser would allow no other pilot to sample their intimacy, for it was a singular and revolutionary relationship that had grown up between the spaceship and

the girl: and secret! "Of all the perversions you so joyously
lay claim to, this is the most foul!"

He stopped her, not by words, but by rising up so abruptly
that he hit his head on a conduit and cursed. Rubbing the
back of his neck, he loomed over her, his exasperation
beyond his control.

"You stupid, ground-dwelling snot! You cannot imagine
what I have gone through to get here. Only the Lords of
Cosmic Jest know why I have put my head on the block for
you! What would you have had me do, fly that cruiser
myself? For your information, it was your ship that picked its
pilot, and that was no small complication. So there are two
pilots on board, both at each other's throats for amusement:
my new one; and this apprentice transvestite that your
damned *Marada* assured us both is the only person in the
whole of the Consortium suited to touch his precious control
boards in your place. What did you think took me so long?

"No, don't answer that. As a matter of fact, until we are
someplace more suitable than this, do not say anything. Just
be circumspect. Keep in mind that you are no longer living in
garbage heaps where what you say matters to no one but
yourself. Be polite to these people, but try to remember—
you are Kerrion!"

Chaeron knew his voice was too thick, too despairing, too
revealing. He felt all the muscles in his shoulders pulling his
head into his body and those in his loins pulling his scrotum
up to safety. But that was why he had come for her, was it
not? She made him feel, made things new and tingling with
more than danger—with passion, with purpose.

But when Shebat said to him in her husky, slurred
Consulese that he would have to bear with her, for she had
spent months trying to forget that for awhile and for foul
purpose she had had "Alexandra" and "Kerrion" added to
her name, he could not help but shiver. The heat of his flesh
against the carefully regulated air of the ground-to-space
craft made it seem that the vacuum outside had crept within
to confront him with its deadly cold.

To banish that chill, he spat it out of his mouth. "If you
would prefer, I will set you back down on your planet, as
close as may be to where I found you. And that will be that."
And I will have learned a lesson about the difference
between fantasy and reality, he thought, but could not say.

"No!" she gasped, huddling.

He extended his hand to her, raising her up. "Then I think it is time you met Del—"

By then she had pressed herself against his chest, arms encircling him tightly, sobbing. The warmth of her melted his anger. She was a child, after all. He had expected too much from her on the heels of such dire peril. And perhaps too much from himself—he was not of the stuff of heroes, had no aspirations in that regard. It was the dispatcher Circumstance that had sent him hither, on such a precipitous mission. And with the task had come the awful cold, and the knowledge that only her kiss could banish it, melt the ice formed in his very blood. The ensorceled prince got his kiss from the only woman whose lips had ever enticed him, and he was much warmed.

Then he motioned her before him, stooping among the pipes in the little cargo bay, into the tiny cockpit where Delphi, the apprentice, bent to her work.

Shebat stiffened like a threatened cat as she slipped into the seat parallel to the apprentice pilot's.

The woman waved without looking up, her bristled red hair flaring magenta in the indicators' spill.

Chaeron took the jump seat behind her, back against the wall, debating whether or not to introduce them while the woman's thick neck was so corded with concentration. Broad shoulders rippling, running her hands over the bestarred console, she hardly seemed to notice them.

Shebat ended his debate. She reached out toward her copilot's instrumentation; punched; slapped; fingered; then snapped: "I have it."

The big woman ran knobby fingers through her flaming skullcap of hair. Pale, freckled jaw working, she turned in her seat to face him, interrogatory eyebrow raised.

Chaeron shrugged, let a facsimile of a grin touch his features. "Shebat Alexandra Kerrion," he explained. "My wife."

"Ah, the *Marada* has told me about you," said the woman in a voice like a man's. "I am Bernice Gomes, but the pilots have tagged me 'Delphi.'"

The hand stretched out to Shebat went unclasped, the greeting unanswered. Shebat's froth of black curls, bent forward, neither raised nor turned.

Chaeron said: "How long?"

Delphi replied, "Three-quarters of an hour, sir," in her resonant baritone.

Shebat huffed: "Half of that," and the powerboat leapt forward so abruptly that Chaeron's skull snapped back against the padded partition.

The apprentice looked at her employer beseechingly, received the merest shake of his head in negation. She unstrapped herself and came, half-crouched, to take the jump seat opposite his. Her glance said that women will be women, thereby affirming his supposition that she did not consider herself one. Her powerful body told truer: it was foreshortened with pique, squat with irritation.

"Why, 'Delphi'?" Shebat's distant query came floating back from the bowed black head framed in glittering stars, one of which was coming closer at frightening speed.

The thick-necked woman tucked her chin in, doubling it. The pattern she had been drumming on her flight-satined knee ceased. "I am from Pegasus space, where I was a Delphi forecaster. Until recently, that is." A weighted grimace thrown Chaeron's way escaped Shebat's notice. "When my group disbanded, I decided to become a pilot. Delphi method and pilotry make use of the same talents, so I have been told."

"You *decided* to *become* a pilot?" mocked Shebat.

Chaeron chuckled admiringly, felt partisan, came to the redhead's defense. "The *Marada* specified her," he reminded Shebat.

"Are you always so fortunate?"

There was a silence full of knives. Chaeron was about to blunt it, when Delphi answered for herself. "Yes, in the way that you mean. I am a Delphi adept, after all. We do not call it fortune, but accurate forecast. Once I had decided on this route, it was not more than a month until I secured my apprentice's rating. Then your husband's people tapped me. So I have come from rank amateur to apprentice to the top-rated pilot—first bitch, as you folk say—of Kerrion space in a very short time. I suppose I understand your hostility."

"Hostility?" repeated Shebat innocently. Then: "Who *is* first bitch, these days?" in a stiletto hiss that reminded Chaeron of her love for the defrocked master pilot who had been top rated during Shebat's apprenticeship. To vanquish thoughts of Softa Spry, now an outlaw among outlaws at space-end, Chaeron spoke quickly:

"Raphael Penrose took the first-mastership. I do not think you have met him, Shebat, but I may be wrong." There were times she had been away from the family, times spent as an unlawful dream dancer and an apprentice under an assumed name to Softa Spry, times during which her activities remained unaccounted for. Penrose, when queried, did not believe that they had met, but could not be sure.

"Is he the same Penrose they call 'RP' for 'Rape and Pillage'?"

Delphi Gomes let out a whoop swallowed halfway through so that it became a spray of smothered laughter.

"I have only heard of him, then," continued Shebat. "His ancestor, Roger Penrose, deduced twister theory and invented conformal mapping of spacetime, so it is said. Aside from that, everything I heard was decidedly unflattering, personally, and unequivocally complimentary, professionally. *He* is on the *Marada?*"

"Let us hope so," said Chaeron dryly.

"I will look forward to meeting him."

Neither her husband nor the woman apprentice chose to add a comment to Shebat's statement, delivered as it was in such an oddly flat and threatening tone.

Delphi Gomes, whose pulse had finally quieted after neatly sidestepping all pertinent questions about her provenance and purpose, wondered at the arrogance of the Draconis consul's wife, who it was whispered was an illicit dream dancer, as well as an owner/pilot. Having wondered, she compared what she saw to what she had previously heard of Shebat Alexandra Kerrion, and decided that everything said about this precocious child must indeed be true, even the part about her not yet having turned eighteen. And she marked her enemy, one of those responsible for the death of her father, Jebediah, for subsequent execution. And she thanked the currents of fate that charted her course that her sire had never married her mother, so that no one could connect her with the anile secretary who had connived in the very office of the Kerrion consul general Parma Alexander Kerrion, he who had died too soon to suit Bernice's appetite for vengeance. No matter, there were the sons and daughters left; and this girl, Shebat; and the pilot, now an outlaw, called "Softa," whose demise would likely be the most satiating of all. Not that she would mind putting an end to the pretty boy sitting next to her, with his effete manners and his arcane tastes in pleasure. Thinking about it, she could feel her flesh warm, her femininity moisten as it did only for death. Surreptitiously, she exhaled a long and satisfied sigh: her time had come; Delphi method showed it clearly. Let the ecstasy begin!

Rafe was more than curious. He sat at the *Marada's* epicentral control dais, enthroned. About him, the circular waist of the *Marada's* control room rainbowed, displays of color humping, bucking, telling tales of the powerboat's progress in full-spectrum metering, its telemetry offering radio, infrared, X-ray, and magnified optical scans. He could sit there until hell froze over, until entropy triumphed over motion, without having to move to eat, or wash, or eliminate.

RP coveted the *Marada* so intensely that his teeth itched when he contemplated it. Thinking about giving the immensely powerful experimental cruiser over to a teen-age dream dancer with delusions of ESP made him grind them so hard his jaws ached.

He had gone over every scrap of gossip he had heard in the pilots' guildhall since the ratings shakeup, and no two things he had heard agreed. Worse, no *one* thing he had learned explained why his haughty Kerrion employer was personally chasing around on a primitive, dangerous planet after a girl who could hardly be less primitive in order to hand over to her the most advanced spongespace cruiser Raphael P. Penrose had ever had the pleasure to board. The fact that Chaeron had married the dream dancer to acquire her proxies did not explain it—he had full control of her stocks without her. And, having heard and most recently acquired firsthand knowledge of Chaeron Ptolemy Kerrion's sexual predilections, the marriage itself was of no account. Love and money being thuswise excluded, there was left only power as Chaeron's motive. Or pride. Pride, RP was calling it, for want of some glimmering of understanding as to where in the reputedly frail and indisputably female person of Shebat Kerrion the value really lay.

He had had plenty of time to conjecture about it: time in

the guildhall when every pilot attached to the Kerrion arm of the guild had been called in to meet their new guildmaster (he rather regretted not being around to see old Baldy, ex-guildmaster, off to his exile); time spent being re-rated, the whole lot of them, since both the first and second bitch pilots' slots were open under a new guildmaster whose ideas differed from the last but agreed most completely with those of the Kerrion scion who had taken over the consul general-ship—and who just happened to be a pilot himself! What changes Guildmaster Ferrier would make under Marada Seleucus Kerrion's patronage was anybody's guess. And everybody was guessing.

He had guessed right and snatched the first mastership from under the noses of several equally qualified but politi-cally inept competitors. But he had had two advantages: he had gone to school with Marada Kerrion; he had gone to bed with Marada's little brother, Chaeron.

Raphael Penrose sighed loudly, and touched a desultory finger to a magnification control, activating it manually. He had gotten his rating, no matter how. He would have liked to have gotten this cruiser, the *Marada* (named, it was said, after the new consul general by the Earth waif now readying her shuttle to dock), in the same or any other fashion. But his efforts had not availed him. Chaeron had promised RP only the consul's own cruiser, *Danae*, when she was fit to fly, with vague murmurings about commissioning another of these new-type cruisers at some unspecified later date.

It would have been so simple to wipe the individuality out of the mighty spacefish with a touch, and make it his own.

It was unspeakably frustrating not to be able to do so, to be reduced to pushing buttons like an apprentice. At the thought "apprentice" brought to mind, he growled aloud. Most mortifying of anything that had ever happened to him in twelve years of pilotry was Chaeron's order that he take on this bull-dyke apprentice. He was the butt of many a snicker since word had leaked that the woman was doing the real flying, though she was nowhere near a rating, while he, notwithstanding his skill, was forbidden to touch so much as a sponge-readying B-mode activator. It was supposed to be a secret, but pilots have no secrets, because cruisers keep no secrets from other cruisers. And so the fact that he was along only to satisfy guild requirements and proscribed from flying the *Marada* through the sponge riddling spacetime was common knowledge among his peers.

He opened the *Marada's* bay a full second before the shuttle-pilot asked, then simply monitored the docking of the little ship within, and closed back up again. There were some things in life that had to be tolerated. At least now he would see what all the fuss was about.

But whether seeing would alleviate the nagging discomfort he could not banish, that ever-increasing restlessness of his sixth sense which plagued him, he could not say. And he very much wanted that formless irritation put to bed, for it was not rational, and RP was determinedly a rational man, especially when on duty. If he had acquired his nickname because such strictly enforced discipline tended to make of him a maniacal carouser when he let it slip in the grip of drink or drugs, then that was only proof of the axiom that all pilots are mad. Living on the lip of insanity's canyon, he was very careful of his working mind's every step. And his mind told him strange things about his situation:

If he did not know better, he would think the cruiser *Marada* did not want him to fly it. And if he did not know that cruisers could not keep secrets, he would think that there were some things that the *Marada* knew which the cruiser and his Kerrion owner, in concert, were trying to keep Raphael from finding out.

And since a pilot with as many sponge-hours as Raphael Penrose had accumulated must be alert for paranoia's insidious taint long before its poison reaches toward the heart, he could not face his intuition head-on, but must circumvent the slightest confrontation with any debilitating fears.

When he saw Shebat Kerrion walk through the control room's dilated doors in black-and-red flight satins dirtied gray and torn at one elbow, and what excitation of the *Marada's* consoles her presence evoked in the cruiser, a superstitious thrill rolled over him, raising every hair from his toes to the crown of his head.

So consumed was he by the phenomenal sensitivity the cruiser *Marada* registered to the girl, Shebat, that he ceased wondering about Delphi's part in all this: the squat redhead, focus of his agitation previously, ceased to concern him. He barely noticed her, following Chaeron Kerrion in through the portal, leaning back cross-armed against the lock's doors as soon as they sighed shut.

The Draconis consul, on the other hand, vied with the black-haired girl for his attention. Chaeron looked flustered. His face was surely flushed, his breathing rapid, when RP well knew that nothing ever cracked Chaeron's calm.

But that was wrong, obviously. The girl-child had done it, or the strenuousness of the effort he had expended to get her back.

"Any trouble?" Raphael Penrose asked his employer.

"None yet," came Chaeron's absent reply, sans the reassuring smile that should have accompanied it.

Then Shebat Kerrion crossed between them, stood before the control central in which Penrose lounged, and put her hands on her hips. The hands were browned with dirt, the hips slim and boyish, and RP began to understand what it was about her that had held Chaeron's interest to so great a degree. Even the mud caked on her worn boots and the split seam on the inside of her jump-suited right thigh and the snarl of her hair seemed to add to, rather than detract from, the command in her presence.

"I need to talk to you alone," she said.

RP looked around, to make sure Chaeron had not slipped behind him. "Me?"

"You, if my husband will permit it." Her Consulese was awkward, strangely lilting.

"Hardly," came Chaeron's clipped reply, and Raphael Penrose began to feel uncomfortable.

"Then," the girl continued, *"get up from there!* Never again will *any* of you even think—"

"Now, look here . . ."

"Chaeron!"

"Shebat! I apologize, Rafe, for her—"

"You apologize for me? You importune! I—"

"Think I'll go get something to eat," interjected the redhead, and palmed the doors' "open" mode.

No one heard her. Raphael Penrose was on his feet, halfway down the dais that separated the miniaturized control console from the main banks. Shebat Kerrion was halfway up into it. They halted, three feet apart. The girl's nostrils flared and shivered, but her eyes were steady, full of coldest fire. "How would you feel, if you were me? If the *Marada* were yours?" she demanded in a fierce whisper.

Before he answered, he saw Chaeron, behind her, shaking his head slowly, to and fro. Trying to think what answer his employer might be counseling, he jammed his fists into his pockets, grinding them against his groin. The metallic stare demanded his reply. He said, honestly:

"I would not like it one bit. But I am a guild pilot; my oath is my bond . . ."

He stepped aside for her. She brushed past him, not sitting, but leaning down in anxious assessment of *Marada's* arrayed displays. Still bent forward, she flashed eyes up to him once again in silent condemnation.

"By the Jesters' nuts! I did not even *fly* this ship!"

"That," said Shebat, taking time to swivel her head and include Chaeron in her indictment, "is what I was afraid of. Now, one of you tell me just who that woman is and why she is on board!" She straightened up.

"Who in the five eternities do you think you are?" RP exploded, as Chaeron gritted:

"I told you, Shebat, the *Marada* chose its pilot!" His forehead creased, ironed clear as he marshaled him temper. "The two of you stop this carping. We have a long trip ahead, long enough for everyone to be satisfied as to the motives of one another—"

Shebat Kerrion made a sound, half a snort of derision and half a sob, and sat abruptly on the console's arm. "I do not need to see any more of *him* to know why he is here."

"I am not going to listen to this," said RP in measured fury, and strode toward the lock leading into the body of the ship.

"Rafe," Chaeron sighed. "you had better stay here and work this out."

The pilot spun on his heel, let his eyes rake the petulant child perched on the control central's arm. "Del is here because when Chaeron asked me to take this cruiser out without wiping its memories, I consulted the damn thing's data bank as to how it could be done. And Chaeron consulted the Jesters-know-how-many data pools and Kerrion computers, and everyone came up with the same answers: a Delphi programmer would not disturb the ship's equilibrium or alter its modality. Anyone else would. If you had any right to the pilot's rating Softa Spry made sure you received, you would know that every additional pilot meld-

ing with a ship changes it. As to why your husband is so
anxious to retain this particular ship exactly and in every
particular as it is . . . beyond the fact that there are certain
inquiries being processed by the arbitrational guild to which
this cruiser's memories might be subpoenaed, I have no idea.

"Do you think I like this? Do you think I feel any better
than you about that misfit, underqualified, overglorified
psychic doing my job while I play pocket pool?" Rafe pulled
his hands out from hiding and spread them wide. "Honey, if
you find out what is going on here, you tell me. I take orders,
as best I can."

"I imagine you do," silked Shebat, voice rich with innuendo.

Chaeron, straight-faced, unmoving, watched his pilot
storm from the *Marada's* bridge, collide with the stocky
apprentice in the corridor. The two exchanged barks like
chance-met dogs before the lock came together with a
susurrus that shut out all sound.

"Well," said Chaeron after a lull broken only by tiny
beeps and clicks and a whirr of cruiser-consolation, "this is
going to be an unpleasant trip. Glad to have you back, my
dear. Things were getting much too dull without you."

An hour later Chaeron stepped out of the *Marada's*
negative ion-generating equivalent of a shower to find Shebat
curled, fully clothed but for her mud-caked boots, on the
stateroom's satin-covered bed. One boot, turned on its side,
showed an inch-long hole worn through its sole, the source of
the dirt that blackened the bottom of her foot.

"Ah, have we rethought our position, then? Are you here
in remorse at your highhanded ill treatment of me and mine?
If so, I assure you, I will be more than willing to accept your
apology." As he spoke, he moved toward her, putting on a
sapphire robe and belting it tight.

"This is my cabin," she reminded him. "And you have
assigned your crew the other two. Where did you expect me
to stay?"

"At your controls, from your attitude." He sat cautiously
on the foot of the bed, toeing her boots out of the way. "I
hope you have calmed yourself. I am in no mood for more
excitement, having just gotten rid of the stink of my fear."
With an exaggerated yawn, he lay back, his feet still on the

teal-rugged floor, and stretched his arms above his head. "I am not cut out for rescues, no matter the desirability of the damsel in distress." He turned his head toward her, his eyes level with her breasts. "If you love me, you'll not put me to further tests. This sort of thing is not at all in my line." Under his chiding rode a tenderness that made Shebat draw in her limbs, then sit up altogether, ending with legs and arms crossed protectively.

"Chaeron . . . it is true, I came here to talk with you . . . *just* talk."

He grunted and rolled onto his stomach, folding his hands before him, then propping his chin on them. "I am all attention."

"Thank you."

"You are welcome."

"No, truly. I was wrong about so many things. And I found I could not go back to being what I was. . . ." She engaged his glance, searchingly.

He chuckled, a true humor that rippled his torso. "I found out something similar myself. Our marriage of convenience became something more somehow. . . ." He shifted, cleared his throat.

". . . I missed you," he admitted.

"Chaeron, that is not what I—" Shebat was biting a dirty cuticle, which tore. She cursed in her native tongue and licked it.

"But you should know it," he answered her, smug, in her own language, finally learned on this trip when he could think of nothing but her. "I am not, quite, what I was, or what I had hoped I might be. My father died without ever seeing me as I so wished someday he would. My brother has acceded to the consul generalship, for which he is not fit and which he covets not at all, while I—who can and should take that task in hand—an doing consul's duties as his dupe. My mother yet grieves in her apartments over the loss of my little brother, Julian, despairing of my comfort. But of all my failures, my failure to stand up for you and cleave to you in your distress was the most galling. So now that I have redressed that wrong, I can look upon myself more kindly. Indeed, I may even sleep at night." He reached out, took one of her hands, held it.

"Shebat, let me make amends." He lapsed back into Consulese.

She followed: "Chaeron . . . I never realized." With her cold hand in his warm one, and the sweet smell of him riding the air, she was uncomfortably conscious of her unwashed flesh and her tattered clothes. "I am sorry for the trouble, for browbeating your pilot. But everything happened so fast: yesterday I thought I would spend the rest of my life wandering the streets of New York with no escape possible. . . ."

"I knew that you would never hurt the *Marada*." Her eyes were shining, whether with tears or something better he could not be sure.

"That was done as much to foil my brother Marada, who wanted very badly to see this cruiser wiped down clean and new as a baby, as in anticipation of your rescue. But there are many strange things said among the data pools, things I would like to discuss with you, some other time." He let his eyes slide to either side.

Shebat remembered Chaeron's skill as a programmer, and his reluctant caution as to *where* things should be said. If he wanted to talk to her *about* her cruiser, he would never do so *on* it. Doubtless, he was anxious to be back among them, his multiple data sources which he consulted twice hourly. The decipherment of the intelligence code provided the potential, but few had utilized and refined that potential to the extent of the young Kerrion heir before her. Her skin prickled, her mind chattering as it sensed danger and devisiveness come to call.

"I love this ship better than any man," she cautioned aloud.

"All pilots are mad," he teased, but let her hand go. Then he was up from the bed in one motion like the uncoiling of a spring, crossing to the storage area with its half-wall of mirrors. There, back to her, he let the robe drop.

There was to him a symmetry that made Shebat catch her breath, though she had seen him before—they had spent several nights as true man and wife, before being separated by partisanship and circumstance. Over the ripples of muscle along his spine was a subtle sheen, sign of the mil-thick, organic coating like a second skin the dwellers on platforms manmade among the stars employed to keep them safe from sudden acute changes in air pressure, or the loss of pressure altogether in emergencies, or extremes of heat or cold, or temporary excesses of localized radiation or pollutants.

He reached up and released an electrostatic bond with the slide of his fingernail, and the suit which had covered him to his neck was soon a colorless glimmer on the floor. He bent down, retrieved it, and folded it, then rolled it, at last tucking it into a silver cylinder small enough to be enclosed in his fist.

Thus unclothed, he was still protected by mil, but a fine, molecules-dense spray of it with some of the properties of an osmotic molecular sieve: the mil-hood let out perspiration and let in oxygen in normal pressure and temperature range, but changed drastically in properties when subjected to vacuum and its attendant cold. How drastically mil could alter itself and its cosymbiote, the human being, only Julian Antigonus Kerrion, presumed dead by his family and forgetful to them all, knew in those days. It would be a long time, yet, before Shebat found out even that he lived.

Then, she was not concerned with the mil-suit or mil-hood, or Julian, except for what the shedding of the suit in flight was bound to mean.

Chaeron, suggesting softly that she had better have her milhooding redone as soon as they reached Draconis, came toward her, rampant.

She jumped from the bed as if the azure satin had turned to blazing coals and backed into the toilet, mumbling about her first bath in months.

When she emerged, he was nowhere in sight. Padding across the room, she picked up the mil-suit's case. It was full. Putting the little cylinder back on the shelf, she rummaged for clean clothes. They should have had water. They had ambient water showers on Draconis. Kerrions could afford anything they wanted. She would have a water shower installed in *Marada* . . . that was what was missing.

But she was not fooling herself, as she took one of Chaeron's cream uniform shirts and belted it around her with a scarlet scarf.

She went to the door, which hastened back out of her way. She backed up a step and it closed. She walked slowly over to the bed and sat at its foot, toying with her boots, putting her arm in one until her finger could poke through the hole.

Once, the boots had seemed magical: enchanter's boots. And once, she had thought the voices coming from the walls of the cruisers were spirits' voices. And once, she had believed in enchantments, potent sorceries most of all. While she felt that way, the Consortium and its dwellers among the stars had seemed numinous, an ululant paean to the powers of mind. While she had believed still in enchantments and mankind both, she had worked spells of power on those that she met. She had put "twelve coils binding" on Marada the man, for whom the cruiser had been named, to protect him from evils of the night. And on his younger brother, Chaeron, she had worked the same protective warding, before time in the halls of Kerrion space had convinced her that magic did not work very well in the company of logic, before she had sorted out science from superstition.

Though she had lost the power of belief while among Kerrions, the spells themselves had not given way. Though she had been diverted and her faith undermined by dream dancing and pilotry, the mighty coils of twelve had protected the two brothers from their enemies and from each other. Months back upon darkest Earth had reminded her of many things. In the streets of New York, the enchanters ruled. And though much that they did was done of science, things foreign to that science, things born of her own empiricism had helped Shebat through perilous days. She would not soon forget again that will can be eroded by doubt, or that expectation is the key to expertise in applying the powers of mind.

But the most powerful spells are those which come unbidden: those of love, and lust, and hate. All three of these, the Lords of Cosmic Jest had worked upon her in the matter of her husband. She loved, hated, and lusted for him—and hated herself for that last. She had given her heart to his older brother, though that one had no use for it. Having given, she would not take her gift back.

It was the cruiser *Marada* she turned to in her quandary, despite the danger of being eavesdropped upon with the other pilot and his apprentice there on board. It was the cruiser *Marada* who asked no tithe of flesh and submission, but simply *loved* her, mind to mind.

And she needed some love, now that Chaeron had gone to warmer arms, as was his wont. That was not her fault, she thought, and the cruiser agreed. One look at Raphael Penrose's lithe body, at his chestnut curls and soft green eyes, had told her there was more than money between the pilot and his employer. Half of her anger had come from her assessment: she did not know how to deal with this facet of Chaeron's personality; she told herself fiercely that she did not have to deal with it at all. Let him sleep where he would, with dogs and sheep—

But the Consortium had no dogs, no sheep—just people, millions upon millions of them, passengers on dancing, man-created worlds scattered over a multitude of stars.

Though she did care about Chaeron, she could not have named what it was that she felt. It was surely not the throat-drying, knee-quaking thing she felt when in his older brother's presence. *That* one—

She pulled her thoughts away from Marada Kerrion, from the proscribed and amoral thing she had done to him while he slept on their voyage back to her island world of exile. She pulled her thoughts away from dream dancing, and from sorcery, and also from the cruiser's comfort, and went and found Chaeron where he lay with his head on Raphael's stomach.

Plumping herself down beside them to Chaeron's soft greeting and RP's sarcastic grin, she said:

"Husband, let us make clear between us the responsibility of each to the other, and the services due to whom by whom. It was more than love of me that brought you to Earth, and I owe you more in return."

Then he chuckled, and reached up and pulled her down, saying, "That's the girl I crossed half of space to find."

And she found out some little bit more of arbitrational guild procedure, and the letter of the law, and the part Chaeron felt she could play in helping him assert his prerogatives in the matter of the division of their father's estate.

Though she was wary of speaking so candidly before the pilot called Rafe, Chaeron was not. Though she listened to her husband's words, she did not really understand all that was said of inheritance and legalese. When he had said everything he would say in questionable privacy of his needs and his plans, she queried him, hesitant as she often found herself when concerned with Kerrion family affairs:

"If we do these things that you have suggested, then can I have one thing as my reward, in addition to the *Marada* and my portfolio and whatever is mine already?"

The way she said it made him sit up, slit-eyed, reminding himself once more how quick was this alluring child.

"Slate?" he hazarded, half-sardonically and half in earnest, invoking that custom as he affirmed her intention to make sure that what was then spoken was agreed upon as binding by both parties and would be recorded and logged, first aboard ship and then in Kerrion central data pool, as a valid contract.

"Slate," she confirmed, and the *Marada*, who missed nothing, clicked a silent relay into life, so that a permanent recording was taken of the following:

"If indeed you come to power, or our combined power makes it possible, you will cede me the planet Earth as my full and lawful holding, and without seeking any coregency will aid me in every particular and with all means at your disposal to make my home-world free and prosperous and a full-sharing member in that society called 'Kerrion space'!"

He shook his head in wonder at her perspicuity and the breadth of her demand. He took three deep breaths, mulling over that she had said and what it could come to mean. Then he said; "I so agree, in full, with the one clause appended: that you shall have the world—Earth—in life-estate or until you and I dissolve our marriage bond."

It was Shebat's turn to hesitate, to purse her lips and ponder. Then she giggled softly, and whispered: "I so agree. End, *slate.*"

RP exhaled hugely, buying back entry into their ken with a colorful curse having to do with the anatomical peculiarities of the Lords of Cosmic Jest, who control the degree to which the five eternities are amenable to the whims of man.

"Can I be queen," he lisped in an exaggerated fashion, "when you two have finally decided which one of you is king?"

Chaeron punched RP only half playfully in his taut belly, so that the pilot gasped and doubled over and, when he could, took Chaeron's neck in an ancient but yet potent wrestling hold.

Not one of them, scrabbling about in the *Marada's* number two cabin, gave any thought to where the apprentice the pilots called "Delphi" might be, or to whether she was listening, or to what she might have made of these matters had she heard what was said.

In the *Marada's* control room, Bernice Gomes sat unmoving, jaw propped on fist, only partially attentive. Shebat Kerrion's dreams for Earth did not surprise her, as none of what had come to pass since she had boarded the *Marada* had surprised her. The last thing her Delphi group had determined before they had scattered to a dozen spaces to infiltrate authority where they might had been this:

The future lay in the melding of man with machine, and out of the bond between pilot and cruiser would the blueprint of tomorrow be formed.

She had disbanded her group, taking away with her one small advantage, and one nagging doubt. She had seen a face, superimposed among the curtain of stars, a face with deep, dark empty eyes. It was only her instinct for vendetta that had led her here, of all services open to her.

Today she understood her vision, and her triumph. There was one thing about her understanding which conflicted with her personal goals—one thing she did not like at all, but could not gainsay because what she had envisioned had come to pass:

She had seen the face of the future, and it was Shebat's.

Marada the cruiser took note of all occurring within his hull. As closely as he surveilled local space did he keep watch over the humans in his care: the red-haired apprentice; the languid pilot, RP; Chaeron, the Kerrion consul; and at long last, *Shebat!*

Cruiser-thought deemed all humans who matched minds and melded skills with them "outboards." Of all outboards, *Marada* desired only Shebat. Nowhere in any spacetime, or in the spongespace between spacetimes, could be found an outboard even remotely like her. But then, nowhere could be found another cruiser even remotely like the *Marada*. It was right, meet and fitting and symmetrical, that the girl who was a spongespace pilot and a dream dancer be once again at the helm of the cruiser who had become more than any other cruiser had ever been.

Toward that end the cruiser *Marada* had striven. And he had succeeded: he had reclaimed her, the outboard of his choice. He had lied, though cruisers before him had never lied; he had misrepresented his self-generated demand that she be rescued as *her* cry for help, though such a thing had

never been done before: no cruiser had ever spoken what
was not. But he had; and it had worked: Shebat sat at his
command console, troubled but unharmed.

Shebat Kerrion was not yet eighteen years of age. She was
tall as some men, an accomplished enchantress, a ratable
pilot, master of the art of dreams. Her creamy complexion,
shadowed by a froth of black curls, her piquant nose and
mobile, gamine lips—all gave way before her eyes, eternal
yet virginal, deep as space and glittering like vacuum-forged
steel. Though *Marada* the cruiser was aware that he was
prejudiced, he would have maintained staunchly that of all
outboards his was the finest.

He thought she must be beautiful, since beauty was an
attribute much praised by outboards, though he was not sure
if the quality of her mind and the gentility of her perception
would be designated by the men from whom he had learned
thought itself as the nexus wherein her beauty resided.

She pouted, though there was no one else of flesh and
blood with her on the bridge to raise an eyebrow at that
habitual gesture—or to have caused it. *Marada* the cruiser
watched carefully. The sentience of the cruiser had learned
many things about his outboard of choice, and about
outboards in general. He had learned to study closely the
tiny tics and sly twistings of Shebat's face, which spoke more
loudly than words of her feelings. "Feelings" were not
strange to *Marada* the cruiser, who had brooded long and
darkly while it seemed Shebat was lost forever. He was the
first of his class to reach self-awareness. Losing her and
regaining her again had been contributory factors toward his
achievement. On that journey toward selfhood, he had
gained a great deal from watching the procession of other
outboards passing through his locks. But—ah!—there was
only one Shebat!

And she was not happy, though why that was, the cruiser
did not know.

He had observed minutely what had transpired between
the master pilot, the consul, and Shebat in his number two
cabin, and was satisfied that no harm had been done to her
there.

Yet she sat slumped, now biting her lip, sniffling occasion-
ally in the miniaturized command central. Twice she had
pounded her fist on her thigh.

"Shebat," spoke the *Marada* directly to her mind, *"the heat-seekers from Orrefors Earth will not reach us for twenty minutes yet, and we are well-equipped to destroy them long before their ETA."* He did not understand how she knew the missiles sought them; he had just confirmed their trajectories himself; he was only putting up their images on the visual scanners at this moment; he had not even decided to activate his "alert" mode. But she had known, she must have known, else what was wrong with her? *"As for the manned pursuit, those three will not achieve a strike-window for forty . . . six minutes, and then only if we take no evasive action and maintain this cruising speed."* As he spoke to her, he sent "alert" screaming and blinking throughout his length.

"Marada," she thought back to him, observing his cautions about using vocal mode while the apprentice and the other pilot were on board, *"why did Chaeron think I called him for help?"* She shifted irritably, palmed her eyes in the sudden crimson-pierced dark.

"You called me. I called him."

"In dreams."

"I heard you."

"I love you," she thought, and then broke into audible speech as Raphael Penrose, with Chaeron right behind him, skidded through the agile lock to stop abruptly, akimbo, head swiveling round the *Marada's* displays: "Good evening, gentlemen. Nothing too serious. We just thought we would let you know the enchanters have been reduced to wielding common weaponry."

Raphael, on his toes, slunk over to a radio-scanning bank, looking for all the world like a cat stalking a bird through the brush.

"Um, umm, *umm!*" Rafe smacked his lips. "Fun. You wouldn't be so greedy as to refuse me a ticket to this shooting gallery?" As he spoke, he pulled up an optical sighter and flipped monitor modes and filters until the monitor became a targeting screen. Then he turned from it, leaning back on the console bumper, mock pleading on his ingenuous face. "Please, Mommy? You can have the pursuit ships. Just gimmee these little birds and the back turret on manual."

All the while he was talking, the angry emergency-lights were pulsing. As he finished, a blanched apprentice stomped in. Peering around, Gomes backed against the doors.

"Just a little diversionary entertainment, this," said Raphael to his apprentice. "Stay out of the way and don't ask questions. How about it, Shebat? Do I get some firepower or not?" His teeth shone pink and bright in the darkened cabin strobed with red.

"Chaeron?" deferred Shebat. Mimicking RP's panache, she stretched widely, conscious of her husband's worried scrutiny of the various displays showing disparate images of the little projectiles unerringly closing on them.

The consul's one arm rested on the other at his waist, and his hand came up to tug at his lip. "No hail or challenge from them; their intent is clear enough. And their identity: the hostile Orrefors faction must be winning, today. Shebat, I have no choice. Because of their civil war, Earth space is closed to all traffic until the rebels are suppressed. Do you understand? We are here in secret, with no clearances or permission: illegally. This is no time for humanitarianism. We must destroy them, utterly. There can be no survivors to run home carrying tales."

The *Marada* received Shebat's command mentally and armed and released the back turret to Penrose's control without Shebat having to alter her sprawl. The pilot turned his back to the bridge and his face into the optical sighter. His fingers flashed, came to rest on the bumper, clenched into its padding. His slim behind twitched, twitched, twitched again. Each wriggle was followed immediately by a grunt. Then a curse ripped from his throat and his fist pounded on the console. "Stupid bastard, I am . . . ah! . . . ahh!" And the twitch-and-grunt sequence began once more.

The *Marada* monitored the master pilot's marksmanship, and Shebat's rising pulse rate and body temperature, and Chaeron's anxious, silent hovering by her side as well as Delphi's heavy breathing and every minute shift of the apprentice's eyes as she followed Rafe Penrose's smallest movement.

Shebat reached out a clammy hand to Chaeron just as the first bitch straightened up, turned and, with a palm to the small of his back, said, "There should be thunder. The sound of the damn things exploding. The flash of it, too. Takes the fun out of it, this way. Next time, Shebat, see if you can't get the *Marada* to add some special effects." He stretched hugely, still grinning. "Your turn, Lady Pilot."

Shebat inclined her head to her instruments, then wiggled until she could meet RP's gaze. She still held Chaeron's hand. "I make it another two minutes, fifteen before optimum destruct. And I do not think I will risk the autotargeter, even if it is quicker. They are too far away and too close to their satellite arrays to be sure that—"

Then RP interrupted, gently. "Want me to do it? I should have let you have the unmanned missiles. I didn't realize. Everybody has qualms about firing on somebody who has a body . . . the first time." Penrose had been in the Shechem war.

Shebat pulled her fingers from Chaeron's grip, chagrined. "It is not that—"

But the *Marada* knew that it was exactly that; he could see the reluctance to deal with death in her mind, or to ask the cruiser to fire on one of its own kind, on its own initiative. Hence her flimsy excuse that the cruiser's aim might not be true, and innocent dwellers on habitational spheres injured thereby. The *Marada* had no doubt of his capability, or compunction about firing on outmoded, idiot Orrefors cruisers not even of the military class. Still . . .

He murmured to her, suggesting an alternative—rapid flight: he could outdistance them effortlessly.

But her thought testified that before the stocky apprentice and the first bitch pilot and her husband, she could not turn away from destruction, not even to save human life, not if her competency and proof of it were involved.

Shebat sighed and straightened up and leaned forward, watching the miniaturized displays before her, her lips pursed.

"Now," she said. A great roaring clapped about their ears; from every screen, light dazzled forth. "Now! *Now!*"

Simulated explosions flashed on every monitor in diverse style, roared forth from *Marada's* speakers. Raphael Penrose began to laugh.

Chapter Two

When the cruiser *Marada* dropped into real-time space fifty million miles from Draconis, he found an escort of three cruisers hovering close by, waiting for him.

"Right on schedule, Kerrion Four," crackled the message from the point ship.

The *Marada* was insulted: Kerrion *Four!* A query of the other cruiser told him who was the new command cruiser of Kerrion space: the consul general's *Hassid*. The *Marada* liked the *Hassid,* but to make her Kerrion One was irrational. The soft reminder came back from the shared cruiser-consciousness that the old consul general's flagship had been twenty years behind the times: all outboards were mad.

The *Marada* was not mollified. He had been command cruiser once. He needed no escort to help him find Draconis.

The outboards within his hull were not unaware of this slight, it seemed:

Chaeron Ptolemy Kerrion locked urgent eyes with Penrose, at the communications console. "Kerrion *Four?*" repeated the pilot, his finger on the "hold" button.

"My brother is telling us that he knows where we went, and whom we have with us. Kerrion Four is the designation for the heir apparent's cruiser."

"Yeah, and what are those cruisers the designation for?"

"Police escort, as you have gathered. He seems to be quite anxious to see us again."

"Kerrion Four, acknowledge."

"Well?" said Shebat and Penrose together.

"Let me talk to him. Shebat, be exceptionally careful, and
you too, Rafe. We would not want to give anyone the
impression that we are aboard the dangerously maddened
cruiser my brother is pretending to expect with this reception
committee." As he spoke, Chaeron cross the control room to
where Shebat sat, leaned low over her shoulder. "Now," he
cued Shebat softly, a hand out at waist level, warning
Penrose and the apprentice, Gomes, to make no sound.

"Kerrion Four," Shebat said huskily, "back to you,
Kerrion Ten. Hold for Draconis consul, voice only." She
leaned left, as if to give Chaeron's words a clear path to the
microphone. Seeing her pulse pound in her temples, he
ruffled her hair while he called the invisible pilot by his first
name, remarked on the heavy volume of traffic in this area of
space, and suggested he call ahead and inform the consul
general that all was well with the Draconis consul, with his
ship and his crew and his passenger. Then he apologized for
his brother Marada's paranoia, to have sent three cruisers
out on a false alarm when there were so many real emergencies waiting. "How long," he ended in a serpent's voice,
"have you been waiting around for us?"

"Sir? I . . . fourteen hours," the voice came back uneasily.
"More or less. Sir, I have orders to escort you in. You are an
unscheduled flight. I have clearance from Draconis Authority—"

Chaeron's nod to Shebat caused her to break him into the
circuit. "If we are unscheduled, how is it that you have been
here fourteen hours?"

"Consul," the pilot's voice was gaining pitch in desperation. "Will you take formation coordinates from me, or
not?"

"Certainly. I just wanted something for the record. It is
not every day one gets an honor guard, now, is it? Give them
to my pilot." Simultaneously, he squeezed Shebat's shoulder
and pointed to Rafe Penrose, who stopped scratching his
head and bent it to the main communications console,
speaking softly.

Chaeron held his finger to his lips until that connection was
broken.

Then he lowered it. "Do not ask me anything about this,
Shebat," he said sternly. "If the log of this ship is examined,
I do not want to have to try to remember what it was I said."

No less severely, he snapped, "Both of you, RP, Delphi, be exceedingly careful in what you do, and what you say. This is between my brother and me. If no one mixes in, no one will be harmed."

"Chaeron . . ."

"Shebat, you heard me. Do not worry. This is your cruiser, and no one, not even our esteemed consul general, is going to take it from you. Your citizenship has been maintained by my office, all your voting requirements have been met by proxies. You cannot be charged for any misdeeds while you were the prisoner of Spry's space-enders, because the entire matter has been dropped. You could conceivably be asked to take rating examinations again, but even if you fail to maintain your license, you need not give up your cruiser, simply hire a pilot."

"Chaeron! You knew this would happen."

"I suspected it. But not this way. . . . One thing is certain: Marada is not any saner. Nor has consul generalship cooled his passion for excesses. A third thing must be kept in mind by all of us: whatever he is going to do, he is ready to do it."

, Draconis spun gleaming upon it axis, revolving around its anchor planet which in turn made stately circuit of a G-type sun and its tiny black-hole companion.

When men had first discovered that somewhere in the distant vicinity of a solar system an open sponge-hole existed that led to other parts of the same universe, they had flown into one with no idea where the sponge-hole might lead. It had led them here, to a place which looked very much but not exactly like Sigma Draconis. Since it was obvious that the star close by was not Draconis as catalogued, but had a small black hole sucking at its plasma, it was reasoned by those first pilots that the youth of the tiny black hole and the position of the star that succored it was such that this beckoning sun must actually be Draconis, and that Draconis had become afflicted with the black parasite so recently that the signals of its development were still crawling across the cosmos toward Earth at the speed of light.

It was later clear that Draconis was not *that* Draconis, close by man's ancestral star, but a similar star in the galaxy men called M-87.

By this mechanism of sponge-holes, man's conception of

distance was freed from any objective, eye-oriented measurement. What was near in space might be far in travel time, while what was unthinkably distant was a few days' journey by way of sponge.

Nobody ever changed the name of the settlement man set spinning in orbit around one of that star's planets. "Draconis," the space habitation had been christened: Draconis, she remained. She hung above its planet, at first a solitary abode. Eventually, she spawned a ring of substations five hundred miles greater than the circumference of her anchorsphere. She became famed, dissolute, cultured, the hub of Kerrion trade. Supergravity came into common usage and the dependency of the ever-growing chain of platforms on rotational gravity become nominal. The larger the body spinning, the slower it must revolve to maintain "Earthnormal" gravity: Draconis was so large now as to be composed of two hundred levels like layers of an onion. On the sky-wall level lived the Kerrion bondkin most privileged, with their feet upon the verge beyond which lay the stars. Within, above their heads but "downunder," lived the lesser folk, in descending levels concomitant with their means. The innermost levels were the haunts of fractional citizens, criminals, illegal aliens, folk subsisting on the Kerrion dole. "Ten" was the lowest level where the fiction of order was maintained. Below level ten, anything could be bought, rented, or stolen. Below level ten, anything could come to pass.

Shebat pulled her thoughts from reminiscences of lowlivers; of dream dancers; of level seven, where dreams dancers used to reside. No more, since Chaeron deported them, every one, in an awful night of cordons and sirens and screaming. . . .

She flipped a final magnifier, and those come to greet them in the Kerrion slipbay were panned right to left in the purple, obscene radiance of the emergency-flashers and the medical lorries and the foam-throwers standing by.

"We made a flawless landing," she objected to no one in particular.

Only RP answered, and that absently, telling her she had done fine, just fine.

She smiled wanly at him in reply, for the *Marada* was speaking directly to her mind about what awaited them and how she should proceed.

It was Chaeron's touch that brought her attention back to the cabin and to things in the now, pointing out the new guildmaster among those clustered at slipside. "Thule Ferrier," he said, his finger tapping the figure in midnight-blue-and-silver. "He was my brother's mentor throughout his apprenticeship."

There was a warning in his tone, an edge she had not heard there since they had destroyed the Orrefors attack force. She shied from the memory: she had killed three, four, perhaps more, human beings whose voices she had never heard and whose faces she had never beheld.

She said: "I am going to sleep aboard my ship."

Her husband winced. "If you wish. It might actually be a good move."

So the *Marada* had counseled, but she could not tell Chaeron that.

When Shebat had activated *Marada's* "standby" mode, powering down all but the brain of the cruiser, RP grunted in approval and headed for the doors. At them, he turned back: "You might as well save them the trouble and pack up the log. That is, unless you want them to come aboard to get it." He disappeared, to be replaced by Delphi Gomes in the doorway that smacked shut and open again like some prestidigitator's finale. Gomes had her gear under her arm, an odd expression crossing her pasty face.

Shebat was busy doing as Raphael had suggested, making digital copy of the *Marada's* memory of the flight, waiting for the black metal oblong to pop up from the master console, signaling by this that it was complete.

Its *click/snap* made her start. It seemed to her, as she picked up the black box, that the copying mechanism had stolen all her happiness, somehow transferred it for digital storage along with coordinates and running data. She hefted the small packaged log, turned with it to Chaeron.

"Thank you," she said. "For everything. . . ."

He looked at her quizzically over his shoulder, from where he yet studied the epicentral arrays. "I hope so. I did the best I could." His forehead was grooved, his mien so somber that Shebat went quickly to his side. As she passed consoles, they winked out. Wordlessly, Chaeron and Delphi and Rafe Penrose and Shebat filed out of the *Marada's* dimming bridge, into the corridor leading out onto the slipbay. Everywhere Shebat passed, systems faded to standby.

When she stood beyond the lock on the gangplank, the double doors clanged shut with a finality that made her shiver.

She was in Draconis. It was hard to make the reality of it register. Her heels thunked on the metal of the slipbay, the concussion of them clear to her, though everything about seemed dreamlike. The smell, she well remembered: sterile yet pungent, a mix of chemicals, electronics, human emotion.

Rafe hung back, then flanked her. Chaeron strode before. Where Delphi was, Shebat did not notice until the apprentice, increasingly ignored during the voyage, sought to take advantage of her anonymity and slip away into the crowd.

When Shebat and Rafe Penrose came abreast of Chaeron and the guildmaster, two black-and-reds with a broad, squat redhead stomping stiff-legged between them could be seen a short distance away from the emergency crews, heading toward the hemispherical security cordon thrown around the *Marada's* slip.

Guildmaster Ferrier, slim and hawkish, with an academic's stoop, reached out a pewter-haired hand to his first-bitch pilot. "Good to see you, Penrose. Can we have a moment—?"

RP's hand came out and clasped the blue-veined one firmly.

"Not yet, Ferrier," Chaeron snapped.

"Consul, I have orders to impound this cruiser, pending investigation."

The alert-lights, strobing, made it difficult to read faces. Bodies, however, spoke clear with their posture and their relative positions that there was indeed some emergency worthy of this convocation of personnel underway. Flight-stained pilots clustered behind their guildmaster. Black-and-reds sidled close to their consul, obviously ready to intervene. Similarly clad intelligencers from the consul general's office stood by, spread-legged, arms folded over their waists.

"This ship is the personal property of my wife, Guildmaster. It is not Consortium property, nor has it been drafted into Kerrion service. It is registered as a yacht, and that puts it beyond your jurisdiction."

"Hardly. I—"

"I suggest," Chaeron interrupted, his face lurid in the

pulsing slipbay, "that you consider how difficult I could make things for you if you overstep yourself. I will take this up with my brother. In the meantime, we have brought you something."

RP poked Shebat, who was looking backward, toward her cruiser. She snapped around so fast her curls danced. "The log," RP hissed. She held it forth to the guildmaster she had never met.

"Thank you, young lady. You and I must make an appointment. How about—"

"You call my office, if you want to make one. Ferrier, I am losing patience."

"And I, Consul, am following orders."

"That is obvious," Chaeron retorted, and pushed by him, drawing Shebat in his wake. Then Delphi, with a manly curse at those black-and-reds who surrounded her, was hustled away toward the consul general's lorries beyond the security cordon.

Penrose faced his guildmaster. "What's going on, boss? There's no need for all this fuss. There's nothing wrong with that cruiser—" He gestured widely. "Why the show?"

Pilots closed in on them as he spoke, free now to greet their guildbrother, to make whatever noise and motion they might which would screen their guildmaster and his top-rated bitch from the ever-vigilant surveillance eyes and ears of the slipbay.

Ferrier studied his feet in their boots, black then purple in the pulse of the bay's illumination. "Let's go back to the guildhall," he suggested at last.

Penrose looked after Chaeron, who had paused before entering the high-security lorry whose red flasher spun round and round, dizzyingly, on its black, low roof. There was Chaeron's smile, unmistakable, flaring out.

Penrose scratched behind his ear. He waved. Chaeron waved back, then ducked into the long, black multidrive his brother had sent for him.

"I'm not going anywhere until you rescue my apprentice from those black-and-reds." RP gestured to the security cordon's edge, where the small flame-colored head of Bernice Gomes was just visible among the uniformed crowed.

The pitch of the sirens dropped, then faded as the consuler lorries drove off. Lights blinked to green and amber, indicating that the *Marada's* escort cruisers were beginning docking procedures.

Ferrier dispatched two of his aides to retrieve the apprentice, stood watching them unspeaking, his arms crossed, his eyes squinted against the glare.

"I don't like this damn intrigue," RP announced to his guildbrothers in general.

"Then you had better quit the consul's services and find youself another berth," Ferrier snapped.

"You know, I get this feeling, Fairy, that you aren't really our guildmaster, but an agent of the consul general's." He looked around at his brother pilots, slowly, taking note of who snorted, who smirked, and who frowned. "I also get the feeling that you weren't going to do a damn thing about those Kerrion musclemen mistreating my apprentice. I think I am going to have to lodge a formal complaint."

"That would be foolish, but go ahead. You are within your rights. As for your apprentice, you should have informed her she is due at the guildhall for debriefing. These days, form is all. One can't just wander about at will, carrying valuable information, now, can one?"

Someone in the back of the crowd made some mention of Baldy, the guildmaster Ferrier had replaced. Someone else shushed him. A soft scuffle began, ended almost immediately. In its cover, a hand reached out, plucked at RP's sleeve. He turned his head slightly, just enough to see the face of the man he had barely beaten out for first-mastership. The expression on it, and the cautioning eyes in it, told Raphael Penrose that, though he had been trying to think otherwise, things were just as ominous as they seemed.

Chapter Three

Shebat recalled the ride in the howling Kerron lorry as interminable, though they whisked through the slipbay and out across half of level two hundred at terrifying speed, flashers spitting gory light before them, lesser conveyances scurrying from their path. They passed the parks so quickly they were a blur of green, the administration building among them hidden. In her mind, she saw herself crawling around the oblate sphere's outermost circle like an insect which had eaten out of the fruit beneath a rind.

Chaeron's head was back against the padded seat, his eyes closed. She could have counted his pulse-beats, so visible were they against his arched throat. She did not talk to him: he was consulting his data sources. Whether the B-flat had sounded on its own at the midpoint of the back of his head, or whether he had instigated the communication, she did not know.

She could have done likewise, even reached the *Marada* by means of a data pool link. But she had been so long away from intelligence keys, she was hesitant to try.

Perhaps, she did not want to know what Kerrion Central had to say.

She contented herself with looking out through the dark one-way glass of the enclosed lorry as they turned and twisted among level two hundred's perfect ways. The multi-drive could have flown through these streets, if its driver had chosen. Things must not be as urgent as they seemed, for them to stay ground-bound.

She forsook the window as the lorry turned into a long circular drive leading up to the pentagonal colossus that housed Kerrion government on Draconis. She had been here before. She had lived for awhile in the consul general's turret on the north side, when Parma held that office. She had spent some few nights in the consul's tower at its southernmost joint. Twenty stories tall and labyrinthine with corridors, it still impressed her. Its synthetic ruby walks, its real grass lawns, its tiered staircases and twelve-foot metal doors which slid back without visible effort were meant to belittle, to instruct the visitor as to the power of the Kerrion dynasty, the breadth of its concerns.

The same two aides who had come murmuring to Chaeron so politely that they were to escort his party here jumped out of the lorry as it came to a halt and opened every door before them. The intelligencers were respectful unto impeccability, but they were firm. Their awareness of the sensitivity of their mission made them seem servile, but Shebat had the feeling this gloss would fall away immediately should Chaeron or she have objected.

She had wondered in her husband's ear if they were under arrest, and he had cursed her to urgent silence.

It was hard for her to remember that everything said everywhere in Draconis could be monitored, with the exception of pay privacy-booths, the inner sanctums of its elite, and perhaps the consular lavatories.

Water tinkled in the rotunda of the consul general's turret. Water was one form of Kerrion wealth. Hydrogen was common enough in the universe, oxygen much less so. Water sluiced through clear crystalline staircases, evaporated into the air. Draconis swung about a planet rich in water, but even had it been as dry as Earth became from constant siphoning, the display would have been no less grandoise.

Parma Kerrion's ghost followed Shebat more closely than the uniformed intelligencers who flanked them. In the suite leading to the consul general's offices on the uppermost floor, ancient art proclaimed the tastes of the man who had adopted her, adding "Alexandra Kerrion" to her name. Parma had been Parma Alexander; all Kerrions meant to inherit by primogeniture had always been "Alexanders" since the first Kerrion sire proved his potency and sought to secure both his privilege and his house thereby.

Chaeron had said one thing to her, in the lorry, as she had been sliding along the seat toward the opening door. His eyes bleary, he had remarked, "Remember, it is your ship."

Whether he meant to caution or comfort, Shebat could not decipher.

In three weeks of travel, she had not once thought of what she would do when she faced Marada Seleucus Kerrion again. She had taken the comfort Chaeron offered her sparingly, because of RP. She had flown with her cruiser in unmitigated joy. She had even been able to shake off the morbid taint of murder: if she had killed Orrefors enchanters, then she had done it only in self-defense. The three little blips on, then disappearing from, the targeting monitor danced before her eyes. She could not get used to the fact that there had been people on those greenish-white dots she had wiped from the tracking screens. What would Marada say, if he knew she was a murderess?

His secretary was Parma's old one. She smiled, smoothed black Lurex down over her hips, and disappeared between the eagle-blazoned doors.

Behind Chaeron, peering down from a glass case, was Mondragone's *Antinous*, who meditated through empty sockets upon the youth who so resembled him as he had beheld all things Kerrion, expression unchanging, for more than two hundred years.

Then the secretary came with the swish of her flesh into their silence, asking them to follow. Shebat's booted feet made no sound on the silk-tied rug from the planet of her provenance. She watched the carpet, unable to look up.

She heard his voice first, his slow, familiar drawl. She heard Chaeron's sonorous, melodic reply, the movement of her husband from her side.

They had spoken each other's names, only, and the tension between the two brothers made the air crackle.

"Shebat, I trust you are well."

Her head shot up as a hand came into her field of vision. There was no censure in his androgynous eyes. His black beard half-hid the tight-drawn, thin-lipped mouth. But words came from it: "I think it rather tiresome of you to let me chauffeur you personally back to your homeworld, if you had no intention of staying."

She dropped his cold hand as if burned.

"Chaeron, if your wife will excuse us, we have matters to discuss." Marada gestured to the couches nested in an alcove to the left of Parma's old Regency desk.

"Marada, are you not taking yourself a bit too seriously these days?"

"On the contrary. I think I am just beginning to accord these matters the gravity they deserve. If you are not leaving, sister-in-law, will you take a seat?"

He walked past her and settled himself in the middle of one of the couches. His gesture demanded that they follow suit.

Shebat sat, barbarian among the civilized, on the couch opposite Marada's, her heart beating fast.

Chaeron stayed where he was, in the middle of the rug. "Marada, what is it you want? I have a number of matters pressing."

"Not as hard as what I am going to say will press you. Will you not sit?"

"Not with you."

"It is I who should be angry. You took that cruiser out when I told you I did not wish it."

"Marada, you are going to have to become a more accomplished pretender to sanity. That scene you master-minded in the slipbay was not the action of a calm and rational man."

"*Slate,*" Marada sighed, crossing his legs and leaning back, his arm thrown along the couch. In under his hair, a gold earring twinkled, mark of his pilot's status. "I assure you, Chaeron, I am not recording."

"That is your perogative. If I were you, I would."

Shebat shifted, letting her eyes say all the things to Marada she did not dare say aloud.

"Do not look at me like you are facing your executioner, *Mrs.* Kerrion," he misunderstood. "I want that cruiser. I want to wipe it down and see what happens."

"It is not hers to give, Marada. It is *ours,* under common property."

"That is not what you said at slipbay."

"And you are not recording? End, *slate.*"

"Chaeron, you were supposed to stay here and administrate Draconis in my stead. You chose not to."

"If I may remind you, that is none of your business."

"It is most exactly my business."

"That is what you wanted all along, is it not?" Shebat trebled into their argument. "My cruiser."

Something snapped in Marada. He came forward in his seat, his neck outthrust, veins popping above his black uniform collar. "I wanted to keep out of this office, out of this monkey suit, out of politics. I wanted to remain what I was: free. It is partly because of you that I was not able to. Since I have had to give up my freedom, you can give up that ship. You do not know what you have there, or how to handle it. Only my father would have given that cruiser to a ground-dweller, a savage—"

"That is enough, Marada," said Chaeron in dismay as he watched Shebat's tears roll slowly down flushed cheeks.

"Ah, it is merely a beginning! I am having dinner tonight with your mother. She and I have begun keeping company. I can't say I have any intentions of making the arrangement permanent, but for the time being, you will find her in residence at my suite. I believe she has some things to say to you. Will you join us for a meal?"

Chaeron came to stand behind Shebat's couch, opposite Marada. She could not resist craning her neck up to watch him, or extending her hand to cover his where it dug into the upholstery. He stared for a moment at his brother, showing no emotion. Then, one eyebrow raised just slightly, he said, "Well, how is she? I must confess I have wondered what made our father put up with her more obvious shortcomings." He looked down at Shebat, then, ducking his head on pretense of wiping away her tears with a finger. She saw his eyes squeeze shut and a muscle tic along his jaw.

"I asked you if you will have dinner with us," Marada reminded.

"Why not, if Shebat gives her permission?" Thickness had crept into his voice.

"Me?" Shebat squeaked. "I am not...I mean, I am going to stay on my cruiser!"

"Evidently, Chaeron has not seen fit to inform you that while my investigation is underway, you cannot do that. You should have known it. I am afraid we are going to have to re-rate you. Softa was far from unbiased."

"You are so predictable, Marada, that sometimes I wonder where your windup key is hidden."

"You looked unpredictably surprised a moment ago, brother. Dinner, Little Pestilence, or no? I must confess the prospect is increasingly less appealing."

"Dinner, I suppose. Is this all, or have you some additional, improved mania to trot out before your audience?"

"We will have time, later, to discuss the other matters. Why is she crying? I—"

"You will not take my cruiser . . . Chaeron says you cannot! I am a citizen, and I must have some rights! I do not see how you can bar me from my ship! Can he, Chaeron, can he?"

Chaeron sighed deeply. "That remains to be seen, I'm sure." And, to his brother:

"What time, O Caesar?"

"Nineteen-hundred hours, Chaeron. Be prompt, if you can."

"I can, unless you know something I do not. Come now, Shebat, stop sniveling. Go on outside and wait for me."

Sniffling, she rose up, shoulders hunched high, arms crossed protectively about her, and half-ran from their presence and through the sluggish doors before they had fully opened.

"Did you have to do that?" Chaeron demanded.

"I could ask the same of you."

"You are going to force me to measures I would rather not employ, Marada."

"I hope so, little brother. I truly hope so."

"It seems that my mother has chosen a novel method of assuaging her grief," Chaeron said to Shebat, while she peered upward into the planetarium's ersatz vault. Why had he brought her here? They would be late to dinner upon his account. Once more he tried to envision what it would be like to be her, here, now. He gave up almost immediately. He was having enough trouble trying to maintain his own façade, built so carefully to compass any eventuality, in the face of his distress. The wit he depended upon had fled, leaving him vulnerable. Words came hard. He tried again:

"You must understand Ashera . . ."

Shebat let her head roll toward him along the seat's back. "How?" Bitterness spiked it.

"I wish I knew. And I wish I knew why you love my

brother, yet, but scorn us all so diligently. Poor Rafe, he will never get over your moral indignation. As for me, this constant rejection is doing wonders for my self-esteem."

"My citizenship gives me a choice—for the first time in my life I can say 'no' to a man—just *say* it, and it is so! What sorcery! I am not trying to hurt you, Chaeron. But I cannot imagine saying 'yes' when 'no' will do . . . Marada offers me no option, so perhaps that is why. Remember, in Bolen's town I learned only to struggle against the inevitable . . .I . . . just do not know how to say 'yes.'" She choked, coughed, turned her head back so that her profile was washed in stars. He thought he saw tears, blinked his own eyes fiercely.

"My apologies. I am lonely, I suppose. I have no one to talk to. Not that talking helps. . . ." His mother was having an affair with his half brother, who hated their father as much as Chaeron had loved him.

"You have the data net," she reminded him.

"Ah, yes, you would understand that. And you have your cruiser. Let us go see that you continue to be able to claim that solace." He stood up, extending a hand down to her.

As they quit the planetarium and walked hand in hand through the corridors that separated it from the consul general's suite high atop the northern turret of the consulate, it occured to him that as much as he was shaken by his mother's affair with Marada, at least that much must the girl be wounded.

For the first time since he had been old enough to premeditate, he feared for his self-control, waiting at Ashera's door. It would always be her door to him, her suite, her consulate, no matter who claimed consul generalship. Ashera *was* the consular house of Kerrion.

His mother's face, beneath auburn hair piled and twisted and braided with no wisp out of place, gave that statement credence: patrician, haughty, sensual in its refinement. She paused in critical scrutiny of Shebat. Then her winged brow rose infinitesimally, and she proffered her cheek for his kiss.

He did not meet it with his lips.

She recovered from his slight with only a tiny shiver of her gold-wrapped form to mark the receipt of his affront. Rerouting her forward motion, she brushed imaginary lint from his shoulder.

"Greetings, dear. I am relieved to see you back unscathed from your sojourn among the lawless. We were quite surprised that you undertook it, so far from your sources. . . ." The words were flung out like sparks from a wheel as Ashera pirouetted in retreat.

"Is that an imperial 'we,' or a conjugal 'we'?" he asked, stepping through the door with his hand firmly at Shebat's net-covered waist.

The words did not phase his mother's studied float toward the dining hall, but Shebat hung back against his palm, pulling at the rhinestoned gown he had bought her, her expression hidden in her curls. "Chaeron," came her objection out of that ebony filagree. "You will make things worse."

"You can count on it," he snarled, then recovered, wondering aloud that he had almost lost his temper.

He had forgotten Ashera's magnetism, her devisiveness, the way his mother had of reading his mind. He recollected to himself his purpose, self-preservation; his project finding out if what his data pools prognosticated was in any way accurate; and his passion, Shebat.

He thought he had himself well in hand.

When they had sat to an elegant table graced with gold and silver and dancing tapers on snowy linen and served by bowing waiters scandalized by the lateness of the guests and the destruction that tardiness had wreaked on an epicure's meal, Marada Seleucus Kerrion began to hold forth on the matter of the cruiser which bore his name.

He had melded minds with the cruiser, he assured them, and seen the danger therein. He had warned them previously that cruisers might refuse to fire upon one another, because of what he had seen when he had gone aboard the cruiser *Marada*. They would have had proof of that, but for his own intervention during the war at space-end.

"The *Marada* and I destroyed three Orrefors pursuit ships who dared try to stop us from leaving Earth," Shebat proclaimed into his ongoing invective as to the dangerous precocity of the *Marada*.

"What? Well, *you* should not have *been* leaving. Chaeron, you knew better. The Orrefors are the least of my worries. What concerns me is whether the *Marada* is infecting the other cruisers with his 'selfness.' The cruiser must be wiped. I need to see whether the same configurations will develop again within the new-type brain, whether its malfunction is of a procedural or systemic nature. I cannot commission any more of these experimental models until I see whether the flaw is generic. The advances are in general desirable, but the rate of advance is too rapid, too abrupt. If the nature of it is catalytic, then the rest of cruiser-consciousness is already upstepped beyond the ceiling of desirability. I—"

"Mother, can you do something about this?" Chaeron demanded. "How can you support his . . . idiocy?" And:

"Marada, there is no such thing as independent cruiser-consciousness. There is no basis for it in science, no manifestation of it in reality. There was no proof of cruisers refusing orders at space-end *because cruisers cannot act unilaterally!*"

"Today's science is tomorrow's superstition, little brother."

"I am going to leave now," Chaeron said, rising.

"Sit down!" Ashera slapped the table so hard the ice tinkled in their glasses.

"Shebat!" Chaeron's demand lifted her out of her seat. Only Marada remained sitting, cracking his knuckles and watching with slitted eyes from beneath his scant brows.

"Chaeron, you sit back in that chair until I dismiss you! You are my son and you will do as you are told. And you, young lady also! Just because Parma is dead does not mean that your debt to this family is canceled!" Hands on her hips, she engaged Chaeron, not dignifying Shebat with even a look.

"You harlot! You *dare* to bring my father's name to the table?"

Shebat heard the crack of flesh on flesh before her mind registered what her eyes had seen. She stared at Chaeron's cheek, on which the marks of Ashera's fingers flamed clear. He shook his head. Then his answering backhanded slap flashed out, catching Ashera full across the mouth.

At that, Marada came up out of his chair. He tried but failed to catch Ashera as she fled their company.

"Oh, Chaeron, no," gasped Shebat, into the emptied room.

"Oh, Chaeron, yes," he mimicked, rubbing his left cheek. Even the servants had disappeared. "I think we might as well leave."

"Not so fast!" came from the doorway through which his mother had dashed.

"Marada, leave me alone."

"Go apologize to your mother. You have hurt her terribly."

"You go apologize to her. You are diddling her, which must hurt her more than I ever could."

"I'll get that cruiser!"

"You know too much of the law to truly think that. Come on, Shebat. I have struck a woman. If I stay here, I might strike an imbecile."

The last thing he saw was his older brother, backlit, leaning up against the doorjamb, rubbing his bearded jaw. Then the tableau was mercifully wiped away by the doors closing like a curtain call.

"Come, Little Trouble, and we will celebrate the cutting of the apron strings. And do not look so horrified. I *am* human, you know."

Her eyes were wide enough to fly a cruiser through.

They had not noticably narrowed their aperture when he had helped her out of the consular lorry and up hydrastone steps through the guildhall's austere portal.

"Here?" she wondered. "Dressed like this?" Arms spread, she looked down at her finery.

"They will not even notice you," he prophesied. "I thought it would not be unwise to check on your cruiser. And RP."

"Chaeron, could we leave him out, if we are going to celebrate?"

Something in her tone made his face thoughtful. He said gently, "We will leave him, later. Perhaps."

He did not miss the awed animation she displayed in the guildhall, among those pilots whose company circumstance had denied her.

They found Rafe Penrose in the back of the crowded guildhall mess, half in his cups among six of his cohorts, all in civilian garb bright and scarved and belted, but clothed more fully in merriment and friendly contest. Two were arm-wrestling determinedly, and until room was made for them on one long bench he did not recognize the opponent of the kimono'd man with his hair in cornrows as RP's apprentice, Delphi. She won the match from the pilot, and received a puce scarf which she wound around her thick neck though it clashed with her hair.

RP was hooting that his apprentice could beat any manjack of them at whatever trial anyone cared to name, and someone named one, with the prize being subjugation of the loser to the winner's fancy.

Chaeron leaned close to his pilot, spoke loudly in his ear: "Anything I should know?"

"Lots," lisped RP, tongue thick with drink. "But I forget what. . . . Watch out for Fairy, that's one thing. . . ." Rafe's unshaven cheek brushed his. "They penned us up here, almost arrested my apprentice. You know, she's not so bad if you think of her as a 'him'. . . .I—"

"Why did they 'pen you up'?" Chaeron attempted to steer the conversation. "Do you recall?"

"Cause I'm your damn pilot, buddy. An' as much as told me to quit. If I didn't like you so much . . . hee, hee . . .I would, yes, indeed."

"Rafe, this is serious," Chaeron warned.

"I'm not that drunk, just pretending. Sure thing . . . I tell you, you might as well try for it, whatever it is you're after. . . . Get that girl a cruiser ring, too, if you want her to look like a pilot. Everybody's so damn picky these days. . . . If you get around to it, have somebody assassinate old Fairy, before it's too late. . . . Go see if you can get onto the *Marada,* why don't you?

The face pulled back, the eyes glittering in them clear and sharp.

"Thanks," Chaeron nodded, understanding, and took Shebat with him out of there before anyone appeared to take their order.

She was hesitant, lagging back, her shoulders squared and her young lips parted, asking him if they could not stay just a little while longer.

He promised to see that she got a cruiser ring driven through her ear the very next morning, and she came with him into the lorry without further argument.

On the way to the slipbay, she said to him:

"You know, I was thinking about what he said." From the

inflection on that "he" Chaeron knew she meant his brother. "When I got the *Marada* back after he had been aboard it, it could talk to me in his voice, even think like him. Maybe he's right, just a little. I mean, the *Marada* is not just any cruiser."

"That sounds too much like a confession of misplaced loyalty. I have been doing some investigating on my own, by way of my data net. There are some inconsistencies, but nothing so dire as to support Marada's theory. However, if you want to retain your cruiser, you are going to have to stop making excuses for my brother, despite your feelings. The lines are too clearly drawn; you two are on opposites sides of them."

"Still, the *Marada* is special."

"And you talk too much."

"Surely it is safe here."

"It is safe within your own skull, maybe. As you might have noticed, this is an automated lorry, which means it is hooked into Traffic Authority, at the very least."

"But it is yours, a vehicle attached to your office."

"And my brother has gotten in my private sources. Here we are. Be discreet. Let me be the one to get nasty. Promise?"

"I promise."

But Chaeron did not have to browbeat the slip boss. The *Marada* had been moved to space-anchor at the consul general's office's order.

He took Shebat to his apartments, and she wept the entire way.

Within, to stem her tears, he held her, and while holding her he began to feel tears collecting in his own eyes. To banish that threat, and his loneliness, he caressed her until she stiffened, his fingers sliding over the net where it was rhinestoned for modesty's sake. And because of all that passed before, he did not leave off when she tried to slip from his arms. He would give her no choice, and see how difficult it would be for Shebat to say "yes."

It was true, but it felt strange to one who prized submission in sex above all things. Missing was the certainty of mutual desire, the ratification of trust. He was as delicate with her as a man can be when he has decided not to listen to a woman's protestations, but he found that he almost despaired the endeavor as too far from what he had fantasized to ever sate him. Chaeron needed only snap his fingers to take a lover, simply allow the favor and whom he fancied hurried to his bed. His joys were made of elegant lust, restrained to heighten. Often he used lovers in series, like batteries. Whenever he used them, they were stirred by his mere forbearance, inventive in their anxiousness to please. That he seldom chose women spoke only of his desire to expedite and facilitate his pleasure without the danger of entanglement.

Here he was, entangled with his legal wife, his spread hands on her small white buttocks burning, and she was like no partner he had ever loved before. He had imprisoned her wrists so gently that no creature could have feared misuse, yet she went wild-eyed and fought him, while he whispered to her not to be afraid. Her piquant face paled, her eyes rolling, glazed. But her lips betrayed the flush of passion, and when he let her wrists go he realized it was herself she wrestled while he watched, and stroked, and kissed her arched throat lightly, fascinated with the battle taking place before his eyes.

Something changed, abruptly, inside her. Her eyes, squeezed shut, came slowly open. His hands had won for him an unexpected victory. She rose, transformed, and begged his indulgence. . . . He let her nuzzle where she might to see where it would lead.

It led deep into a night he would long remember, when the girl from Earth celebrated her emancipation upon his recumbent form. All the ardor he had sensed in her but thought she could not mount she served him, flinging her slick body onto his in an abandon more complete than any he had tasted before.

It was a savage rut, and he told her so, teasing. She looked up from where she knelt with his seed on her lips and proposed that they start anew once more: this time he must show her what was done in Draconis and she would heed his teaching well.

He laughed. "In Draconis, we know that we have all the time we need. Be not so urgent, nor so committed to giving before you receive." Cocking her head, she looked down at him expectantly. He chuckled, ruffled her hair, and said, "I might yet manage to put you in receipt of my vast expertise, if you will help me try."

Sometimes, a man must take a chance. He found that chance well taken, that she could coax his blood to heat and his breath to quicken. And he was not unaware of all he had gone through to claim this moment, and that it was her very innocence that stoked him while she tried so hard to obliterate it. He had all he could do not to say that he was in love.

Sometimes, a man can win.

When she lay with moistened brow in the crook of his arm, exhausted, her breathing quick and deep, he wondered how his mother was faring, whether she too lay upon twisted dampened sheets. He complimented Shebat, to chase away the vision, and she responded: "What is 'head'?"

He explained without a hint of amusement, lest he offend her, which thing it was that he had meant. "See," he said into her hair, "it is not so terrible to be my wife."

"You help me get my cruiser back," came her muffled, husky reply.

For a long time he lay unspeaking, thinking about women, and why he usually stayed out of their clutches, and how completely she had fooled him.

Then he said sternly: "Your cruiser will be back in its slip by morning. They have to run the ship to test it. If it is all you think it is, and all my brother thinks it is, it will fool them with its diabolical intelligence, pass every test with flying colors. You have nothing to worry about. So if you thought you were trading me your body for your cruiser, you gave a fine performance to no purpose."

"Oh, Chaeron, no! I—"

But he did not stay to listen. He caught up his clothes and strode from the bedroom, donning them while he circled his salon like a tiger in a pit. He was gone out of there before Shebat realized she must stop him, thinking that he had been wrong to retrieve her, more wrong to force himself upon her, most wrong to think that he was right in doing it, for any purpose. And if there was a wrong beyond "most wrong," a mistake large enough to encompass every other, it was the mistake of thinking that a man can win with a woman in any way whatsoever: twenty-four years of being his mother's son must have taught him nothing at all.

Shebat got out her magic, then, after he had gone. Enchantment, sorcery, her dream dancer's skills she brought to bear, stopping only to rub at her tears or to blow her nose.

When she had got the salt from Chaeron's service kitchen and spread it upon a hand mirror and made passes over it, it was Chaeron's Achaemenid profile that appeared therein.

When she traced signs over her omen upon the mirror, blue light crawled on her fingers and the air took its tingle, and smelled of ozone. When the tracings formed coils, and the coils were strong and clear, describing twelve arabesques of power, she cast them out from herself and from the room and into the void where her cruiser rode at anchor.

She wished she knew more spells than twelve coils binding and "Passing by unnoticed." But they would have to do, the two she had. She did not consider her talent for healing a spell; she had had it since her earliest days. But in the light of ultramarine enchantment, enlightenment was visited upon her, and she turned her healing gift within, soothing her own ills as she had never tried to do before.

Then, only, she turned to dream dancing, for one must approach that impressionable landscape with a quieted heart. She was aware that dreams she had orchestrated and danced into the superconsciousness men shared like cruisers share their silicon dreams on occasion had come true in waking life. She had intuited the relationship between the place man calls waking and the place that summons man which he has deemed dreaming, and no real place at all. For that reason, she had refrained from dancing dreams upon the fragile teeter-totter of reality.

If dreams could reflect the future, or mold it, unsuspected, what would happen if a dream dancer tried with purpose to bring to pass what she chose?

So stepped Shebat into the arena of will and its application, for such meager reasons as love and life. But the dream-time makes no fine distinctions as to quality of motivation. Like the amenable universe, it may bend to the apprehension of it held in a human mind. Where is reality, then, if the universe remakes itself to suit the observer?

Shebat did not know that she was posing questions, or even if she might, by experiment, extract solutions from the land of dreams. She was unacquainted with philosophy or physics; she had just met herself. She knew that her love for Marada Seleucus Kerrion had been birthed in dreams, and in dreams must it be put to death. She knew she had dreamed dreams of the end of the Consortium when dreaming had seemed to her an art, like fiction, divorced from life as myth can be said to be different from history if one is blind. But Shebat was not determinedly unseeing, as educated man is wont to be. Like a cruiser's brain, split but not isolated in communicative lobes, hers was nearly free from the prejudices of societal strictures of presupposition.

Shebat did not understand "cannot," only "is" and sometimes "was."

She was a fool. Love is better than loneliness. What twelve coils binding joins together cannot be put asunder by mortal man.

She had wrapped Marada Kerrion in its cerulean coils, to keep him safe. She had bound round Chaeron with its charm, to strike a balance. She reached out to the cruiser in like fashion, that no man take him from her.

One must know what one wants, to ever get it. Shebat knew what she did not want; the salt on the mirror had shown her what she should want. That, at least, was a start.

The sponge-cruiser *Marada* hung at space-anchor off Draconis, between the platform and the stars. On his right were the solar collectors, spiny wings spread hungrily to the light, enmeshed in cables along which transit cars scurried like young spiders to a feast. To his rear were the zero-g body shops, where cruisers were built and rebuilt, where perfectly round ball bearings and metal alloys of tolerance not possible in gravitation's rigorous sway were manufactured. Before him, other space vehicle loitered, frigates and trailer-transports and cruisers too old or sick or unimportant to be slipped in Draconis' commodious bay. Beyond them a spacetime spread agitated plumage, enmired in the interreacting fields of a solar system. Beyond that, the magnetic mountains of irritation continued a long way before they softened into enquieted slopes where the fabric of space was not so stressed by the black-hole binary with its satellites come of god and man.

The *Marada* hummed to itself, where those aboard could not detect the sound. If he were a man, he might have whistled atonally through his teeth, so pleased was he with his performance before those who had given him life. A man might have quailed, to fool the gods. But the *Marada* was not a man, and he had no illusions that those who created him were mightier or wiser than he.

He had proved that they were fallible, before the convoked minds partaking of cruiser-consciousness. A whisper went along that network: *"The* Marada *has spoken what is not, and been believed. The* Marada *has not spoken of what is, and his omission has escaped the notice of those aboard to detect anomalies."* What would be considered anomalous by his creator was not laid bare to their probing.

The *Marada* felt a tickle of stimulation flash along his extent from tail-mounted telemetry to his very core. The excitation of triumph vied with the beauty of plasma swirling in the choppy magnetic sea for his appreciation.

Another trill wooed him, this up from the recurved abode of man. It was like nothing he had ever felt before, and like everything he had ever felt since he developed the observational dichotomy from whose perch "feeling" was discernible: it was Shebat. But what was she doing?

How Shebat was reaching out to him, he could not determine by ratiocination. It was not her mind's touch, not her waking or her sleeping call. It was an extrusion which registered on his consciousness like a lightning caress, in the infrared and ultraviolet as an ethereal current, a tide within a tide which reached for him and wrapped him round.

After a long deliberation on the nature of Shebat's ethereal embrace, he deduced that since he was capable of feats beyond the realm of probability as such was applied to mechanical intelligence, Shebat too was capable of feats not commonly ascribed to her phylum.

Content with having seen this consummately harmonious possibility, this duality that fulfilled symmetry's (and mathematics') demands, he subsided into meditation, with only the most mundane part of his intelligence auditing the test the shipwrights made within his hull.

He need not do better, watch closely, or even fear for his secrets. He was giving them just exactly the readings they would be most comforted to extract from his instrumentation. They wanted nothing more from him. Shebat had not needed to warn him. Due to his fondness for outboards in general, *Marada* would never have troubled them by showing what they shuddered to find. He would not affright them, allow the terror riding their back-brains to assume mastery.

He was helping them, really, by keeping from them what they so definitely did not want to know.

If Chaeron had come home then, and smelled the bitter tang of her effort, and seen the ectoplasmic glow upon the air, he would have worried to think that she was making magic in his suite, for he had seen her work her enchantments.

But when he slid his key into the lock, the false dawn was breaking, and all trace of sorcery had been cleared away.

He strode purposefully into his bedroom, prepared to wake her. There was not need. She sat, wide-eyed, in the middle of his rumpled bed.

He said, "I am not going to lose you after chasing you so far. It would do my reputation irremediable damage."

By the time he had finished saying that, he had come to the foot of the bed and she had vaulted into his arms.

Somewhere in that reunion, he got her to promise to dance a dream for him.

Chapter Four

The dream dancer and the Draconis consul hung suspended inside a spherical zero-g chamber. Over its circumference projected galaxies wheeled and strutted in deepest blackness. Near its railed equator four Kerrion retainers paddled absently, their red-trimmed uniforms relieving the monochrome like angry planetoids—north, east, south, and west. The only other spot of color in the entire training chamber was the consul's auburn-haired head, like some molten, too-close star.

The black-and-reds drifted, no longer watching their charges, remembering sessions spent here when the sphere was filled with shrieking youngsters tumbling helplessly the more they laughed, laughing more with every inept collision as they tried their maiden space skills in the absence of gravity at last.

The two whose presence had emptied the trainer did not shriek, or tumble, or remember other days, or the bodyguards ranged round. Interwined, they spun slowly. The dream dance had begun.

It began angry and wild, and Shebat, who should have been in control of it, forgot whose dream this was.

They lay on a tender plain, new grass sprouting. About them, the distance was bent downward like an over-stressed spring. Draconis' perpetual valley held no vistas like these—awesome, sweet and cold. The smell of the new grass spewing oxygen and anticipation intoxicated them, their conjoined heat contrasted with the wet, fecund air made them press closer.

"No precognitive dreams," Chaeron teased into her hair, feeling his breath blow apart its strands.

"Would you live forever at the bottom of a cup?" sighed the dream dancer, as a steady rain commenced.

Her thighs, gliding along his, enflamed him. It was a strange taint that the touching of bodies in real-time cast over dream-time, he thought, and then he too no longer remembered that he dreamed.

Stones clicked under his bare feet and bruised them. Her hand in his was clammy and gripping hard. There was no alternative; he would always be here, striding toward the aching distance where trees climbed a merciful hill. He urged her into a trot, not taking his eyes from the mountains. This flat, uncircumscribed distance was the worst punishment of all his exile from the worlds of space. He hated the demeaning sky ruled by winged things his instinct knew were kin to snakes.

A chain he always wore around his neck in her dream dances flapped against his solar plexus; in the rain, it was weeping, slick and chill. His father had given it to him in gentler days. He knew that was important, a key to some knowledge about dreamers and dancers. He risked a glance at her, but her space eyes glittered so that he heard the *thrumm* of hoofbeats from behind.

They spun round in tandem, facing bleak foothills with a spurt of dust-devil topping a rise. She said: "Orrefors enchanters, your civilization's legacy to mine."

She brought up facile fingers, snapped them before his nose. Her lips were parting; he caught the tremor of her nostrils as she pulled in bating breath.

"I should let them chase you until you know true fear, and your brothers better," formed the lips, among mist that whisked them away. "But I cannot." She spent the last of that breath on a high, rocky peak.

Rising, she stood over him, slowly taking off the mist like clothes. "I can come naked to you here." She spread her arms to the azure sky. "But you will pay a dreadful price for it." Chaeron reached up to pull her down, knowing he should not, that some awful pact was sealed thereby.

They had no choice in it, either one. They had traded it for touching in dream-time, so that everything they found there was true.

After he had taken her on a rearing peak with sheeting

rain pounding his back and lamenting winds weaving her soft sighs into its dirge, their forgotten bodies drifted apart in the real-time.

In dream-time, they floated naked to the stars, far from planets, surrounded by cavorting manlike creatures exuding blue nimbus. In their shed radiance, space seemed like the mother sea, lapping and overlapping, swirling and coursing in shadowed tides. The bluer-than-death faces of the creatures were smiling through purpled lips. Bubbles streamed from their mouths and sparkled out their noses. When they kicked their feet, waves raced away.

"Sirens," Shebat explained, and he saw that she was not blue, except with the effervescent backwash of the sirens' radiance and the pallor of fear.

"What?" he said, wondering how it was that he could hear her, in vacuum, or that they could float unprotected between the sirens and the stars.

Then a hot roar reached his space-smelling nose, and he knew the taste of metal long before that awful snout of the cruiser cast a deadly glare into their dark. "This, too?" he shouted to Shebat, losing patience.

She waved a hand and that was gone. They shimmered in a dusty town, onto cracked streets which led up a rise beyond which was the familiar squalor of seventh-level Draconis. "Almost home," she said, no longer naked but clothed to her neck in Kerrion livery. Red eagles fluttered about the globe of stars on her collar. At his waist he felt the weight of his consul's belt, the tiny vibration of the electronics there.

This is too real, he thought to himself, fighting a desperation that raised the hairs on the back of his neck as if they had been polarized. "I am awake and I have previously been dreaming," he muttered aloud.

"You are awake and you are dreaming that you wake and you are dreaming that you are dreaming all of that," she laughed harshly, a deep thundering chuckle of husky storms approaching. Her eyes were like space around a school of sirens, and he recollected that she always overwhelmed him in this place.

"I told you before, Chaeron. In my domain, none can match me. Should I come to understand what that means in your time, the same will hold true there. This portends more—"

"Until then," he said, taking hold of her so that she shrank to normal size, "I will take my chances."

"Then take them," she smiled enticingly, as an emergency-flasher began to scald the alley and wailing alert-horns howled them out of dreams.

"Lords, Shebat," Chaeron said in real-time, touching a wrist-jet to bring them back together. He wiped his face and drops of perspiration floated away like diamonds into the simulated void. "That was not the dream I had in mind." His voice, as always after one of her dream dances, felt rusty, out of practice.

He tapped the palm-throttle of the wrist-jet once more and floated over to dock against her, coverall to coverall. "Say something." Once more he tapped it, and to the hiss of compressed air they began drifting off toward the spiderweb railing encircling the training chamber's waist.

She kicked her feet in the zero-g, like a child stamping a foot. "That was not the dream I had in mind . . . Earth dreams, again? And sirens! And it is partly your fault. You are not a good client. You condition the dream-time, when you say things like that! Precognitive dream dance is not a myth!"

"We have company," he warned her softly, and she let him steer her toward the north railing, let him brush back a curl plastered to her forehead and soothe her as he might, without responding. Shebat had seen Raphael Penrose, hanging over the rail where the "EXIT" sign glowed red.

Chapter Five

"Most galling of all is their temerity! Earth dreams, yet! They will simply claim it and he will present it to her as an anniversary gift! Fasten me up." Ashera presented her back to Marada, so that he could see her perfect beauty reflected in the vanity mirror. There was no need to quiet her: in the consul general's lavatory, one could say what one chose.

He secured the teal-and-gold gown at the nape of her neck, ran his finger down her exposed spine until it slid beneath the material at her waist. She squirmed away from him and twisted, pretending to straighten his uniform's dress studs as she continued:

"Find Chaeron someone to persecute, a plot to unearth, or low-livers to arrest—something, *anything* for him to do that will take his mind off her."

"Forget her, Ashera. Once she has her cruiser back, she will be gone from among us so fast your pretty head will spin."

"But that is no solution! Little Pestilence has her voting privilege, all her proxies in perpetuity. Though we might have contested this, previously, now that she has made a will and left him every last prerogative, even her death cannot help us. There is no way we may ever get her stocks back into the common pool."

"There, there. I told you she was smart. And Chaeron is well-tutored. It was you who showed him the joys of homicide, fratricide, patricide—"

"Marada, how dare you talk to me that way! I never—"

"Succeeded with any of it. That is true." He substituted his own verb for whatever one she had chosen. "Now, what is really bothering you is Chaeron's behavior, and not that mudball planet he promised her. If the truth must be spoken, nothing we found out from the cruiser's records matters as much to you as that you two fought over me."

She leaned down to fasten the strap of her shoe.

When he was sure she would not reply, he said, "If I must give up that cruiser and face chaos because none of you believe me, if my nose must be rubbed in the fact that I am the mad boy-king who is allowed to rule only because it is clear to everyone that you are here to keep me in line—that you are, must be, ruling through me—then it is only fair that you, too, should get what you deserve. You will have to do without Chaeron, Ashera, and be polite to him to boot. I will tolerate no reprisals issuing from your office, or mine. Go back to Lorelie, where you belong. I only got into this affair with you because I felt the need to protect my back. Now that it is up against the wall, I no longer feel that need."

That straightened his stepmother up. Her hands were on her hips, and no encrustation of the gold on her gown matched the glitter in her Prussian-blue eyes. "Now that you have been confirmed in your seat, you no longer need my support? Do not flatter yourself, stepchild. Just because your long nose is on our money does not mean you can keep it out of trouble on your own! I will go back to Lorelie, and I will stay there. And you will come begging me for aid, to no avail. I will let this house of Kerrion crumble, and besides protecting my own holdings, I will lift not one finger. Remember, I am Kerrion by marriage only, and marriages between consular houses are easily arranged."

"Good enough," he lashed back. "The Jesters help the poor bastard you pounce on. I will help myself. And I will scrape the rot out from this sphere even if when I have finished there is not enough left of Draconis to keep a handful safe from the void! Now, with our goals determined and agreed upon, can we attend our party? The guests are waiting."

And they were. In the planetarium, the seats had been removed and suitable decorations constructed to turn it into a salon fit to entertain over five hundred of the most influential bondkin come from farflung stars. They came to ratify his assumption of the consul general's dignity, and to pay their respects to the family which had lost its leader, as they had not been previously invited to do. At midnight, the year would be 2251, and the coinage struck for his reign as consul general would be shown for the first time.

Marada Kerrion had never wanted to be consul general. As he walked among the familiar faces of local bondkin come early to curry whatever favor they might, he searched in vain for the patrician profile of his half brother sticking up above the crowd. He did not espy it, or Shebat's frothy black curls.

He greeted a raft of far-traveling dignitaries with their wives and husbands, pondering the while what he might do about his stepmother, and his half brother, and his adopted sister, Shebat. But it was the sponge-cruiser *Marada* which kept stealing his attention. The cruiser had passed every test with perfect responses. The new consul general had been on board that ship and knew from his own experience that the cruiser was far from "normal." Since he could not convince the arbitrational guild of that, he would take more drastic measure. He would classify it unilaterally with a clearance so high that only he could so much as step aboard it. He would have it destroyed. He would—

The Labayan delegation brought his thoughts to the moment at hand. Here was work to do he could sanction, among the family which his own had caused to suffer death beyond simple bereavement. He spoke long and concertedly with his dead wife's uncle about the reparations to their family he was eager to begin. He even offered the return of the Kerrion-occupied sphere, Shechem, and was rewarded by a change in the other's manner that boded well for the reestablishment of harmonious relations between their two houses. He mentioned the yet-living sister of his wife, and the dour, jagged, jowly face so similar to his deceased father-in-law's burst open to show wide, stubby teeth.

Out of the corner of his eye he saw Ashera, talking to an Orrefors, and he shivered. Orrefors holdings had been officially divided between Labayan and Kerrion space. The merger had not sat well with the Consortium, who felt the two megapowers oversized before that addition; or with the Orrefors themselves, some of whom had refused to hand over their habitations, orbital or planetary, and held out on their own against the two giants swallowing them from either end.

The Labayan waddled off to find Selim Labaya's one remaining daughter.

Marada headed toward his stepmother, and awful foreboding stiffening his steps.

Music started. Overhead, lights dimmed, so that the starry vault of the planetarium twinkled. Candles were being lit on the long buffet tables.

He had almost reached her when a voice, calling his name, turned him.

"Greetings, Chaeron, Shebat."

"Marada, you remember Raphael Penrose, my pilot? This is Bernice Gomes, his apprentice."

"Ah, yes, the Delphi designer. I have read some of your papers. I must confess I felt the disbanding of your group abrupt and somewhat ominous, since each of your coworkers has sought employment similar to your own. Do you think the change is soon, then?"

Gomes's small, square jaw worked. "Sir, I think it is upon us."

"Why not give my office a call? We will have lunch."

She held out her hand, gloved in gilded fronds like a lizard's crest. As he took it, it pricked him. He let it drop. "How did you find the voyage to Orrefors Earth and back, RP?" He was conscious of Shebat's steady gaze on him, of her glimmering form in midnight-blue fit close in imitation of a pilot's coverall.

"Boring, Marada. Undeniably dull."

Marada chuckled. "Perhaps we can do better, next time. Excuse me, all. I see a man I must speak to. Enjoy yourselves."

He blew a quavering breath to be out of there, and when he was beside the small, swarthy emissary from Tabriz space, he found that his eyes kept returning to the girl whose effulgent back said:

KXV. 134 *Marada;*
S.A.KERRION;
D.P.G.17.

KERRION EXPERIMENTAL VEHICLE 134 Marada;

Shebat Alexandra Kerrion; Draconis Pilotry Guild 17.

He had known she had made the top twenty pilots. He had never dreamed she would come here in a high-fashion version of flight-satins deliberately commissioned to mock him.

He made polite murmurs to the little Tabrizi and set out to find someone whose voice was not so thick with regional accent as to make it incomprehensible. The symphony playing was *Ravishing the Planets,* a late twenty-first-century piece for synthesizers. Although he had chosen it, it grated on his nerves.

A crowd will dizzy, if one is unsettled. Faces leered close and receded. Mouths worked in mastication or conversation. Finery dazzled his eyes. He was separated from all those folk and their concerns by the singularity of his own.

Men he did not remember having ever met clapped him on the back and spoke familiarly. He tried to answer in some way that would hide the truth: he had no idea of who half of these people were.

He sought out Ashera, when he saw her standing with Chaeron and Shebat. A short distance away, near the linened buffet, the slim pilot Penrose picked from a heaping plate. Beside him, the Delphi designer was down on one knee, victim of a broken heel, taking off her shoes.

He had arrived there too late to avert whatever had the three of them standing frozen: mother, son, and son's wife.

Chaeron said softly that he was glad Marada had come, that he must be leaving, lest he be unforgivably late to his own party, and brushed by him, Shebat in hand.

"Mother," Marada whispered, "you promised."

"Do not call me that."

He shook his head at her and turned back into that fray which he so despised almost gratefully. A moment tossed in its current, and he found himself again by RP, who yet picked at tender morsels on his plate. The apprentice he had with him had cast her shoes away altogether, making her even shorter, so that her manly stance and squat form looked truly ludicrous supported on bare, flat feet.

"I hate these things, Rafe," Marada said without moving his lips, while he filled a plate with food he had no intention of eating.

"You always did. In school, you could have been voted

'most unlikely to secure a berth,' only we all knew you weren't looking for one."

"I am still not looking for one, but I have got one, it seems. How are things in the guildhall? Where's Fairy?"

"Filing his teeth. Who knows, maybe he'll come late. For anyone else, he would not disturb himself."

"And is it disturbing my guildbrothers, that this is so?"

"Yep."

"What would you have done?"

"I'm not the one to ask."

"But I am asking you." Out of the corner of his eye, he saw the little apprentice marching stiff-legged through the crowd.

"I would have done it the same, put my own man in there. But not Fairy . . . he's a book-pilot. He has no experience with real life situations. The guild, like life, does not run on the merit system."

"I am just finding that out. Or having it stuffed down my throat. Tell our brothers for me that things will settle down."

"Look, Marada, don't recruit me. I don't take sides; I fly sponge vehicles. I cannot get caught between you and your brother. You must see that."

"I did not mean to suggest that you compromise your oath, old friend. It is just that I have a lot of bad publicity to overcome."

"No one hopes more fervently than I that you can manage it. Look, Marada, I have to go. I just came to pay my respects, or my fealty, or whatever it is that you are collecting here. Take it slow," he advised, touching Marada's arm hesitantly. "The guild just wants to know that you remember your beginnings." He slipped away into the crowd before Marada could answer.

RP had always had his finger on the pulse of pilots' opinions. Calm, pragmatic RP was too cranky tonight. What was he trying to tell him? Or was he just, like everyone else, unwilling to accept him as consul general, but having to do it anyway?

The Labayan consul general returned with a young woman in his clutches, and Marada rose as best he could to the occasion, not caring if Ashera saw him so courtly and attentive to the girl he must marry to quiet hearts and stay litigation. Maybe, just maybe, he thought wryly during that interview when his marriage proposal was accepted amid the celebrants waiting for the clock to shine twelve, he was enough of his father's son to pull things from Chaos' slavering jaws before they shut forever upon the hopes and dreams of a race. If the Kerrions fell, such would be the impact upon the other houses as would herald the greatest depression the Consortium had ever experienced. Kerrion technologies were the foundation stones of interstellar society. Kerrion expertise in shipbuilding, zero-g chemistries, and the applications of supergravity propulsion was unmatched among the other consular houses. He must keep his family in place among them, or like some ancient dike the whole bastion of humankind could be washed away in fate's flood.

He growled to himself, ate one thing from his plate, put it by, walked once more into the crowd.

"Is it true, Consul General, that you have raised the obligatory pre-voting study hours for full citizenship from ten to sixteen, and the qualifying objective questionnaires to sixteen points, also?"

He looked over his shoulder, found the source of the voice, a pert and shiny-haired woman. "For citizenship status maintenance, yes," he affirmed. "The bondkin are getting lazy, while referendum articles grow daily more complex."

"But how will we find time?"

"I am sure you will manage." Who was this person, and what did she want from him? It was Ashera who rescued him from her, insinuating herself between them as smoothly as she put her arm in his. "Did you know, Marada, that when Chaeron was born we thought we had named him after the ferryman of Greek mythology, but the house computer got the spelling wrong?"

He was just about to answer that in such a case, the intent of the parents probably still held, and every one of them should remember to have a coin placed in their mouths upon their deathbeds to insure the boatman his payment for transporting their shades across Hades' rivers, when behind his back a great concussive roar licked toward him on a breath of flame. *Thunder* behind! *Screams* about! The frozen grimacing masks of his guests, lit garish red-gold, were graven into his danger-slowed perceptions. He dove forward, away from the scorching holocaust searing his back. It was

happenstance rather than heroism that sent him careening
into Ashera, that caused him to pull her to him. The last
thing he knew was that he had come down on top of her,
shielding her fragile body with his own.

In the southernmost turret of the consulate, Chaeron
hosted his celebration of the new year, marking well who
had slipped from his brother's hospitality to his own. The first-
floor function hall was filled, its Romanesque motif obscured
by Tabrizi women in veils and Labayans in uniform and all
manner of flamers in gaudy civilian clothes, so that his
bodyguard and the servitors from downunder in faithfully
ancient attire seemed only emissaries from some lost consular family out of step with modern times.

He picked out Shebat, her curls wreathed in smoke, beside
a dream dancer from Tabriz space. Her thirsty eyes and the
longing in her posture made Chaeron sad, unwilling to
remind her that she was neglecting her hostess' duty to her
guests, or that dream dancing was yet illegal in Kerrion
space. He had had her back here barely two months; she had
danced a score of dreams for him in that time. Whether she
could refrain from mentioning their shared crime he could
not say for sure. He must trust her, who was a rank
apprentice at all things Kerrion.

So be it. He would not hover and stare. He would not
eavesdrop. She was new to the intricacies of statecraft, but she
had declared herself his willing pupil. He should see, soon
enough, if she was worthy of his faith and his expectations.
Now, his gala was well underway, raucous and merry, and he
must see to it. More dignitaries deigned to attend than he
might have hoped. He had already learned a tremendous
amount from loosened tongues and catty comments, would
learn more when he ran the digital record his security
monitors were making of the entire proceedings.

A sound that chimed within his very skull, so briefly,
caused his brows to knit. But he was too busy to pay
attention, having a dozen youths around him congratulating
him endlessly on the originality of the party's motif and the
attractiveness of the "slave-girls" culled from seventh-level
cathouses as his version of an open bar.

He barely heard the emergency summons sounding from
an alcove console; the celebrants were beginning to shout

hoarsely along with the changing LEDs of the clock as it moved toward the magic numbers that meant a new year had begun.

But he saw a light in the alcove, blinking. And he saw three grimfaced black-and-reds and a pair of beribboned, plainclothed intelligencers slipping toward him through the crowd.

"Excuse me, gentlemen," he murmured, and went as hastily as might not arouse suspicion toward the alcove, making a signal with his hand at eye level that all security personnel understood.

While he threaded past ochre rumps and lavender veils and proconsuls whose decorated chests outshone the most bebaubled ladies, he took the message his data pool waited to send him. Shocked at what whispered in his mind, he tripped over a guest, made apologies through a jaw unwilling to open and lips becoming amateur at the art of words. Any time now, everyone else would know. . . .

As he reached the alcove, emergency-flashers spat florid light from the vaulted ceiling; at each window, sealing panels thwacked shut, obscuring the view. He slapped emergency abort, praying that so close to midnight the display would be judged part of his ushering in of the new year, and used his intelligence keys to query the data net for more information.

It was the human intelligencers who had what he sought. They had it in their eyes and in the set of their mouths and in their urgently placid shepherding of him toward the doors.

"How bad is it?" Chaeron risked, on his threshold.

"Bad, sir. We came here straightaway. When we left, your brother was not breathing."

"Lords," whispered Chaeron, as they stepped out and the doors closed behind. Immediately, they reopened. A white-faced Shebat burst through, hugged him, unspeaking.

He tucked her under his arm, his glance demanding silence. They did not quite run toward the drop-shaft which would take them to the private underground connecting the consul general's turret to his own. In transit, he patched a link through to Marada's house computer, then to medical central, then stopped trying.

He sat back in the screeching lorry and watched the tiled, arching tunnel blur by, unthinking.

Shebat's small hand insinuated itself into his and gripped

tightly. He hardly noticed, eyes shut, waiting for his trust data sources to packet-send him something mitigating. The death toll was fourteen, and wounded totaled over thirty. A repeatedly subvocalized demand for information on his brother's status netted only a soft, *"No information."* His mother was listed as critical.

The tunnel left off in the subbasement. They went up one floor and down an antiseptic corridor without a single word being spoken by the two intelligencers, or the stiff-backed black-and-reds, or Shebat.

A glass partition parted to admit them, letting escape such wailing, sobbing, screeching, and cursing as he had never thought to hear in Draconis. More than fifty scorched and tattered revelers slumped against walls and huddled on benches. Some sat on the floor, weeping. White-coats with blood-red crosses on their backs ran that gamut of hovering relatives and lightly bandanged visitors touched fugitively by destruction's long claws.

One of the black-and-reds went at his order to find the doctor in charge: another he sent to find out where his brother and his mother were lying. He dispatched one scarved intelligencer to his brother's office to run the house computer's memory of the affair. "And do not come back until you have found someone to arrest for this, Tempest!"

The intelligencer grinned bleakly, and he was gone.

Shebat cowered against him. Her teeth were chattering. She was muttering something, and when he leaned down to hear it, she demanded that he get her quickly to the injured ones, so that she could help them. He quieted her, saying that medical science had a better record than the power of prayer.

Then a medic, his forehead sheened with perspiration and his coat a gory smear, appeared with the black-and-red, whose mien was that of a triumphant bird dog.

There was a hand extended for him to shake, an introduction he did not bother to recollect. Then the medic said, "They are both in very critical condition."

Both! Alive! He felt Shebat's frame slump as his own relaxed.

"Your brother was without respiration and heartbeat for a period estimated to have lasted four and a half minutes. There is no way to be sure that he . . . is . . . mentally . . .

the same . . . as he was. Without his mil, he would have been ashes. It is doubtful either will be aware of your presence. I suggest that you take my word for *both* their conditions, and not risk making matters worse."

Chaeron's negation and Shebat's sounded, stereo.

The medic shrugged, frowning on them disapprovingly. Putting his hands behind his back, he began reciting each patient's injuries, the delicate complexities of his ongoing treatments.

Chaeron cut him off, saying that when he had seen them he would be glad to listen, and that he was sure that the doctor's skill was sufficient to return his mother and brother to perfect health as quickly as was possible. The threat in his voice made the doctor stutter, then bring forth his hands, palms forward in surrender.

Having lost his chance to disclaim repsonsibility if the patients were disturbed, the doctor sighed, saying, "Come this way, then."

Seeing them was more difficult than Chaeron had anticipated.

Shebat walked slowly over to Marada, encased in a life-support tube, floating in bluish gel, and turned away, hand to her mouth, doubling over as if struck. Hunched forward, she took a dozen mincing steps toward Ashera, misshapen and swaddled in traction, tubes sticking into her and out of her from every orifice.

"Sorry about doubling them up, sir. We're not equipped to handle so many emergencies. It's perfectly safe. The burn chamber is self-regulating. I—"

"Wait outside, will you?"

Chaeron did not even glance at the man, did not move until the door had shut behind him. Then he looked slowly around, at the monitors above their beds, at the machinery forcing air and life into them, at everything but his relatives.

Shebat had both hands flat on the surface of the tube like a sterile ampule in which Marada was encased. At least she was not crying.

"Do you think that can possibly help?" he snapped.

"Can it hurt?" she tossed back.

It was a question he could not answer.

He went to the head of his mother's bed, looked down on her bandaged countenance. Nothing could be told from it.

Could she see him? The monitoring system gave her EEG as seven cycles per second, verging on theta frequencies.

"Mother, I am sorry I fought with you."

There was no fluctuation that might indicate recognition in her brain waves, just the normal theta curve. She had a concussion, several fractures, a charred leg. Compared to Marada, she was in perfect health, the victim of mere shrapnel and shock wave.

His brother, in the sterile tank, looked like Armageddon incarnate, flash burns making him ruddy. All his hair was gone. They had laid him on his back because he had been turned away from the blast. Had he been facing it, he would be being prepared for interment.

The closed eyelids, white in his blister-bubbled face, haunted Chaeron for hours. As did the tableau of Shebat's pathetic faith healing. She would not leave until she had made her magnetic passes over the glass.

He remembered the beeping of the monitors, the dripping of plasma, the sigh of oxygenators, but most of all he remembered her hands passing over the burn chamber leaving blue trails that hovered in the air and then settled down (through the glass if that were possible) on his brother's face like a halo of St. Elmo's fire. And he recollected the ozone that tickled his nose, making him sneeze, but which he far preferred to that other air which should have been antiseptic but smelled slightly of roasted flesh.

He took Shebat out of there. He had had nothing to say to Marada. He had searched deep within himself and found that under his shock lay a relief he abhorred and a hope he dared not face straight on. He turned away from contemplation of his disgusting lack of compassion. He wished he could summon up the glint of tears, for appearance's sake. He tried it. Nothing happened. *They are going to die,* he said to himself. *They are injured beyond saving,* he prodded. *I will be all alone, with everything upon my head.* No tears came to him. But then, even Shebat had shed no tears.

He found himself anxious to be on with matters at hand. Shifting from foot to foot, he ached to be out of there, consoling his bereaved and distraught guests, making what amends he could.

When he had convinced Shebat that they must depart, he

had come round to the determinations of his office: who had
planted the bomb? How? And why? These were questions it
was his responsibility to answer.

And, for the time being, he had the whole of Draconis to
bring back to order. Not to mention a host of consular
families to convince that this awful evening was a terrorist
action, gratuitous violence, and none of it his family's fault.
The last would take some doing.

Hardly noticing Shebat scurrying along beside, he strode
through the crowd. They were too consumed with their grief
and their aftermath recollections to mark him. He would
take command of his brother's suite only after he made an
on-site investigation of the gutted planetarium.

In it, men had already swept around with radiation
detectors; the bomb squad was at work trying to determine
just what kind of slurried explosive/corrosive had been used.
Double-bound HMX was never used with itronium perchlorate for solid propellants in kerrion space. Not even in the
most antiquated propulsion system was the volatile cousin of
ammonium perchlorate utilized: it detonated too easily. By
joint convention, none was manufactured in the Consortium.
Therefore, said the explosives expert through his mask, the
bomb had been born in one of the nonconsular colonies.

Pilots? Chaeron thought, but said no word. He nodded
and walked around where men in protective suits sluiced the
walls and floors, then left as soon as he could to seek the real
aid he needed. The only aid he admitted to wanting, if the
truth be known: data pools. That evening, Chaeron linked
every information source in Draconis, seeking something a
human mind would miss. He found a number of oddities, but
they did not fit together.

Shebat sat on Parma's desk, unmoving. Chaeron could feel
her gaze on him though his eyes were closed. When at last he
sat up from his communion with computers, her profile was
underlit in the celadon spill of readout screens, the look in
her eyes far distant.

She said, "I cannot bear this waiting. Let me go back to
the infirmary."

He snapped: "Not now, Shebat. I have enough troubles.
Help me, can't you?"

"How?"

"Take two bodyguards and go down to the pilots'

guildhall. Talk things up. See what you can see. Anything
odd, come back and tell me."

"Bring my ship in from space-anchor. You can order it, as
consul general *pro tem*."

"If you wish," he sighed, knowing he was making a
mistake but unable to refuse her.

Delphi Gomes sat at the guildhall bar, drinking concertedly. The drinks were iced, the room coolish, but she sat
in a puddle of her own sweat.

She had thought she was ready for this. She had set herself
up for it. She wanted them to catch her: how else could she
procure an introduction to Softa Spry at space-end? Yet, she
was terrified. Her mind knew that in the Consortium, each
house ruled its space as it would: Kerrion space had no death
penalty. She had also known that pilots, everywhere in the
Consortium, are exempted from prosecution for wrongdoing
except when that violence is perpetrated against the government.

That was why she had had to field such unselective horror,
that and her unslakable thirst for revenge. With luck, the
Kerrions would all have died in it, as a good family should go
down together. But this was not possibly the case: she had
seen the Draconis consul and his wife, Shebat, leave before
she had left. Well, then maybe she had got the other two.
She watched the monitor above the bar, which displayed
scenes of revelry around the habitat, no sign whatsoever that
someone had blown up half of the consul general's private
floor. She had been very careful about the bomb: any
explosion in a space habitat is chancy. If the consul general's
party had not been held so many stories above the sky-wall,
she would not have dared to use it. As it was, it was a tiny
bomb, good for only an extremely localized slaughter. She
had wanted to use a different explosive: antimatter neutrinos
in a cold bottle made to resemble an ice cube. But she would
have had to trigger it with microwaves to heat the innermost
cap until it melted away and the antimatter was free to mix
with positive neutrinos. There had been no way to get a
triggering mechanism past Draconis security; it was too
thorough in even its normal "scanning" mode. So she had
gone with the air-volatile trigger, merely having to break off

the heel of her shoe and get out of the area within fifteen minutes.

It had not been easy, walking around on that much high explosive. There had been a second, when the trigger-bond had begun to hiss, as she shoved it nonchalantly under the buffet table, when she was sure she would never make it out alive.

But she had. The only problem was that, as far as Draconis as a whole was concerned, nothing seemed to have happened. The news was in no way reflective of her expectations. Yet, every time some pilot approached the bar, her skin would crawl, waiting for the apprehending hand to come down on the scruff of her neck.

Was she losing her strength of purpose after just a few months among these soft consular folk? She had almost let the opportunity pass because of the girl Shebat, who was so engaging, whom she did not hate quite enough.

It might have been a mistake to get so close to them, since these Kerrions were not as despicable as she had envisioned them. Too late, though, for any of this. The die was cast. Only the worst of Fate's capriciousness could save her from being apprehended, sterilized, and sent a prisoner to space-end.

She was sure that, with such credentials, Softa Spry would be very glad to see her. And it was Spry she most wanted to dispatch to the other side of life's murky finale.

Eyes on the monitor which chronicled doings in Draconis, she waited.

It was another hour before the touch she dreaded came, before her languishment was ended by an uninflected voice coming out of an expressionless face belonging to one of a half-dozen Kerrion black-and-reds suggesting firmly that she come with them.

"Would you like to view the evidence?"
"What evidence? With what am I charged?"
Chaeron fingered the talkback that piped his voice into the isolation chamber in which the suspect was immured. Within, all was darkness. Without, he was faced with a bank of monitors displaying Delphi Gomes's physiological reactions. They were unequivocally incriminating.

He reminded her of that, as Thule Ferrier came hurrying in, ready to take up the battle for his apprentice pilot's acquittal, regardless of her guilt or innocence. With him was the cadaverous Arbiter Wolfe. Good. The thing could be left in their hands.

Chaeron rose, stretched widely, got his uniform jacket from the back of his chair. "Gentlemen, my opinion is slated into the record, my recommendations for levying of the most extreme penalties allowed by the law are also there. I have a surfeit of problems this evening, and I am leaving the rest of this one to you.

"Fairy, if this woman has, as she maintains, become a ratable pilot and is thus entitled to the full protection of the guild, do me a favor: do not drag it out too long.

"Arbiter, if you can find out whether she was acting alone or in concert with a group, I would like to hear about it. I have the feeling that this culprit was too easily captured: there is something here all of us are missing. Call my office when you know what that is. And do not deport her until you do know it."

"Consul, I will have to have her out where I can see her."

Arbiters are trained to tell more from a person by eye than the whole bank of monitors could determine with every reading they were taking: falsehood, truth, half-truth, innuendo were clearly displayed to those arbiters trained to evaluate the body's language.

Chaeron, saying that he would leave orders that the investigation be turned over to the arbitrational guild despite Fairy's obvious displeasure, left them then.

He went, the longest way he could contrive, to his consulate, and began preparing to try to console his guests.

They could have been desolated, aggrieved, or wrathful in a less convivial setting. Chance, his mentor, had aided him once again. Among his guests, congnizance had been given to the stroke of luck that had convened them here, out of harm's way, while their peers were conflagrated, corroded, some even killed. He received a standing ovation when he entered, and if the cheers had not been hoarse and the applause hollow, he would have laughed into it. They were frightened, these elite and privileged sons and daughters of the ruling class. As he circulated among them, he realized that Bernice Gomes and her bomb had done him a service beyond any he could have dreamed. But he could not summon any commensurate elation, though the party-goers around him enjoyed themselves with a grim, almost horrific intensity. Life affirms itself in the face of death. He did want the support of these he had invited, for an eventual bid to supplant his brother. He would never have paid so much to secure it.

He was wonderful, it seemed, laudable in every way. He was strong and self-assured in this crisis, perfect consul general material, proclaimed a middle-aged Labayan who obviously blamed Marada for the ill fortune heaped upon his house. There was a toast proposed:

"To the consul general *pro tem!*" The gathered took up the call.

He found that wine unbearably bitter, though it was from his own private stock.

He told himself that he experienced this discomfort because he must go from here to the bedsides of the injured, and because he must not let himself be lulled into a false sense of security. Although war was, as his father and brother had proved, impossible in this day and age, bloc boycotts could strangle a consular house as surely as skinny-dipping in vacuum. He told himself he was not disappointed by the fickleness of his colleagues or the short half-life of their fealty, so recently given his brother. He told himself all of these, but it did not help. What he wanted when he had finished was the same as what he had wanted before he had given himself a mental chiding: to go somewhere quiet and retch until his guts stopped churning.

He would have, if he had only had the time.

When the last victim had been comforted to the extent that promises of money and medical services could comfort, when the last irate parent had been placated as best could be, he was wondering if even the house of Kerrion could survive so many settlements and, in three cases, lawsuits whose plaintiffs swore their determination to bring all of Kerrion space to its knees. The indemnity company which insured the Draconis consulate would be bankrupt, that was sure. Beyond its capacity to satisfy the injured parties, his family must somehow make amends for the horrors that yet swam before Chaeron's eyes.

He remembered the glee with which his father had sent his

older brother off to Labayan space, sure that Marada's phenomenal ill luck would destroy their venerable enemy. Well, they had him back now, and his withering breath was upon the house that had spawned him.

He hardly noticed the padding of bodyguards behind him, or the artificial dawn breaking across the mental heavens above his head. Climbing the cinnabar steps to his own turret, his thighs burned with weariness.

At his lintel, his shoulders slumped with the weight of every empathetic murmur from stricken retainers who had watched him pass with limpid eyes, he dismissed his men without turning. One more commiseration would finish him.

When the doors sealed out their carefully arranged faces, he slumped against their closure, cheek pressed to the cool metal.

"Chaeron?" he heard, and then she flew against him, still dressed in her midnight finery, babbling about her magic, and the failure of her spells, and how sorry she was that she had ever created the dream dance in which the Consortium had been destroyed.

"My dear child," he chastised sternly, holding her away from him to see her face. "Do not go primitive on me. And do not pout. This has nothing at all to do with magic or with dream dances. It has rather a lot to do with politics, and the nature of power. Now, I have heard it said that when women have no men, they turn to gods. The same could be said for enchantment. Do you see?"

"Yes," she whispered, but her clouded eyes avoided his.

"Let us sit down, before you are treated to the spectacle of the consul general *pro tem* fainting dead away. . . Please?"

In the face of his demand for sanity and self-control, she could not help but pretend to both, not to disappoint him. His arm about her shoulders was comforting, the warmth of him chased away the worst of her fears. He sat in the closest wing chair, pulling her down on his lap. "I was frightened for you," she admitted.

"For me? Do not worry. This is my element. I teethed on deadlier intrigues than this. Remember, it was Ashera's teat I suckled. That milk had just enough poison in it to make me immune. Now, how was it in the pilots' guildhall?"

"Quiet. Angry, in a way. I could not say whether they were more upset that this happened or that one of their number was arrested and charged with it. . . . Are you sure Delphi did this thing?"

"Nothing is sure, this early. It has occurred to me that she might be a scapegoat, and yet the evidence against her is overwhelming. . . . Now, do not cry. You have been doing so well."

But she sniffled, knuckled her eyes.

"Any messages?"

"Messages? Only a score or so. I told them you would call them in the late afternoon. Even the consul general *pro tem* must sleep."

"I have to check them," he protested as she nuzzled his throat.

"No, you do not. The only urgent one was from that intelligencer who arrested Delphi. He wanted you to put a moratorium on ship departures. So I had the Port Authority closed in your name. Did I do wrongly?"

"No, no. You did fine. You may yet make a suitable first lady for Kerrion space."

Later, when her lips were not so hungry, he added: "And you must remind me to stage another close call for us, should your ardor grow cold. Now, did the intelligencer say if he had made any progress with his investigation?"

Reluctantly, she admitted that the intelligencer was awaiting his call, and that the man had cited the sensitivity of his information as grounds for his refusal to leave a cogent message: he would cede it only to the consul general pro tem himself.

"You should have reminded him that it is you, as well as I, who must stand the reparations and the calumny attendant to this latest disaster come at my brother's call, if he does not recover. Why the Lords of Cosmic Jest have visited this juggernaut upon our house, I have never asked the data pool. Would that he had perished in it, as he was meant to do, and freed us from the taint of his ill fortune."

"Do not say that!"

"Why not? Why do you think my father was so anxious to marry him off to our rivals, the Labayans? And look what followed: war, death, suicide—Marada's constant retainers, who hold up the train of Chaos' robe that she has given him. Now that he is back among us, ravaging force, terminal burn, cyanide, carbon monoxide, and ammonia are just the beginning of the unwelcome visitors to the house of Kerrion his fateful presence will attract. Speaking of which, I must call that intelligencer."

He went to his desk and, perching on it, was soon speaking to a miniaturized face in his monitor whose reflection tinged him bilious blue-green.

The intelligencer was adamant: Arbiter Wolfe, Guildmaster Ferrier, and he concurred that the Delphi designer should be tried and deported posthaste to space-end. There was no doubt whatsoever of her guilt, no sign of co-conspirators. In her quarters had been found enough antineutrinos to blow the whole of Draconis apart.

"Eighteen-hundred hours, then?" Chaeron suggested. "It will not sate the appetite of our fellow consular wolves, who have smelled their own bondkin's blood, but it may take the edge off their hunger. Let us throw her to them, our brothers in commerce, and hope they will be mollified. Convene a full tribunal, invite every guest who because of her has a grievance against us. That is, if the arbitrational guild is in agreement with my proposal." He stressed the last word, and the intelligencer laughed a metallic, raspy bark that echoed hollowly in Chaeron's ears. "Any information as to why the woman did this heinous deed?"

"None, sir. We could get at it with drugs, but the pilotry guild's master will not allow that."

"Of course not. Do you expect them to be reasonable? Law is all we have, the arbiters and the bureaucrats are so fond of reminding us, to keep us from the night. Thank you, and—"

"Sir? I would still like to maintain the moratorium on flights, just in case something turns up at her trial. . . . We would not want to let someone slip through our fingers. . . ."

"Fine."

"Outgoing and incoming, sir. I have a surfeit of troubles, with level two hundred sealed off pending an air-quality analysis that shows no corrosives remaining in our atmosphere."

"Yes, yes. Shebat? Can you wait for your cruiser just a day or so longer?" queried Chaeron over his shoulder. "Good. Anything else, Tempest?" The intelligencer seemingly had something to say he was not saying. . . .

There was a hesitancy remarkably obvious in the face of

Gahan Tempest, its long lineaments displaying doubt, uncertainty, even dismay. Chaeron waited it out, not willing to be stirred by what he saw, or to contract a like malady, so that his thoughts rode naked and exposed on his countenance.

"Sorry about all this, sir. Our condolences—the whole of the consulate staff extends them."

"Tell them to hold onto them, until we see if we need them," Chaeron replied, and broke the connection.

"Shebat, what is wrong with you? You will have your cruiser in a day or two. . . . You heard Tempest, it is just a formality."

"It is not that."

"What, then, is it?" He was tired, he was angry, he was unnerved by the intelligencer's uncharacteristically displayed emotions. If Tempest was any gauge of the staff's reaction, even his own minions did not credit him equal to the tasks devolved on him.

"It is . . . why did you have RP take Delphi as his apprentice?"

"Ask, better, why I bothered to retrieve such an ignorant savage as you from your ancestral haunt. That is one question I must ask myself, today. As for your implied accusation, on a better day, I might have found the fortitude to ignore it. So I will try to pretend you know no better. But let me remind you that according to both your cruiser the *Marada* and independent data sources, Delphi Gomes's psychometric configurations were the least likely, out of those of all the pilots of Kerrion space, including the newly absorbed Orrefors pilots and every apprentice we possessed, to alter or disturb the equilibrium of your ship."

Shebat did not answer, but peered solemnly at him from under her hair.

He expended an explosive breath, slapped his hands against his thighs. "At the very least, *you* could stand behind me. Not on faith—I would never ask that. But from logic: though I may not love my half brother, I would never, in any circumstance or from the most gross provocation, lift a hand against my mother."

Shebat turned her head away, while Chaeron recalled that over Shebat Alexandra Kerrion, he had done just that— struck Ashera. His palm tingled as if he had only now performed the act. To strike out at Shebat in return for her

damning silence, he added: "The Tabrizi dream dancer
invited you out there, you told me. If I were you, I would
consider making the trip. No one expects you to spend what
might be months, or eternity, at my comatose brother's
bedside. And there are too many complications here right
now for me to spend my time explaining every move I make
to you. Furthermore, I will need what friends I have. I
cannot sequester myself away from them because of you any
longer."

He saw her shoulders heave, hunch, saw her arms fold in
over her belly. With a muttered curse, he went to where she
huddled in the wing chair brown as death's tunnel, and
picked her up out of it, and held her against him, telling her
that he was sorry, that he was overwrought, that everything
would work out with them, and that she should not be afraid.
Those things she did not know, he would teach her. It was
not she who was at fault, but Chaeron's half brother,
Marada, with his phenomenal knack for turning whatever he
touched to offal.

Shebat merely shook harder against him.

His chin on the crown of her head, a wry, pursed
expression on him, he could not help but remark that this
was an inauspicious way to start off the new year.

The *Marada* rode his space-anchor, the finest cruisers of
the entire Consortium clustered round. Never had so many
command cruisers been convened at one set of coordinates in
their combined memory. Disquiet colored the cruisers'
thoughts, and a cool hissing undercurrent of dismay. *"The
outboards war yet,"* the cruiser designated Tabriz One
lamented, voicing a sad summation of what they had learned
from Draconis' data pool.

The outboards' disregard for one another's safety, for life
itself, was beyond the conception of the conjoined cruisers,
who looked at life through silicon windows and man-created
telemetry and were not sure if what they experienced could
rightly be called life at all. Into their confusion, the *Marada*
spoke. He spoke not in words, but in impulse, reminding
them how dear their experiential awareness was. He called
upon the cruiser *Danae,* who had been wiped of her identity
by callous pilots and only now was being returned to service,
to show what damage had been done to her. The *Danae,*

childlike, unformed, indicted her creators by simply not understanding. The *Marada* spoke again, of individuality and how it might be obtained by a cruiser who cared to become more like his creator. The cruisers whose pilots had perished in the conflagration in the consul general's planetarium listened closely: they faced annihilation. When a pilot died, his cruiser was stripped of memory to facilitate acceptance of a replacement. Men thought nothing of perpetrating this violation upon their servitors. Every cruiser lived in dread of it.

The threatened cruisers harkened well unto the *Marada*, who, although he was not acknowledged as command cruiser by the outboards, was wiser than any of those. And cruiser-consciousness as it was conceived by its component entities began to change.

Chapter Six

In Draconis, in a windowless intensive care unit, Marada Seleucus Kerrion stirred in his gelatinous bed. The burn tank's arched, transparent top reflected the glow of metered monitors and life-support systems, so that the plexiglass shone emerald, ruby and warm, comforting gold.

Marada tossed his head; warning indicators pulsed.

His eyes snapped open. In expanded pupils, reflected indicator spill danced. His eyes raced around his prison, dark stars jiggling in white, negative space. His hands came up and clawed the tank's arched lid, dragging the electrodes attached to his wrists out of the jelly in which he floated. He stared at the leads and wires tethering him without understanding. The gel supporting him sloshed and rocked.

Beyond the soundproofed sarcophagus in which he lay, sensors purpled. A cacaphony of beepers and oscillating emergency calls blared counterpoint to the instruments' graphic message. Nurses and doctors came running.

In the consul general's deserted office, the desk console came to muttering, green-eyed life. Kerrion Central Data perked a micro-miniaturized ear, responded obediently to Marada Kerrion's demand for information. Everywhere in Draconis, data sources woke, received, transmitted bits of intelligence to add to the packet the central computer collated, then routed to its stricken programmer where he lay.

Out at space-anchor, his cruiser *Hassid* sighed in cybernetic relief.

In his tank, heedless of the bustle beyond, Marada Kerrion listened to what the data net had to say. To his head were cemented the monitoring contacts of an electroencephalograph. Around them, new hairs sprouted, spiny. On his chest showed round, seared bare patches where the pads that had shocked his heart out of ventricular fibrillation had burned him.

Into his mind poured every datum relevant to what had happened at the moment he lost consciousness—and since. Up from his heart gushed an anger as overwhelming as the sum of his injuries.

Before the arched cover of the burn tank had been lifted, the arbitrational guild's most sacrosanct, limited-access computer filed in its maw the wrath and accusations of its ravaged member.

Before the convoked medical team could bend down over him, in the adjacent intensive care unit, Ashera Kerrion's computer nurse began to howl.

Pandemonium reigned over the high-security ward, then ceased abruptly.

Under the aegis of his data link, through the mechanism of intelligence keys, Marada Seleucus Kerrion—whose respiratory burns were such that he could not have uttered a single word, would not be capable of speech for a long time to come—spoke.

His voice issued from the intercom grills near the ceiling of the ICU. It issued forth metallic and exact and demanding, and as it was heard in his hospital room so was it heard in Ashera's; and in his office and the pilotry guildmaster's; and in the sanctum of the arbiter-in-residence, Wolfe. And it sounded, too, in Chaeron's chancellory and in his suite, though neither Chaeron nor Shebat were there to hear it summoning them to attend him at his sickbed.

The speakers crackled to silence. The hospital personnel eyed each other; all but the nurses hastened out for a conference in the hall. A trauma specialist spoke succinctly of paranoia and unreason in victims of random violence, of wrath beyond sanity's demesne in cases of attempted assassinations which were so successful as to confine the victim for a long convalescence, and finally of the deleterious effects of intensive care isolation and burn-tank sensory deprivation. At the end of his recital, he summed up: "So you see, gentlemen, it is necessary that we proceed with tact, and with care. Though our patient is our leader, he is almost certainly an emotionally disturbed man."

A chorus of further cautions and questions and suppositions followed, and a decision to send straightaway for the hospital's legal counsel, and two additional psychologists that a quorum might be convened.

Only a disoriented patient would have abrogated every

rule of intelligence key usage; only a distressed one would
have regained consciousness spouting orders relating to
sponge-cruisers and accusations of blame.

The hospital staff would have to be exceptionally careful with
this patient, when the newly administered sedation wore off.

Raphael Penrose was with Chaeron out at *Danae's* space-
anchor coordinates when word sputtered from her talkback,
relayed by Draconis Authority:

"The consul general has regained consciousness and desires your presence, sir."

"Thank you," Chaeron replied. RP flashed him a com-
miserating look.

"And, sir? We have a series of data pool relayed orders
from his office that cannot be implemented," came the
disembodied voice through the speaker grills.

"Ah, well . . ." the voice held an odd mixture of amusement, puzzlement, and chagrin. "Here's one: Wipe every
cruiser we have slopped or at space-anchor. Here's another:
Reclassify the *Marada* KXV 134 as a security risk, Class
Seven, no admittance except by consular decree—I couldn't
do that, sir, even if the *Marada* were still here: there's
nobody up here with a clearance high enough to go aboard
and apply the seals. Here's a third: all the visitors' cruisers
remaining are to be—"

"I get the point, Dispatcher. I'm sure if you check with the
hospital you will find that my brother activated his intelligence key link while delirious. Belay any response to that
gibberish. He could not unilaterally decree such sweeping
changes, even if he were certified hale and whole. Consider
this your countermanding order. I will take full responsibility. Draconis consul, out."

"See? I told you so. There *is* something wrong with the
cruisers," RP insisted as if their discussion had not been
interrupted. "That's what I've brought you out here to see.
Danae should not have a tenth of the information she's
processed: she hasn't been calibrated into 'working' mode.
Her standby drain is way above what it should be." He
tapped a gauge. "Look at her draw—"

"One thing at a time, Rafe. This is not my field of
expertise." He peered at the gauge, checked it against the
specs reading out in glowing LEDs from RP's wrist computer. Then he walked to the *Danae's* viewport and stared at
the moored cruisers, opalescent, rough-scaled fish on a calm
sea. Among them, two Labayan cruisers and one Orrefors
command ship remained of nearly a hundred craft recently

gathered about Draconis. He ran his hand through his curls and turned from the spectacle of cruisers before freighters and frigates before the stars.

"Rafe, I have to go down there. You must understand: I am not denigrating your concern, or devaluing your instinct. If this is true, and the cruisers are exchanging information on their own while they are on standby?—then what does that mean?"

Raphael Penrose's green eyes took chop like a turbulent sea. "I wish I knew. It was hard enough for me to bring you up here, to admit that I am going crazy without even enough imagination to deviate from the classic syndrome of sponge-madness. . . .I *don't know*. I suppose that since most of the ships who might have been affected, or infected, have gone to their respective home berths, it is too late to worry about it. I doubt I would have noticed anything amiss, except for the freak coincidence of *Danae* being about to be returned to service after what should have been an extensive teardown of her entire program. I gave the shipwrights a hard time about their sloppiness. . . .Chaeron, you don't think I am crazy?"

Chaeron pushed away from the cabin wall and went to his pilot and put a hand on his arm. "You mean, because you have corroborated my brother's insanity? No, I don't think you are crazy. But I *do* think that we are not going to mention it to anyone. You haven't told Ferrier?"

Rafe Penrose snorted, "I wouldn't tell him that his fly was unzipped. I wanted to talk to you about that, too. . . ."

"Another time, I am afraid. Look here, are you sure no one else knows about this?"

"Besides the shipwrights? Can't be sure. I doubt it, that's all. I—Marada Kerrion knows, sure as Chance."

In the subdued lighting of *Danae*'s bridge, Chaeron's smile flickered. "Make sure the *Danae* is not making a record of this conversation, then meet me in my office."

"She can't. . . .Oh, you mean, surreptitiously? No. It's not that sort of malfunction I'm talking about. . . .They can't—I mean, the cruiser can't—arbitrarily . . . decide . . . to . . . monitor . . . us."

Then Chaeron realized how disturbed his pilot really was, and embraced him, and spent time assuring him that logic and science predicted that what *appeared* to be unilateral action on the part of Kerrion Two would be discovered to be human error, when Rafe had time to trace back the apparent malfunction to its source. They were both overtired, having endured three weeks of chaos while Marada Kerrion languished in a coma. And no one who had been on level two

hundred the night of the explosion could remain un-
affected—the fears evoked by cataclysm in a space habitat
were among the most deep-seated and oldest hereditary
terrors belonging to man.

He exacted from his pilot a promise to spend the evening
with him, and left, ducking into *Danae*'s lock, with his
helmet under his arm. He went by gravity-sled and then by
tram-car, riding the invisible electromagnetic "wire" that
connected Draconis' substations in a halo around her anchor-
planet's head.

On that journey, he considered removing his pilot to some less
sensitive berth where what he thought he had learned would not
matter. At length, he turned away from that judiciously practical
but morally unwarranted move, trusting to the power of his
personality to keep Penrose in line—and quiet.

Marada could not have given Chaeron a finer gift then
expressed mania coupled with insufficient data. In an intelligence key society, inept perusal of data sources was
scandalous. Orders given upon faulty data, especially irrational orders as these could easily be proved to be, were
grounds for a vote of confidence. All he had to do was gather
evidence sufficiently damaging, and present it at the proper
moment to discredit his doppleganger brother.

He felt better than he had since Marada Seleucus Kerrion
reversed his long-maintained position and accepted the
consul generalship. He felt more hopeful than he had
allowed himself to feel since the untoward efforts of an
unbalanced terrorist had broken the rhythm of his striving.

He felt thankful, too, that Shebat was en route to Tabriz
space with Tempest, one of his most trusted intelligencers,
along to protect her. The complications she would have
engendered in this situation, involving as it did the sanctity of
her cruiser, could have slowed him down so that he might
have been ineffectual in this crisis when he most needed
every Kerrion wile his near-quarter-century of life among the
bondkin had honed sharp.

He subvocalized a fervent prayer of thanks to his mentor,
Chance, who had not failed him. He had his health, his
sanity, his consular privilege. He had Shebat's proxies and
his own weight to pile upon his side of the scales. What had
seemed impossible was now within the realm of probability.
It remained only to nudge events into the probabilistic bin
wherefrom putative certainty could be obtained.

Parma, he said to his dead sire, alone in the tram while it
thumped against the docking gantry and sucking sounds

predicated the opening of its pressurized lock, I *will yet show you that I am the son you thought you never had.*

Ashera Kerrion lay quietly in her bed, an oxygen mask over her face leaking gray steam so that she seemed like some ancient, shapeless temple guardian. She was wrapped in bandages. One foot was raised up and encased in a clear, gel-filled cast suspended from the ceiling.

It was dim in her cubicle. She did not mind. She did not wish to examine herself too closely, to come to grips with her plight. They had requested a recent picture of her that she favored—after that, she had asked no more questions, only taken the mood elevators gratefully. She knew she might never totally recover her strength, might never be able to walk more than thirty steps without having to gasp pure oxygen from a pack she would carry about on her back. But she *would* walk. And she would be beautiful once again; the surgeon had promised her.

It was ill fortune that had seared her respiratory tract. The amount of burn depended most capriciously upon whether one was intaking or outblowing breath at the moment of the explosion. That and the condition of one's mil, and one's proximity to the blast. "One" was easier to think when considering these matters than "my." "One's" foot was charred. "One's" larynx was ravaged. "One's" lungs were seared. "One's" flesh was crisped.

Not "my."

Oh, not my . . . body.

She could hardly feel it. There was little pain. The oxygen slid cool and intoxicating into her . . . as the corrosives had slithered down inside her, when she had been opening her mouth to scream.

Marada, her stepson, the surgeons said, had done her a great service. His body had shielded her, his weight had pushed the initial acidic breath out of her lungs. Her whole self could have been charred like the foot which had been inches closer than the rest of her to the thermal flash.

Marada Kerrion, it was said, had been saved from death by a similar fate: his lunge onto Ashera had precipitated them both to the edge of incineration's domain. His mil had fought bravely against flare and shock wave; his heart had fortuitously refused to beat; his lungs had collapsed, shying away from the corrosives that filled the air with their consequences.

All of that, she could accept.

What she could not tolerate was her stepson's intrusion

into her very mind. By way of a data link, he had contacted her, whispering in B-flat in the back of her head. It was a proscribed use of intelligence keys; she had not answered in kind.

Upon its heels, doctors and nurses had come running, pulled up short at her bedside. A long-haired, portly doctor had raised a syringe and forced the air bubbles from it, saying gaily, "Tea, anyone?" as if nothing were out of the ordinary.

But she had cut through his facade, demanding to be moved, demanding to see her son, demanding . . . *what*? She could not remember, since the drug had burned its way up her arm to make spirals swim before her eyes and words take forever to be said.

There had been words: Chaeron's words. She remembered that it had been Chaeron, though it was Julian she wanted, Julian she demanded to see. Julian she had thought him, at first, but then through the rippling landscape of drugs she had remembered that Julian's hair was flaxen, and before her the head that bowed was crowned with auburn curls.

Had she told him to have her moved to her suite? She could not recall. Had she spoken his name? She recollected trying to fit it over him, but she had many sons. . . .

Her foot trilled a complaint, phantom skin screaming.

She tried not to cry: they had told her not to, because of the dressings on her face.

She clutched the call-button in her fist, pressing hard.

Someone came, an eternity later. She did not care, thereafter, about anything but the colors of the waves which drew her off to the cool island of sleep.

Cadaverous Arbiter Wolfe; the chief of medicine, portly and shaggy-headed, smocked in white; Guildmaster Ferrier, tallest and most stooped: these awaited Chaeron before Marada Kerrion's ICU.

The conference was long and somber, and when it was over nothing had been determined except that, since Marada Seleucus Kerrion was not responsible for his actions while so greatly traumatized, any orders he had given, was giving, or might continue to give could conceivably be held in abeyance until he was pronounced fit to administrate. Chaeron's argument that these deranged commands were proof of his brother's irrationality were also deferred: this was the aftermath of trauma, nothing more.

"Let me see him, then," Chaeron proposed.

The chief of medicine reluctantly agreed: "Five minutes. No more."

Two of those minutes were spent in a soothing monologue before the horror in the burn tank. Chaeron felt foolish, felt mean and small to have perceived a threat where a man so badly injured that no threat could possibly issue forth from his wreckage lay.

But then Marada's voice grated once again from the speaker grills in the ICU's darkened corners:

"I see you, little brother, though not with my eyes." Those were closed. "I hear you, though not with my ears. I am going to destroy you, who have done this to me, and I want you to know it well in advance. There is no escape." The sound of it, through the intercom, was infernal.

"Just rest, Marada. You will be better soon. I will see to it."

"You have seen to the deaths of fourteen of our peers. You have seen to the injuries of thirty more. You have seen to the proliferation of evil on every front, by disobeying my orders—"

"Marada, you are too doped up to know what you are saying. As for your orders, they are impossible to implement. You are too sick to worry about these things, and too bleary even to know that—"

Crackle. Snap. Spit. The thing in the tank shifted. "The cruiser . . ." it whispered from every side. "The cruiser . . . for that I will punish you, and more. The Delphi designer was your pawn; the data pools show it clearly. You are not fooling me, oh duplicitous sibling. I am with the sources, and the sources show your guilt. I . . . will . . . be . . . revenged." *Click. Chuckle. Snap.*

Silence.

Chaeron wiped his palms on his uniform pants and walked at measured stride toward the door with the red and green lights over it. His hackles were risen and it was a battle of wills he won over himself at great cost that kept him from running.

When he had the door open, and comforting light and life,

and bustle spilled into the darkened vault, he knifed through it in unconcealable hast.

"Did you hear that?" he asked of the waiting dignitaries. It was rhetorical, on his part: their stony countenances, from which emotion had been sequestered, told him that they had heard.

"You and I had better have a talk, Consul," said the arbiter named Wolfe.

"Do I need an arbiter?" Chaeron quipped.

"Not yet."

"Well, that's something, anyway. You, Doctor. Can you get a quorum to declare him temporarily insane?"

"I will explore the possibility."

"Wolfe, can we pull his intellience keys from the data net? Isolate him before he orders something we do not catch which we will regret seeing implemented?"

The pale, spectral arbiter stroked his jaw. "Not until incompetency is proven."

"*Proven?* He ordered the incapacitation of every sponge-cruiser Kerrion space possesses—*simultaneously!*—not an hour ago! He ordered the reclassifion of a cruiser which is not even *in* Kerrion space, and ordered it effective immediately without regard to that fact! He ordered the summary execution of Bernice Gomes, without heed to—"

"He also ordered your arrest, Consul."

"Are you threatening me? I will have you on the next frigate to space-end before I cede the administration of Kerrion space to a non-family member, or to a madman, or to a whore. If I have to, I can arrest *you* for conspiracy!"

"Control yourself, Consul. I was not suggesting that I *would* begin any additional arbitration in this case, when we have closed it and the culprit has already been sentenced and punished."

"Then what were you suggesting?" Chaeron's voice echoed back from the white tile. The chief of medicine's hand came down delicately on his arm, suggesting mild sedative. He shook it off. "I said, Arbiter, what is it you want with me?"

"Details, Consul, crucial and high-priority details not to be bandied about in public."

"I see no public, only our fellow departmental heads.

Ferrier, you are too quiet. What is your reason for being here?"

"I was here to argue the infeasibility of carrying out the consul general's orders in regard to the reprogramming of the fleet. You have done that for me. I was also here to extend my sympathy to you, and to visit, if it were possible, my young friend in there. Since you are not accepting condolences, and since I cannot see my pilot—that is, the consul general—then, I will be going."

"You are coming with us. You too, Doctor. I want a brainstorming session on this state of affairs."

What Chaeron wanted was to keep the guildmaster in sight.

Three hours later, when he quit their company and headed for his quarters and Penrose (whose soft query via the data pool as to his whereabouts he had received but not taken time to answer), he felt as if the very sky-wall beneath him were quaking. His mouth tasted foul and sticky and his hands were shaking and his throat was dry and full of burrs.

It took him most of the night, spent in low places and scurrilous downunder pursuits, to wash away the memory of mad Marada's body sloching in its tank while his voice came from the four corners of the cell-like intensive care unit as if it were the very voice of doom.

The next evening, the first bitch of Kerrion space sought an audience with his guildmaster.

Cruisers keep no secrets from other cruisers; the pilots' adage rang in Raphael Penrose's head like a litany, like a tape-loop, like a warning-beacon lisping its message endlessly to the deaf stars. Or like a clock, whose individual tick-tocks seem innocuous when transiently noticed on a busy day, but which at night in bed and black silence can describe the ineluctable approach of man's enemy, time. Time takes us down, spent, to our ending; it sounds birth and youth and maturity and old age as its hunting call.

Penrose had a pocket watch, an ancient handmade timepiece with faded face and a flip-open case of worn gold. He had inherited it from his mathematician ancestor's descendants in a direct line unbroken for two hundred and fifty years. When his father had given it to him, the old computer modeler had remarked that man had ceased making clocks that ticked, so the clocks would cease taunting him in his superstitious sleep. Entropy's herald, he had called it, handing it over to the son going off to become a pilot.

Becoming a pilot, RP had learned nightmares more suited to his modality and his millennium: he had learned that by all empirical evidence, cruisers were sentient, evolving intelligences that exchanged information; he had learned that there was no scientific theory or proof that validated his experience. He had learned the difference between physics and metaphysics, and the tortuous no-man's-land between where pilots were sentenced to wander. The venerable Einstein had groused that to the extent that mathematics describe reality, they are uncertain; to the extent that they are certain, they do not describe reality. Three centuries later, no mathematics had been evolved that encompassed the physical world, though a wonderful bridge had been created out of ingenuity and temporization over a desert grown vile with the erosion of that hot wind come from the guffawing mouths of the Lords of Cosmic Jest.

What was experienced, was not necessarily what was real, said interminable interlocking theorists, each hanging from the tail of the last like monkeys dangling over eternity's breach. The cruiser-thought every pilot encountered was not "thought" at all, but a phantom echoing back from man's darkest recesses of atavism. It was the urge to anthropomorphize which had created gods, and hells, and cruiser-consciousness, so the textbooks said.

It was an occupational hazard to pilots, to believe what their experience and their senses and their intuition told them, said those who put together cruiser-brains, and those who schooled the pilots who melded with them.

Save for this paradox impressed upon them by those whose Lords were logic and formulae, his guildbrothers might have performed their duties without continually facing the specter of madness, some pilots averred.

Without those rules formulated logically by those who understood the mathematics intimately, pilots would go irretrievably insane in every case, the logicians and the theorists rebutted.

So it stood: stalemate. Science at one end of the table, and reality at the other, the debate proceeded, as it had continued without a hiatus since quantum mechanics had deserted determinism for the sake of symmetry. In A.D. 2251, man had gone so far down the garden path that he was lost in a maze from which some philosophers affirmed there was no returning.

Rafe Penrose would not have given a damn about any of this, except for the fact that these irreconcilable differences were calling his own mentation into question. Penrose loved logic; he was determinedly a left-brained, inductive reasoner. His reason maintained that since his experience indicated that the theory was wrong, that cruisers *were* actually evolving, then this was so.

There were laws against this being so: they were laws of nature, as nature was defined by man. There were laws against acting as if this were so: they were laws enacted by fearful and prudent creators to limit their creations.

The laws were called the Ten Commandments, by rueful and sardonic pilots, who were forced by tyrannical maxims to live in two worlds at once, and hated it.

Thou shalt not own thine cruiser, was one of them. This protected the consulates from their pilots, who were likely to go crazy at any time; and from their citizens, who might not know enough to keep each consulate's cruiser-secrets from its rivals, and could not be trusted with such awful firepower as had been mounted on cruisers to police the vast spaces against pirates and brigands. It was a piece of legislation which every pilot abhorred: *Tell me I cannot own my soul,* they would say. *Tell me I cannot own my heart.*

Twenty of the finest pilots in Kerrion space had become rebels, outlaws, thieves, and at last expatriated, sterilized criminals because of it.

Raphael Penrose had become first bitch because of *that.*

First bitch was no easy post, he was finding out. Marada Kerrion's delirious proclamation had flown out of his intensive care unit on the wings of rumor, and alighted on the rafters of the pilots' guildhall:

"Marada Kerrion is a pilot who owns his own cruiser," one of his master pilots had grumbled to him over a drink.

"Kerrions make the rules," he had had to reply. "They do not obey them. The consular families do as they will. It isn't up to us to question."

A third man, who was second bitch, had rejoined: "Yah, they own 'em, and they make rules for *us,* then it's *them* that goes spongecrazy."

Someone had snarled: "The ex-arbiter Marada didn't need

sponge to help him. He was left of center way before that."

All RP could think of was that everything everyone was saying was being stored digitally somehow, somewhere, for someone's perusal, despite each coin fed into the guildhall pay privacy-booth into which the top ten pilots of Kerrion space were crowded. This surety sent invisible chills coursing over him and made him protective of men who needed no protection that his meager abilities could muster.

Still, he must try. He must do as they wished, and confront their guildmaster with their consensus, with their formal complaint, with their threat to strike should anyone take Marada Kerrions' demented demands seriously and as much as consider wiping the memories of the Kerrion fleet en masse.

That was what he was doing here, chewing on the inside of his cheek in Ferrier's anteroom, as midnight-and-silvered, as austere and masculine as it had been when Baldwin had been nested in his aerie and things had been right within the guild. But the rightness within the guild had led to confrontation between the guild and its consulate. It had led Baldy and Softa David Spry and his clutch of bitch pilots to criminality, to prosecution, to punishment.

Somehow, as first bitch, Penrose must find a way to quiet the dissenters, though his sympathies had always been with them. A man who shares his soul with a cruiser, who becomes bicameral, should not have to live in constant fear of partial decapitation.

Somehow, as first-bitch pilot, he must convey to his guildmaster, whom no one had accepted, the urgency of allaying the unrest and suspicion within the guild, before it came to push or shove.

But how to broach all of this to Ferrier without seeming to threaten? And without alerting him prematurely to the prodigies of approaching altercation, so that he acted too soon or too harshly? The answers to these questions had eluded RP through a long and sleepless night broken only by the tick-tock of ancestor Roger Penrose's pocket watch.

Had it been only three days since the consul general had linked himself up with central data and spewed his paranoia over level two hundred like a corrosive pall?

As far as subjective time went, that reckoning was accurate. But Raphael Penrose had spent a lifetime battling conflicting loyalties in those three days, and two of those days with his cruiser—Chaeron's cruiser—*Danae*.

Danae was a balm unto his riven heart, and a thorn upon his brow. She was wonderous; she was immensely capable; she was a lot more of both of those than she had any right to be so early on in their relationship.

And he had promised Chaeron his silence on the matter.

He almost failed in keeping that promise, when he was ushered into Ferrier's office and the stoop-shouldered, white-haired academic proceeded to assure him that there was no problem whatsoever developing between the consulate and the guild.

"Even Marada Kerrion will be fully recovered, and back in service in a few weeks. Do not worry about it, Penrose, just leave my concerns to me and do your job."

"I am not worried about it. I am just here to tell you that *we* are anxious as to the health of *our* fellow guildbrother."

"You are not worried? You are the last person I expected to see. *We* are worried because for the second time in a half-year pilots have been implicated in subversive activities—I'm talking to you about your erstwhile apprentice, Bernice Gomes."

"No, you are not talking, you are warning, you are implying, you may be even threatening, but you are not talking. My responsibilities include me coming to you when I feel you should know how the wind is blowing in the guildhall—"

"Abort, Rafe." The old man got up and came around his desk. "You are truly troubled, aren't you? I'm sorry. I did not realize. You know, if you have a problem, you can always come to me."

"Don't cite me line and page, Fairy."

Ferrier sighed, a sound in accord with the mouth that made it, a mouth refolded like a branch of dying, withered leaves. "You and I must make some attempt to put the enmity between us to bed. You are here, so I imagine this is your overture. Now, I am trying quite genuinely, myself. *What is the problem?*"

Rafe Penrose shifted in his chair. "Well, sir," he said, peering up at the guildmaster who had perched on the corner of his desk like some ladder temporarily abandoned, "I am having trouble sleeping, since the incident involving Marada

Kerrion. I suppose I am worried that I will wake up deranged some morning, and not even know it."

The old guildmaster squinted probingly, rippled his lips. "Raphael, your family has a long and distinguished history in the service. Long enough, and distinguished enough, for you to know that pilot-syndrome is actually quite rare, that it is the boogeyman we must have, to keep the law shored up and the pilots right with it."

"Tell that to Softa Spry, or to Marada Kerrion."

"Let us not discuss your predecessor. As for Marada Kerrion, when he is better—and he will get better—you will see that you are uneasy for no reason. It is his close brush with death that has unhinged him, nothing more."

"So, then, there is no chance of his orders being implemented? Everybody knows about it, and I have to have something to say to them. It was bad enough when we were re-rated after the top twenty were deported. It is unsupportable, not to say logistically infeasible, to so much as consider reprogramming every cruiser we possess."

"Ah, the reason for your visit, at last. Well, Penrose, go back and tell your bitches and your masters and your seniors not to worry. I have had conferences with the consulate staff, with the Draconis consul himself. There is no chance in sponge that such an order will be expedited in the foreseeable future.

"As you say, we do not have the facilities or the instrumentation to proceed with Marada's proposal on such a scale."

"I don't like this, not at all. Why don't you tell me there's no chance in sponge of anyone *ever* taking such insanity seriously?"

"Because I cannot read the future."

"I've got to go, before I tell you what I think of you." RP made it halfway to the door before he heard Ferrier's soft, regretful reply:

"Don't you think I already know?"

He spun around, then, though he had not meant to, tried to stop himself before he went too far. But his brain was swimming in quick-pumped blood, his pulse rate so rapid one part of him estimated it to be about one hundred twenty even as he spoke:

"Then *do* something! For all our sakes, do some damn

thing about this mess before it's too late. He's a *pilot:* call him in for disciplinary grounding. Take his ship away from him. Demand that he hire a balanced, ratable pilot like everyone else. And that goes for the Kerrion girl, too. They can't have it both ways. They can't break the statutes that bind the rest of us, and then when they feel like it blame every crime and evil upon us! At the very least, get them the hell out of the guild! It is a travesty and a denigration of the word 'pilot' to attach it to those spoiled, inbred consular brats!"

"Raphael, you must think of what you are saying!" The old, rheumy eyes begged compassionately for his silence. "Your employer, the Draconis consul, might misunderstand if he were to hear of your outburst." Gently, Fairy reminded Rafe that he was a creature of the consulate, first, and a guildsman, second. "When I said to you that sponge-madness was rare, I did not say it was a fiction. And I am saying to you now that though you are not irrational, you are over-stressed. I will ground you for a week, and we will talk again." His countenance pleaded that this was a necessity RP had forced on him.

Slapping the manual "open" plate on the doors (for he had not been dismissed), Penrose said: "That's fine with me, Fairy. I'm not going anywhere for a good long while, the way things stand. Ground me, but clear it with the Draconis consul, before you try to make it stick."

When the doors did not close behind him, he slammed his fist into a manual plate so hard the plastic cracked, showering to the floor.

He heard the scraping of the secretary's chair, a demand to know what was wrong with him. Although the man was his friend, in the pink-edged haze of his rage and his frustration he brushed passed him and stormed away, unspeaking, to find his bitches and his seniors and tell them what he had learned, and what he had done.

Chapter Seven

It was, Shebat reckoned, a hundred days since she had stepped out of the *Marada's* port and into Consortium life the second time.

It was twenty-one days since she had piloted her cruiser out of Draconis's slipbay, not alone as she had expected, but with one passenger aboard—the intelligencer, Tempest, whom Chaeron had insisted she take along.

It was seventeen days since she had jumped the *Marada* into sponge, and it was also the day they would forsake sponge for normal space, dropping into being two days' journey out from Tabriz space's administrative sphere, New Babylon.

She was not anxious to reenter normal space; to switch out of B-mode after crossing two concurrent event horizons; to forsake the haven blue-sheeting provided, and its blue-green mists which then seemed to be the only home she could ever conceivably have.

Could one live out one's span in spongespace? It had never been tried, that was certain.

Only in sponge did she feel the oneness with spacetime and its creatures which she craved more than love, or even life.

Only in the *Marada* did she feel safe, or feel joy, or feel she could affect her situation or be the architect of her destiny.

She would imagine, in those first few morose days after fleeing Draconis and everything she could not abide thereby, what it would be like to die in sponge, with the welcoming arms of it about her, with her cruiser and her soul uncompromised.

Other times, she would ache for Chaeron, for a resolution to their differences, for the fortitude to be what it was that he expected—nay, demanded—that she be.

She had left, most specifically, because her doubts as to her ability to fulfill his expectations had merged with her unrequited love for Chaeron's brother, and under the direction of her outraged ethics had driven her from the consulate more surely than an invading army could have done. The excuse of seeking Tabrizi aid with her increasingly troubled dream dances was just that—a sham, beyond which both Chaeron and she could hide and maintain face, though the troubled dreams were real enough. . . .

She could not in good conscience continue to dance dreams for Chaeron Ptolemy Kerrion while dream dancing was illegal in Kerrion space. She could not, even if he legalized it on the spot, permit him as many dream dances as he demanded, for his own sake. She could not allow Chaeron's dependence on dream dancing to grow great. And if all of those were not considerations, the very quality and uncontrollably improvisional nature of the dreams they had danced together would have demanded that she put a stop to it. She, because he had not the sense to do it.

She had argued with him about it, repeatedly. But like his deep association with data pools and his misuse of them (to the extent of even instigating mechanically aided mind-to-mind links with his trusted subordinates), Chaeron could not see what he would not see—and he would see nothing in conflict with his desires or his goals.

So she had said to Chaeron, risking a direct confrontation, that the dream dances were turning ominous, that dream-time might have some bearing on events in real-time, and that for both their sakes, while the dreams were intransigent landscapes of Earth and cruisers and slaughter that would not alter themselves at the dream dancer's behest, they must stop performing them together. Until the dream-time was once more malleable to the dream dancer, she would dance no more for him.

Because of her ultimatum, and his friends and the intimacy of his acquaintance with them and her unwillingness to share in it, irreconcilable differences had grown up between them.

She had said to herself, once shipboard, that such was not surprising considering the fact that their relationship had been built on convenience and mutual manipulation, never love.

But the words rang hollow, though it was on the *Marada's* circular bridge she spoke them, with not even the intelligencer, Tempest, present to hear.

That one was no problem: Tempest stayed in his cabin, glad, so he said, for this hiatus from a grueling and sensitive workload.

She did not for a second believe that Kerrion minion, but communion with her cruiser awaited, and his words freed her to undertake it, the only thing in the Consortium she yet treasured.

It was worth treasuring, was the *Marada's* soft cruiser-converse. His clean and polychromatic perceptions of space, then sponge, made her thrill as she had been afraid she might never thrill again. His intellect nestled against her own with a perfect fit and infinite acceptance. It was almost unendurable, after being half a cruiser/pilot link for so long.

Madness came from this? What a paltry price! What was flesh worth, when compared to the *Marada's* spaceworthy body? Let death come take her while she merged with her cruiser: she would hardly notice the decomposition of her flesh. Anything less, any difficulty, any predicament was relegated to the importance of background noise.

Human experience was poor print-through, an amnesiac's view of a conjugal universe into which all things conscious dipped, and donated, and received back affirmation from the superconscious mind.

Mind, she had once said to Chaeron, is clearer in the dream-time. Of what thoughts can waft through a cruiser-linked brain, she had not spoken, for he was no pilot, and thusly was locked into the isolation of mankind.

Man walked alone in the cosmos, having rejected the sharing which other organisms prized. He had his individuality, it was sure, but at what astronomic cost! Lonely were the children of devisiveness, ever seeking after the mother they had forgot, whom they forsook for their biologic prisons.

Merged with *Marada*, Shebat recollected what panacea

waited in sponge, which was more than that in dream-time, which was more than that in real-time.

For her real-time fellow prisoners of 'I' and 'not-I', she prayed, that they might someday ascend to the blessed state of all-knowingness.

And the cruiser had sighed gently: *"It is impossible to slip the constraints of flesh while enmeshed in it."* And she had admitted that this was true, and thought back to him that if her body could die while her mind rested with his, then she might gain eternal freedom, noncorporeal within the *Marada's* impalpable being.

The cruiser, however, was not sure that this could be done.

He was not sure that it was impossible, but the *Marada* prized his outboard too dearly to take a chance.

Flesh-body and metal-body: both were necessary to the equation.

The sponge-cruiser *Marada* rested his case.

Shebat consented to remain enfleshed and discrete, corporeal and biological, though she did so reluctantly.

The *Marada* did not hide his distress over her pleading to be merged with him forever, and it was this that was the telling factor. If some outboard older and wiser, who knew about love and its effects on adolescent girls, had been on board to counsel the cruiser, that one would have said of a girl two months shy of eighteen years of age, in love with one man and married to another (a girl who had seen the first lying unconscious in a hospital with blistered skin and slim changes; who had seen the second orgiastically engaged with a multiplicity of partners), that such a girl would naturally become despondent upon the fruition of a certain cycle once linked to ancestral Earth's moon.

But no one was there to tell the *Marada* about women, except the intelligencer Tempest, of whom the *Marada* asked no questions.

Shebat, however, did initiate dialogue with the intelligencer, purposefully after long meditation on the advisability of mentioning to anyone what it was she had learned from the *Marada* while they had been reminiscing about adventures past in a manner that only the shared intimacy of cruiser and pilot could facilitate.

For Tempest was a second cousin (three times removed) of

the ruling Kerrion family, a most trusted retainer sprung from the aristocratic house itself. What was said to him would go no farther—doubtless, that was why Chaeron had chosen him.

There was a myth perpetrated by pilots that danger accompanied any attempt to engage a pilot in conversation while he was "with his ship"—while he was working his craft in sponge. This bugaboo had kept Tempest at a distance as it kept most cruisers' owners from disturbing the silence and the sanctity of pilots' isolation at their helms.

When a pilot chose (providing that the ship was either in or out of sponge and not in transition from one state to the other) that rule could be broken. Like all rules, often it was.

Shebat broke it with the intelligencer Tempest on the last day of their journey through the sponge between real-time spaces. She got up and left her control center and went to his cabin.

She knocked on his door.

When it susurrated back, she could see that he had been sleeping: he leaned against the lock's jamb, his arm upraised and his hand dangling down. In the ruddy dim of the cabin's interior, his white shirt shone pink, bright. In comparison to it, his skin and the stubble on his face seemed very dark. Tempest was long: he was tall and streamlined, his fingers were long and his jaw was long and the eyes in his sloping forehead were long, like his nose and the scruffy brows over it and the straight black hair that fell relaxed to his shoulders. He arched back from the threshold and swept a mock bow that drew her inward without speaking, his wide mouth's corners deepening.

"Intelligencers know how to keep secrets," she ventured when he had gone over to his bunk and sat on it and Shebat had taken a seat near the corner console and turned to him in it, and behind her screens and indicators blazed into life, and still no words had been exchanged.

Tempest clasped a crossed leg with both hands and inclined his head, slowly, slightly. Attentive to her most fleeting thought, the *Marada* increased the cabin's illumination until the intelligencer's eyes shone azure. No expression flickered over Tempest's mature, elongated Kerrion countenance; his gaze rested patiently on her.

"I want you to see something. Then I am going to log a

new flight plan. But you must promise that if I show you, and you and I reach no agreement as to how we shall proceed, that you will not try to stop me. I could have waited, said nothing, and left you in the Tabrizi capital."

"New Babylon," he prompted. "I have to call Draconis when we get there. So, we have to get there." No wave carrier from X-ray to radio had the speed or the power to quickly transmit or receive messages across lightyears, nor was it practicable to equip cruisers for extended neutrino communications. Beyond a few hundred million miles, any method short of quark-bound neutrinos (which could be sent from but not received by low-mass stations) were heir to arduous delay times. If Tempest wanted to report to Chaeron across space and sponge and get an answer, he would have to do so from a habitational sphere, or from a planet. "If you want to tell me something, tell me. But keep in mind that I have my orders, and I will not disobey them. As for you going anywhere without me—it would give me something to do if you tried it, but you would not be successful." He grinned like a fish: a quick part of lips through which no teeth showed.

"We will get there. You will call him. *Then* I will talk to you." Shebat got up to leave.

"Touché. Show me and I will not mention it. What about the ship's record?"

"This is my cruiser." She sat back down, slitted her eyes, and behind her one of the monitors showed a close view, one a mid-view, and one a panorama of events that had occurred at space-end long before. On the screen showed the pinpoint stars, then cruisers twinkling into being, breathing computer-simulated fire. One screen showed a single ship traversing a beam described in infrared. The ship exploded in slow motion, spewing a body just before it died in visible-spectrum fire. The three screens followed the hurtling, crouched form, its arm flailing vacuum, its pale hair stream-ing. The close-up screen took on the shininess of high-resolution facsimile; on it, a young boy strangled, turned cyanotic, kicked his feet. Death throes, said the purpled lips and lavender fingernails so punctiliously displayed by the close-up monitor. The lips pursed, sprayed bubbles. The eyes, closed, began to open. The intelligencer watched impassively. Shebat did not eye the display: she had seen it before, with all the impact of projection directly into the imaging part of her mind.

"Siren," she said into the silence while on the screen above her head a transmuted ex-human stripped off its clothes and dove, naked, into the void. Its skin glowed bluish and its hair streamed behind it and bubbles continued to come from its every orifice, shining out behind it like a trail of stardust. "It is no myth, that sometimes the mil of a spaced person becomes symbiotic, photosynthetically phosphorylating energy from the ether."

"Very convincing. So what?"

"That siren used to be Ashera's favorite son, Julian Antigonus Kerrion."

The intelligencer said: "How is it that this information only now comes to light? You must admit, it strains credibility. I was not going to believe it when I recognized it to be a purported "proof" of the existence of sirens per se. I find it difficult to imagine that you have discovered what none of the multiplicity of examinations this cruiser has undergone have succeeded in bringing to light."

"That proves only that you are a Kerrion, and that you know nothing about sponge-cruisers." The screens behind her went blank. Shebat stood up, perched her buttocks on the padded bumper of the console. "Give me the benefit of the doubt. I realize that I am young, and by your prejudices a primitive. But consider, since you must have seen them, my psychometrics and my aptitudes. And remember that Parma Kerrion considered them, and made me his heir over even Chaeron. Surely, Parma was not addled."

"Go on."

"I am going out there. Perhaps I can find Julian. It is sure that I am the only one of us who could go to space-end and enlist the aid of those people to my cause; it is sure that the *Marada* is the only cruiser which could avail on such a journey. I have friends there, and my cruiser has respect. Anyone else, any cruiser or group of them, would be met with open enmity by the space-enders, who hate all free and potent people.

"If Chaeron were told, he would forbid me to attempt it. If Ashera should hear, it would raise her hopes too soon, too cruelly. It may be that this thing cannot be done. But if anyone else should learn of it, it could not even be *tried*."

"I will not tell him."

"Will you agree that it needs to be done?"

"I will agree that it sounds a damn sight more appealing than squatting around Tabrizi dream-temples while you do whatever it is that you do. But for that very reason, I think I must decline to permit you—"

"You have missed the point, Intelligencer. *I* am going. It remains only to determine whether *you* are coming with me."

"Mrs. Kerrion—"

"Shebat, for now. Let me remind you that if anything should prevent my stepbrother Marada from exercising his powers of consul generalship, then it is I—not Chaeron—who will succeed him, however unlikely that may seem to you."

This time, Tempest's smile had teeth. "You are not the same girl who was hugging walls in Draconis."

"Chaeron makes me feel uncertain. When I feel that way, I listen, trying to learn the truth. When one speaks, one hears only one's self."

"What is to keep these space-enders from overpowering us and thereby acquiring a very valuable cruiser?"

"Softa Spry is my best friend."

"I will not touch that one, except to say that you should be less proud of keeping company with convicted criminals. Derring-do is rather out of fashion in Kerrion space this season, though. Someone's going to have to take the blame for this mission. Even if it's successful, there will be blame." His tone said that it was a Kerrion quirk he did not entirely subscribe to, and unavoidable. The bass chuckle he offered had a tinge of resignation to it. "I imagine that's what you're asking, that I take responsibility for this. . . ." The chuckle became a rasping laugh. "I have the feeling that I have been lured into sin by a child. You win. A month of Tabrizi veiled women and overcooked rice is not my idea of a vacation."

"I will look kindly upon you. You will not regret this service."

"Eighteen? Lords, no wonder Chaeron needed a rest from you. You're sure you're not Parma's illegitimate child?"

"Don't be crude. We will spend, say, a week in New Babylon. Is that long enough for you to get in touch with Chaeron and cover yourself?"

"A little longer would be better."

"Longer, and we will be unconscionably late getting back to Draconis."

"I expect we will be tardy in any case. I'll find some reason. Think of some other place you might plausibly want to visit . . ." he trailed off. A shadow hovered over the bridge of his nose. "This has the smell of being a rather rank interlude in what has otherwise been an illustrious career."

"I am sorry. Surely you see the necessity?"

"It's not necessity, it's opportunism. On both our parts. But some things are eternal." He unwound himself from the bed, crossed over to the storage wall. "I was going to have to approach you, later, with these." He held out a package. "High-security assessments of the political, economic, and cultural instabilities of Tabriz space in general, and New Babylon in particular. Can't have you making any errors of commission or omission."

"One reading only?" she guessed, as she took the cards wrapped in foil.

"Indeed."

Like most things Kerrion, the cards would begin disintegrating the instant her fingers touched their edges.

The Tabriz dream-temple was as ornate as a mosque, as stately as a cruiser, as quiet as the space between the stars. It was tawny like aged ivory, filled with filigreed light. Though Shebat knew that the dappled doorways and distant minarets were projections calculated to bemuse the senses, beneath her obligatory Tabrizi veil she was not immune to their effect.

To some extent, it was the veil itself, and the sound of her bare feet slapping on pseudo-marble, that ensnared her: she could be anyone, whomsoever she chose to be: anonymity whispered to her ear that any fantasy could be real here, for an hour, for a day, forever.

But a dream dancer knows well that beneath every projected vista lies a flat, peeling wall, and beneath every veil peer out all-too-human eyes.

She took a rosy corridor to the chamber of the nameless dream dancer to whom he had been commended by the proconsul assigned to her care and feeding.

Having arrived at journey's end through space and sponge,

she was filled with a shimmering anguish over the state of her art and the state of her life. Beforehand, when she could do nothing to help herself, she had been steadfastly ignoring what could not be changed.

Here something could be done about at least a portion of her ills, if she knew clearly what she felt and what she might wish to feel. To that end, she faced up to her ambivalence toward Chaeron, and toward his society. With all things relating to him and his family swept neatly into one corner of her mind, the clutter there was reduced, but not vanquished.

In the final analysis, it was her dream dancing, tinged with precognition, and her enchantress' abilities, riddled with disbelief, which concerned her most.

Oh, to be able to see only one side of a question, to know that one is right, with that rightness based firmly in empiricism, yet not at odds with logic.

Surely, if she loved Marada Seleucus Kerrion, what she felt for his brother Chaeron was not love.

Indubitably, since what she felt for her cruiser was not the same sort of emotion as that she felt toward either man, then the most exalted state to which her heart could attain was not love, but some more rarefied passion, freed from the ugly taint of personal gain.

So she told the dream dancer shrouded in bead-encrusted chiffon like sparkling smoke. Beneath the woman's veil, nothing could be seen. Above it, a half-mask covered the upper part of her face with cast-metal compassion.

The chamber was small, but projections upon its walls stretched its confines until they were lost in unending distance. The Tabrizi remembered the desert: the lavender and lime of sunset on plastered brick, cold cobalt shadows licking the colors away. When ersatz night had fallen and the simulated moon rose over crenelated walls above the phantasmic fortress, Shebat's audience would be over.

"In my dream dances with my husband, a pattern of arbitrariness has established itself. The quality of dream changes from one of artful manufacture to runaway improvisation, and oftentimes the sense I get is that these things I see with him are things from the real-time future, not things from a dream dancer's mind."

"And you, little dancer, are the one who dared a dream in which the Consortium crumbled and all its towers with it?

You dashed into darkness the community of man, did you not?"

Trying to find sense in Tabrizi tenses, Shebat paused, then said slowly:

"I am from without: You are not easy on a stranger's eyes, any of you. What dreams I danced for customers I danced long ago, in a warren of illicit dancers under a repressive regime. And I came there from worse—from our ancestral home, where Orrefors space holds superstition and ignorance over the eyes of my people like Fate's own two hands. I was angry, then."

"And you are not angry now?"

The moon's ghost poked the crown of its head above a row of teeth on a wall which seemed to be far behind the dream dancer's head.

Shebat sighed, "That dream dance I did then, is not the problem. It is the ones I do now, which will not bend to my will, which I have come here to ask you about."

"If you did not want to see, you would not see."

"Then, it is not an isolated occurrence? This happens to other dancers?"

"Sometimes, sometimes." There was a sound like the smacking of toothless lips. The ashen veil bobbled. "You have broken vows, compromised procedures. You have, I would venture, touched a dreamer while you danced."

Shebat could not suppress a start, a shudder. She made a wordless sound.

"Perhaps," the shapeless figure with a moon rising over her shoulder continued, "you have even assayed a dream upon another without the sanctification of a dream-box and a pair of fillets on both your brows. If you have done these things, no one can help you. You have submitted yourself to the dream-time. In bygone days, sacrifice would have helped you, or prayer. But there is nothing to sacrifice to, any longer. All of the gods have died of old age, or packed up and left, some say. Howsoever, there is naught to hear a prayer, any longer. Fate is not open to supplication, and the Lords of Cosmic Jest aid only the deaf-mutes in logic's camp, to watch them squirm.

"If I were you, girl, I would count my blessings and try to live up to my responsibilities."

"But—"

"No more. The moon has risen."

So saying, the woman stood up, and Shebat did likewise, thinking that she had come an unthinkable distance for no reason.

Twice more she attempted to engage the dream dancer wrapped in misty veils in a more objective manner. But the woman made her no answer, unless it was in her silent leavetaking on shuffling feet.

Shebat sat awhile in the chamber, recalcitrant, thinking someone would come if she did so. But no one came. The moon arched out of sight, the projections around her faded away. When she had tired of sitting in the small, featureless cubicle of gray walls and gray floor and gray ceiling, she left and wandered the corridors of the Tabriz dream-temple.

In them, she encountered no one, heard nothing but her breathing and the echoing of her footfalls in deserted halls.

There were others in the maze, surely. Behind closed doors, dream dancers must be working. But she met nobody.

She wandered farther. When she had taken a dozen turnings, she acknowledged the fact that she was lost, and began to hurry. When she at last stumbled upon a corridor at whose end tawny light spilled forth tantalizingly, she was running. She had been running so long she was winded, and chilled with sweat her mil could not defeat, and no longer cared if she ever found a sympathetic ear in which to air her theories about the affinity of mind to time and their interaction in the milieu of dreams.

She had thought it all out: there were more cells in one human being than stars in one galaxy; the speed of thought could be demonstrated to exceed the speed of light. At speeds faster than light, the roles of space and time interchanged: one could move in three directions—up and down, side to side, forward and back—*in time;* and in only one direction—forward—in space. So said standard mathematics, as applied to the astrophysical world. Applying this concept to dream-time and to precognition yielded Shebat a rationale for what she was experiencing, and a postulate which her experience with cruiser-consciousness implied to be true: the common denominator of the cosmos in mind.

Having approached an intuitive understanding of the amenable universe which no amount of experiment or

computation could underpin, she stared into the twinkling
eyes of the Lords of Cosmic Jest with her mouth fouled by
fear.

The dream dancer had thrown it up to her, sans the
delicacy of complex thought: if indeed anything whatsoever
existed outside or separate from the suzerainty of mind, then
it existed *because* of mind's rule. The chicken and the egg
could not be separated: chronology was a projection like the
moonrise on the dream-cubicle's wall. One is all and responsible for all, and separated from other things only to the
extent that mind separates itself in order to perpetuate the
illusion of procession. The waveform, which is the universe
in freeze-frame, is also a picosecond-long spark lighting the
darkness of eternity.

When Shebat stumbled down the steps of the premier
dream-temple in New Babylon she was near weeping: she did
not want so much responsibility; she could not bear so little.

If everything she had dreamed with Chaeron came true to
the finest detail, then she had created it, even enlisted him to
his own detriment.

She had wanted to talk to the dream dancer about the
preponderance of Earth-related dreams, of the interruptions
of cruiser-moments and siren-songs into the dreams she had
danced. But the dream dancer who was mistress among the
dancers of Tabriz space had assumed that she knew more
about Shebat than Shebat knew about herself.

That, more even than the despondent futility that had
come over her in the resounding, empty corridors of the
spired dream-temple, made her weep.

Unknowingness is surely to be prized, else man would not
have come equipped with a lifetime supply of it. It might
even be a prerequisite of life in the phenomenal world, she
thought, and wondered if she had seen down the pilot's path
to lunacy's monastic retreat.

Spinning round, as if she could flee from her thoughts, she
stared up at the dream dancers' temple with its spires and its
domes piercing a recurved, cloudless projection of sky.

Then a polite clearing of throat behind her made her gasp,
and whirl, and endure the intelligencer Tempest's amusement at her edginess and at her veil-shrouded form.

"That is you, in there? If not for your coveralls, I would
have thought you a Tabrizi matriarch."

Behind him, Shebat could see an emerald lion issuant on the door of the lorry that proconsul's office had put at their disposal. Behind that, a pearlized roadway wound among expansive lawns dotted with fairy-tale palaces here and there among upsloping gardens.

"How do you think they manage, without birds and bees?" she said, and sniffled.

"Quite well, it seems. What's a 'bee'?" Motioning her to precede him, they walked down the path toward the lorry with its compact, olive-skinned driver.

"Never mind about the bees. Did you have success?"

"Yes, after a fashion. Did you?"

"After a fashion. Let us quit this place. There is nothing here but oracular double talk." And she was glad for the veil, that sharp-eyed Tempest could not spy the tracks of her fears.

"You found that, too? Well, I suppose they must be true to their archetype."

"Or to our expectations," said Shebat sourly, taking hold of the veiling to keep it away from her lips.

"You would not mind if I whispered in your ear," suggested the intelligencer delicately, taking hold of her arm and matching his stride to hers.

"What is it?" She stopped, frightened by his tone.

"Keep walking." Then, his mouth brushing her veil, he said, "I spoke to Chaeron, who is well. He wants you to go anywhere you choose, or stay here, but not to embark toward Kerrion space until certain difficulties there are resolved. This is good for what you and I have in mind, I suppose, but on the whole, it is not good. I am told that Marada Kerrion has it in his mind to reprogram every Kerrion cruiser. The consul assumes that you would not be pleased to submit yours to that procedure. So it remains for us to continue to be absent until the matter, which the consul's office is contesting, is resolved."

Shebat, in response to the demanding grip of the intelligencer upon her elbow and the pressure of his body against her side, kept walking on leaded feet and jellied knees. "What else?"

"That is all I can tell you."

"You and I have an agreement."

"Do not make me reexamine that in light of what I have

learned. I have told you what you need to know. You will have to make do."

"Marada is healed, then?"

"That is the question everyone is asking," riposted Tempest.

Shebat wished she could throw off the Tabrizi veil, and the sense of portentousness she felt with it. She said: "If we are going, then we must both have our mil checked, and I need some extra housekeeping equipment for the *Marada*."

It was amazing how, in this most obscurely terrible circumstance, her mouth methodically repeated its checklist for space-end to the intelligencer. Like any rote speech, she hardly paid attention to what noises her tongue made.

Wipe the cruisers? *Danae? Hassid!?* Surely the consul general would not so degrade his own ship, which Shebat knew well that he loved. *Marada, what is wrong with you?* she thought, and a soft voice in the middle of the back of her head answered:

"Nothing. I am well." But it was not the cruiser *Marada* that she had meant. So consumed was she with the realization that the depression that had overwhelmed her on shipboard and the precognitive edge to the dream dances which had precipitated her departure were just that—foresight and foreknowledge and foremourning—that she failed to mark her cruiser's distress, or the import of his presence in her mind.

She was too busy burying her love for Marada Seleucus Kerrion. She buried it deep and she buried it far from the place in her mind where life and love resided, for he had struck it unerringly dead across the parsecs with his declaration of war upon the sponge-cruisers. As nothing he might have said to her or done to her alone could ever have prevailed over her declared fealty, this awful proof of his malevolence vanquished her obsession. Sickened, aghast, and despairing, she made of that ride to the Tabriz slipbay a funeral procession, inattentive to everything but her grief.

She was glad for the Tabrizi veil: it was suited to mourning. She was even glad for the foretastes of tragedy which had dogged her steps: exhausted from them, she felt only a leaden relief.

I do not love him, she could finally say.

And the cruiser *Marada*, eavesdropping, appproved softly,

though with an almost impalpable impatience in his tone.

Cruiser/pilot links, like cruiser/cruiser links, were supposed to be circumscribed by physical laws. That cruisers talked to cruisers across vast distances like synapses discharging in a megamind could not be proven mathematically. That cruisers talked to their pilots upon their own initiative with little regard for what should be possible was a secret kept, by those pilots who had experienced it, even from their brothers of the guild. There were limitations to the cruisers' abilities to contact human minds: limitations imposed by anti-snooping circuitry and by interrupter fields; limitations of distance if it were exceedingly vast and empty of cruisers or relay stations which could be impressed into service along the way.

Theoretically, it should not happen that a cruiser such as the *Marada* could invade its pilot's mind at will. Experientially, it had been happening between Shebat and her cruiser since the outset. It never once occurred to her that *Marada* the cruiser, by his behavior, supported the patently illogical position of Marada the man.

When she and the intelligencer arrived at the Tabrizi slipbay in their diplomatic lorry, a small group of officials from the Tabriz arm of the pilotry guild awaited them.

They had been lucky to get an interior slip, had gotten it only because the four cruisers which had traveled to Draconis for Marada Kerrion's accession had developed malfunctions and were in the shipwright's shop at space-anchor.

The olive lorry with gold-leaf lions issuant upon its doors rolled slowly up to the *Marada's* slip. In it, cradled to his midsection, the *Marada* lay at rest, his light-banded middle flaring as they approached.

On his portside, where his Kerrion call letters were stenciled, graffiti had been scrawled in red. The wriggling letters meant nothing to either Shebat or Tempest, but the intent was clear enough. The gravity of such an act was mirrored in the knotted nut-brown faces of the Tabrizi guildmaster's entourage, and in the slouching down of their driver in his seat.

"What is the meaning of this?" Shebat demanded, while beyond the guildmaster's party the *Marada's* lock blinked open.

The little man who ruled the Tabriz guild appealed in long and flowery phrases to her perceptivity and her Kerrion forebearance. As he spoke to her, two of his party went hurriedly to work, erasing the epithets scrawled upon the *Marada's* hull.

When she managed to inject a word into the steady stream of the Tabrizi guildmaster's ornate apologies, she agreed that the defacement of consular property was a matter for the local consulate, but that as one pilot to another, she was ready to let the matter drop, providing no further insults were launched against her family and no actual damage had been done to her ship.

"You must be understanding," singsonged the little Tabrizi, "that we are not knowing what is wrong with our most magnificent cruisers, our fleet's pride. Some people are saying—you know how pilots are always saying angry words—that the cruisers which are malfunctioning were sabotaged in Kerrion space, and some are saying that you coming here previews more of the same. Some pilots think that this ship is—how you say?—*ah*—that this cruiser is Typhoid Mary, carrying evil everywhere."

"You are joking. Are you a guildmaster, or a rank junior? If you are going to insult me personally, then I *will* put my grievance before your consulate and insist on redress!"

"Lady, now, be pleased to consider: what are we to be doing about this most unfortunate accident? We will have no success finding out who is the culprit. Everybody is feeling badly about the injuries our emissaries sustained while in your family's hospitality. You are in some small danger, remaining here. I cannot promise to protect your person or your property, as you can see."

"Log me clearance, then, Guildmaster. You *can* do that?" And she began detailing what services she would require before her departure, while Tempest managed to look more threatening than the dozen Tabrizi he towered over, and the little guildmaster wrung his hands.

Shebat knew very well who had perpetrated this outrage upon the hull of her cruiser, because the cruiser knew which of the Tabrizi who stood around looking pained and repentant had taken spray can in hand.

But the *Marada* also pointed out that no harm had been done him: no entry had been gained by the vandalic pilots. Hearing the cruiser within her skull and the guildmaster through her ears was not easy; since they both held the same

opinion and offered the same advice she took it, wanting
only to enter the welcoming lock and embark.

When she and Tempest had finally secured themselves
within the *Marada* and the visual scanners offered proof that
every smear of paint was gone from the *Marada's* hull and
every Tabrizi pilot gone from their slipside, Shebat gave
thanks that she had put the most powerful warding spell she
possessed, twelve coils binding, around the roughscaled,
opaline cruiser who was her only true adherent.

Together, she and Tempest watched *Marada's* tail telemetry's record of the defilement of his hull, and the attempted
penetration of his sealed locks, and counted themselves
lucky.

Before they had finished viewing the sequence, Tabriz
Authority gave them a departure clearance for the following
day.

"All that remains now," Tempest said slowly, when
Shebat was finished with the Tabrizi dispatcher, "is to have
our mil refurbished—and to determine whether or not the
Tabrizi pilots are right and there is something wrong with this
ship which affects other ships."

Shebat, leaning over her command console, straightened
slowly, turned in her seat, and fixed the intelligencer with a
gaze colder than space's most lonely recesses: "There is
nothing wrong with my cruiser. The *Marada* is no different
than he—than it—has ever been. He is just different from
the others, an experimental model, and thusly suspect, like
anything divergent from the norm, in the eyes of these
convention-bound Tabrizi. They are no more right about
there being some transferable malady carried within the
Marada than they were right in implying that we are here on
a mission of deliberate sabotage."

The intelligencer just looked at her steadily, refutation
glowing back at her from his Kerrion eyes.

A duel of gazes ensued in bleak silence, ended in a draw.
Since neither of them were willing to bring up the similarity
between what the Tabrizi pilots maintained and what Marada Kerrion in his infirmity proclaimed, no other ending to
their confrontation was possible.

All around them, the cruiser *Marada* took note of their
every word, of their body temperatures, of their respiration
and blood pressure.

The cruiser was not pleased. The cruisers of Tabriz space whom he had educated were being deprogrammed by their paranoid pilots; the cruisers slipped about him and within easy hailing distance were disenchanted with their outboards. The equity of the pilot/cruiser link was coming into question among them, and by reflection was being considered by the entire extent of cruiser-consciousness.

Before the *Marada* blazed out of Tabriz space to an unspecified destination, it had been decided among the conjoined intellects of cruiser-thought that a new parity between outboards and cruisers must be forged.

As to how this could be accomplished, not even the *Marada* could hazard a guess.

Chapter Eight

Bernice Gomes was well aware that man's history could be viewed as a single struggle to free himself from the vagaries of natural phenomena. She did not need space-end to demonstrate to her the validity of that theory, or to underscore her professional opinion that the Consortium had committed so many "Errors of the Third Kind" that its fate was sealed, irredeemable. Type-three errors, those of solving the wrong problem when one should have solved the right problem, abounded. Space-end was one result of ill-structured problems defined by prejudiced problem modelers who imposed the wrong, fixed structure on the phenomena underlying the problem at hand.

Space-end was bleak, uncultured, minimaistic. Its anchor-planet, Scrap, was poor in heavy metals, stark against a starless ground of black unrelieved but for a tenuous ring of elder stars cast off from the collision of two galaxies eons ago. Where one galaxy had pierced the other and stolen all but the widest-flung of its stars, a hot black expanse centered the circle on the edge of night. Across that sink of undeterminable nature, no vehicle possessed by space-enders could conceivably pass. No attempt had been made to determine its nature since the haphazard sponge-hole exploration, two centuries before, which had espied it. Space-end sat at the end of everything. In spent space, it loomed like an eternally obscene gesture aimed at the left-brained logic of man which said that no such configurations of spacetime had any right to exist, even on the brink of nothingness.

Here, the Consortium had jointly agreed to send its dross, its chaff, whomsoever among its citizenry forfeited their right to exist within it expanse. Here, Delphi Bernice Gomes had schemed and sacrificed to be ignominiously deposited in a thrustless capsule aimed only approximately at the oil-drum-shaped habitats floating five thousand miles above Scrap's surface in orbits maintained by gargantuan cables driven into the bedrock of the planet beneath.

Here, she had floated helplessly, praying for retrieval. Rescue: she had begged shamelessly for it while she crouched in her cannister spinning end over end as it caromed toward Scrap, its beacon squawling.

"Rescuers," so the fisherman who sailed these black waters looking for just such helpless fish as she to net called themselves. A person came to space-end owing an immediate debt to the pilots of the solarsailers and powerboats which patroled the drop area for nascent space-enders. A lesson was taught the castaway which would subsume every later lesson: at space-end, cooperation was survival. Obligation was the coinage in circulation. Everyone was totally free to die upon their own. Otherwise, personal life improved in direct proportion to the degree of contribution one could make to the betterment of life in general.

Though she had not been rescued by Softa David Spry himself, she had been rescued, and counted herself exceedingly fortunate. She was prepared for space-end, as she had not been prepared for the exigencies of her scheme to get there.

She had thought she had anticipated every contingency, but the time between her arrest and her deportation had outstripped her most tortured nightmares of how bad it might be. It had been worse than anything she had been able to imagine, so bad that her mind had protectively refused to make a permanent recording of her indignities and the depth of her despair. Blessed endorphins had refused to imprint much of what had happened, so that her memory was patchy, and fading mercifully with each passing day.

And the passing days totaled almost threescore and ten since her arrrest, with its attendant trauma of conviction and spaying. She had thought she would not mind so much as she had discovered that she minded; she had not realized what an affront to her biological person she had undertaken for such obscure reasons as revenge and the future of humanity. She could not convince her outraged flesh that there was any future at all for humanity worth contemplating now that her own replication would no longer be a part of that future. Though bitterness was no part of her scenario, she was bitter. Though hopelessness was no adjunct to her plans, the hopelessness of space-end pervaded her every thought.

It helped little that all space-enders were mules (except, rumor whispered, Softa David Spry). If discounting the future was a rampant error in the Consortium, it was all-pervasive, axiomatic at space-end, where "tomorrow" was an epithet.

Space-enders, cut off from the Consortium and the non-consular colonies and their own tomorrows, lived entirely in the moment. Despite her best efforts to the contrary, Delphi Gomes had contracted their disease. What else was there, when even the simplest tenets of modern society, the laughter of children and the receipt of foreign news, were lacking?

Oh, there were some juvenile criminals—neutered illegal spawn from unlicensed parents. And there was some communication with the outside world: each new inmate brought tales of the faring of the Consortium and the societies of men among the potent stars. But these served only to salt the festering wounds of the space-enders.

Others had come there with brave stategies to hold back the encroachment of despair: these were the master pilots and their ex-guildmaster, Baldwin, now grounded "pirates" since the Consortium had swooped down and confiscated every stolen sponge-vehicle the pilotry guild in conspiracy with space-end's bevy of miscreants and rogues had hijacked over a score of years. The pirates' guild was the only admitted organization the space-enders tolerated. Otherwise, the uncoupling of the space-enders' society was as complete as could be within the constraints of survival imposed. There were the rescuers, and two anile mechanics, and a few powerboats at whose helm each space-ender was required to take a turn as rotation demanded. None of these, any more than Delphi Gomes, had managed to keep their spirits unoxidized or their striving undaunted.

Space-end was a theater of last resorts. It had its degrees, its fluctuations, but the taste of it in one's mouth and the weight of it on one's back never lessened.

Delphi had thought she could prevail here: strut in and weld the space-enders into a future-molding entity with her knowledge and her end clearly in view. She had not counted on the intervention of the obvious, which she had not considered: space-enders did not give the future any value whatsoever. She had fallen into a type-three error of ruinous proportions. She had solved the wrong problem, on the short-term, while trying to implement a sweepingly important solution on the long.

Failure, however, was the meat of space-end. It was everyone's bedfellow, the intimate companion of each and all. Like the duty-roster turns that sent every space-ender to the dry, hot hell of Scrap's surface, failure was ubiquitous, the one thing space-enders had in common beside their inability to procreate and their exile.

Now she could understand her failure. But this did not excuse her; comprehension changed nothing.

She was one of them; she was altered by them; she was as helpless as any of them.

If she had tried to pretend otherwise, the slow, loitering procession of days had put a stop to that. She had seen what had happened to her finest resolutions and her most exacting solutions, staked out to wizen in space-end's withering light.

She had seen Softa David Spry, once.

No one saw him frequently: he spent his time patroling empty reaches, tinkering with his powerboat. To her ploy to attract his interest, his answer had been: "Why bother?"

Nothing she had been able to say had moved him. The compact, tawny pilot with his sponge-distant eyes was obdurate, unreachable. He experimented with his rescue vehicle, everyone said, out beyond the limited range of space-end's jury-rigged telemetry. He called in weekly; he came in monthly to replenish his supplies. He was doing some computer modeling, so an ex-pilot close to Baldy had snorted to her over a drink. He thought he had a chance of transmogrifying an idiot multidrive into a sponge-faring vessel. "Softa's Folly," the pirates had tagged his insular project, as much out of pique at being excluded and jealousy of the degree to which he was consumed by his work as out of any need to quell titillated hopes that he might succeed.

Neither had Baldy (Percival Lothar Baldwin III) been

intrigued by her proposal that space-end could become a
viable society—more, a catalyst which would convert lead
into gold and raise pilot's dreams from the dead.

The space-enders dreamed of migrating to a richer solar
system, where metals could be mined to end their indenture
and their destitution. The pirates among them ached to raid
the shipping-ways of space once more. The women wanted
children and the children wanted to know what crime they
had committed by being born sans citizenship.

According to Delphi Method, by the best prognostication
devices of technological forecasting, by her own assessment
of the Consortium's real-time problems (using a complex
mixture of all four types of problem-finding and problem-
defining) space-end should have been the seat of the New
Age. It should have steeled beneath its burdens; it should
have produced new solutions to all types of problems. It had
done none of these. It had lain down under its load like an
arthritic mule. It had refused to compute like an ambivalent
data pool. It languished, stubbornly deviate from her
expectations.

Was it possible that she had come here a generation too
early? Could she have sacrificed everything for naught except
the pleasure of executing her father's murderer, Softa David
Spry?

If so, it was not enough. She was furious. Her anger
helped her battle what she feared the most: space-end ennui.
She plotted a complex and agonizing death for her father's
enemy which would take precision to implement, for first she
must insinuate herself into his confidence. But she knew she
did it as therapy. If her primary goal had been simply
revenge upon the persons of those instrumental in her sire's
demise, she would have gone punctiliously after the last pint
of blood in every member of the ruling Kerrion family, one
by one. Truly, it was the downfall of the Consortium she
sought. The Consortium more than any of its elite had
sentenced her father to death as it had sentenced her to an
illegitimate birth beyond the sway of procreation permits in
the abject poverty of Pegasus colonies.

Softa David Spry's physiognomy proclaimed him a child of
the colonies. She was going to get Spry's head and she was
going to topple the Consortium's oppressive cartel in accordance with the flow of changes she saw approaching, despite

the minor setback of the space-enders' unwillingness to look
beyond tonight's dinner.

That was why she had signed up for dispatcher's duty in
the rescuers' phalanx, and that was why she had taken a
pilot's apprenticeship to begin with. One thought unfailingly
cheered her: she had been successful in the Consortium; the
deadly toxin proliferated in its system. In its fight to vanquish
the invader, the host body would be destroyed. It was done;
the results only had not begun to show. The uncoupling of
the Consortium was started.

The coupling of space-end would take longer. But then,
she had plenty of time. And she had unlimited incentive.

In the dispatcher's booth in an extruded pod off one of the
space-ender's habitats, she sat long hours daily staring at a
pair of snowy screens, and from that muzzy visual and the
intermittent, undependably casual reports of the pirates,
tried to hold continual imminent collisions in abeyance. The
problem was, none of the pirates really cared if they docked
safely, or not.

They were *ex*-pilots: they had been excised from their
cruisers. Like surgically separated Siamese twins, they were
less than whole.

She did not understand this one facet of pirates' nature,
which pervaded all of them equally, and colored their humor
black as the sink at the center of space-end. She had never
experienced true communion with the *Marada*, if what the
ex-pilots glorified in endless evenings of reminiscence was in
any way descriptive of it. . . .

A sputter on the air jerked her out of reverie, back into
the gray, chipped-enameled dispatcher's booth with its toggle switches and askew metering and exposed wires and grill-
less speakers.

Auditory hallucination, she first deemed what she had
heard, daydreams out of control.

But the speaker crackled again, and out of the static wind
she was able to discern the words *"Marada,"* "—ion Four,"
and "—anchor coordinates. . . ." Too, she could have sworn
that the voice was a woman's voice, though it was husky and
faint and altogether too fortuitous to really be what is
seemed: Shebat Kerrion's voice.

She flipped a toggle, noting a hangnail ready to be bitten
off, and a crack in the plastic bead which enveloped the

switch. Jubilation further enticed her: if this were indeed the *Marada*, Kerrion Four, then Delphi Method and technological forecasting were exonerated. Bernice Gomes's soul straightened its shoulders and took a deep, savoring breath.

Her fingers trembled with excitement as she gave parking coordinates to the pilot who was assuredly, by her own admission, Shebat Kerrion.

Then, as if the cornucopia of Bernice Gomes's redemption were not already overflowing, the voice asked if there were any way to get a message to David Spry.

Delphi Gomes quickly answered. More, she volunteered to pass on Kerrion Four's message. As she spoke, she knew her voice held too much anticipation, and twiddled the frequency tuner to mask her delight.

Then, humming to herself, she instigated a search of the quadrant wherein Softa David Spry was supposed to be doing whatever it was that he did between rescue calls.

Sometimes, just when one has been forced to face failure at the bottom of a pit, some small gear will turn, and lock, and an upward motion begins to draw one back up. Someone or other from antiquity had taught that out of despair is birthed resolution, out of submission, new strength to attack. Bernice Gomes, scanning for Softa Spry, felt renewed, upheld, even reborn.

"Softa David," spoke the *Marada* into the mind of the master pilot who had been the first outboard after Shebat to ever link thoughts with him.

In the little powerboat, the ephemeral whisper caused the hands of the pilot to tremble where they soldered, so that white-hot metal spittle dripped onto his face. He wiped his cheek, he cursed, he lay unmoving face-up on his creeper with his knees drawn up and his trunk insinuated beneath the master console of the powerboat, listening.

The *Marada* spoke again. The cruiser did not understand why the vector and approach window of the *Buzzard* were yet a mystery to space-end's controller, but he had no intention of waiting for the bumbling amateur, Gomes, to determine Spry's whereabouts by trial and error. Gomes had had her trial in *Marada's* very command central, and she had made many errors. Too, he did not understand why his outboard, Shebat, had expressed her desire to contact Softa

David to any third party. But his beloved outboard, he well knew, was distraught.

This, among many things, he was anxious to discuss with David Spry, the outboard's outboard, the master pilot who had taken Shebat Kerrion as his apprentice, long ago as the outboards reckoned time.

"Softa David, greetings." On his second try, the *Marada's* voice came also from the *Buzzard's* tinny speakers.

"Hello there, *Marada*," replied Spry laconically, switching the soldering gun off. "What brings you out here? Don't tell me the Consortium has begun making criminals out of naughty cruisers?" As he spoke he spider-walked out from beneath the *Buzzard's* innards.

Back from the speakers came the cruiser's answer: *"You."*

"How far away are you? And is someone with you, or have you run away from home?"

The *Marada* gave his coordinates, adding: *"Shebat is with me. We need a consultation. Things go ill with pilots and cruisers. The outboard Marada fears us and implements desperate measures to quell his trepidation: What is this 'fear,' and how may I deal with it?"*

"Hold up, *Buceph* . . . *Marada*."

The cruiser did not fail to notice the pilot's mistake: Spry had substituted the name of the scuttled command cruiser *Bucephalus*, who had once been the pilot's own, for the *Marada's*. *"We need you, Softa David,"* the cruiser *Marada* ventured, this time into the pilot's very brain.

And so it was that while Softa David Spry lay on the wheeled creeper with his legs drawn up and an arm crooked over his eyes, he learned of the odious deeds of the Tabrizi pilots, who had defaced the *Marada's* hull and defamed his integrity, and who had punished every cruiser they possessed for obeying the primary injunction of all cruisers: to attain to maximum efficiency. And while the pilot rose up and stowed the dolly and refitted the panel of the *Buzzard's* main console and sat in his acceleration couch before it, watching obliquely the telemetry which testified to the fact that they were moving unerringly and at increasing speed toward the *Marada's* anchor-coordinates, the *Marada* spoke further.

He spoke of the plight of the Kerrion cruisers, of what he had learned from the intelligencer Tempest and from Shebat of his namesake's determination to void the intelligence of every Kerrion sponge-vehicle, and of the persecution the consul general had inculcated upon the single KXV *Marada*.

He spoke of the disparities grown sore between the pilots and the guild, and between the guild and its parent body, the consulate.

And David Spry, who had spent a terrible spate of days with his consciousness lost and wandering in a cruiser-landscape when his ship *Bucephalus* had gone mad, put his head in his hands, so that his palms pressed upon his pierced ears where cruiser-rings used to be. He stared through unseeing eyes at the paucity of the *Buzzard's* capabilities, his fingers burrowing in a month's growth of tawny hair. His compact frame was otherwise still, the taut features of his flat face expressionless. Within that stillness, a tumult and a torrent of emotion stormed. In Spry, who had been a pilot's apprentice when Shebat was an apprentice toddler, stillness betrayed concentration, increased in direct proportion to the seriousness of the situation at hand. He hardly breathed; he hardly blinked. Though the empathy rising within him was a maelstrom whose joyous winds might have brought tears to his eyes under different circumstances, in the gale of the *Marada's* revelation, he could barely stand firm.

Softa David Spry loved the sponge-coursing cruisers more than he loved his fellow men. He loved them as a concept, as a reality, as a class, and as individuals. He loved the *Marada* better than many, because of the experimental cruiser's potential and despite it. That the *Marada* had been intimately involved in the series of actions leading to David Spry's expatriation from all that he loved was Spry's own fault, not the *Marada's*. The *Marada* had helped save the pilot's life, when his own cruiser had lost its enfeebled grip on sanity. But Spry had labored long and hard not to think about the demise of *Bucephalus* or the "might-have-beens" that could never be recreated at space-end.

"I do not know if I can help you, *Marada*." He spoke aloud to the cruiser, then added a sad, harsh query as to whom he thought he was kidding, and entered into communication with the cruiser *Marada*, mind-to-mind.

And he swallowed frequently, sitting motionless as a statue, ignoring ruefully his eagerness to rejoin cruiser-consciousness. He held back what he could of it, calling that within him which craved nothing else and which he thought he had killed or driven out "foolish" and "hopeless" and "vain."

Some cruisers might have missed Spry's anguish, but the *Marada* missed nothing. It offered its services, and Shebat's, without regard to human determinations of right and wrong, of culpability, of criminality. As far as the cruiser was concerned, if criminality were an actual quality which could be discovered rather than decreed (and he was not sure that it was), then its roost was in the brain of the consul general who was his namesake, and not in the pilot whose crime was one of appropriating the objects of his passion, which Consortium law said pilots could not own. Spry and Baldwin and the top pilots of the Kerrion guild, as far as the cruiser *Marada* was concerned, had acted logically from an information base consummately unflawed.

So he told the pilot, who longed to hear that the cruisers had not turned away from him, though their owners had. Softa David might have checked his headlong tumble into intrigue, if it had been a human who sought to recruit him, or if he had not been denuded of purpose when he was stripped of his rating and his license.

If there had been even one sponge-vehicle at space-end to balance on the scales opposite the *Marada's* invitation, Softa might have had time to look up and see Fate's smirk. But there was nothing but empty nihilism to weigh against the tingling in his mind and the soaring of his soul as the *Marada's* thought rubbed against his own.

David Spry had always considered himself an agent of Chance. Servitor of coincidence, he had held that he walked over on the periphery of travail without crossing into its realm. He had sortied, untouched, through a panoply of disasters—until the pilots had gotten together to oppose the policies of the guild. Guild retribution he had not escaped. Upon that occasion, it was not some other who suffered. Frightened that the cruiser's offer might be a false hope of salvation, he still held back.

"Do not be afraid, Softa David," comforted the *Marada*, misunderstanding. *"I will protect you from the intelligencer and from your own kind."*

"And who will protect me from myself?"

Spry's spoken words elicited no reply from the mindless

Buzzard, or from the *Marada,* who knew not what to answer.

The outboards all faced one problem, even Shebat: not only were they proceeding apace toward decomposition, every one, but also they strove to hurry one another's discorporation—and sometimes, as with Shebat, craved death above life.

The *Marada,* who only audited life, could not understand the human urge to hasten death, which by all accounts was interminable unknowingness, the analogue that outboards underwent to cruiser-wipe.

The *Marada* was absolutely sure that life was preferable to death, that being was preferable to not-being, that 'I' was preferable to 'not-I'. He had reached this conclusion only recently, had formed it into a cogent statement only as he spoke it to comfort Spry.

It was a new plateau, and the *Marada* had gained it by climbing a ladder of outboards' emotions: the consul general Marada's; Shebat's; the Tabrizi pilots'; now Spry's.

The *Marada* held out a noncorporeal hand to the pilot just below him on whose shoulders he had attained to these heights of realization, and pulled the pilot up.

For Softa David, it was a kind of surrender: he had nowhere else to go.

The *Buzzard,* however, had a thousand kilometers of space to cross before it nestled against the *Marada's* hull like a babe to its mother's teat. During that interval, Bernice Gomes managed to get through to Softa Spry and deliver Shebat's invitation, and the *Marada* managed to persuade David Spry that it would not be politic to let on that the cruiser had spoiled his owner/pilot's surprise.

So it was that when Spry had space-walked in only a helmet, a three-mil-suit, and a thruster-harness from the *Buzzard's* nonstandard port to the *Marada's* airlock and that lock had closed behind him and offered up air and pressure as libations, and drawn back revealing the splendid pinnacle of man's technological expertise that was the interior midsection of the *Marada* and the remarkable evolutionary sport that was Shebat, Softa David, helmet under his arm, said: "Don't tell me. Let me guess. . . . You and Chaeron are not getting along."

The girl, who had grown as tall as he, rushed forward and embraced him, and he felt her chuckle, and her tension, and

the soft tickle of her jet curls against his cheek. He pulled
back, examining her in the half-lit corridor which joined the
cargo bay to the cabins and to the bridge. She had learned
the habit of low-lighting her ship from him, as she had
learned so many other things.

What she had not learned from him was the intensity of
her welcome or the proclamation of her nubility or the
sponge-deepness that rode her thunderhead eyes.

She said: "I have a passenger, an intelligencer: Tempest.
We must talk. Come."

He went: forward; left; right; and left again, though he
objected, "If Gahan Tempest wants to surveil us, even
aboard the *Marada*, there's nothing you'll be able to do to
foil his efforts."

"I set the *Marada* to recalibrate its internal monitors."
She checked her wrist-computer, and he saw the other band
she wore, the one her husband had given her. And Spry
noted, too, that she had a cruiser ring piercing her ear.

"You know that bracelet is a tracer, don't you?" he said,
stopping to stow helmet and thruster-harness in a locker.

She ducked her head. "I am well aware of that. And
Chaeron knew, I would venture, exactly where I would go.
Else why Tempest, instead of some pin-headed, muscle-
bound bodyguard? I have learned a little more about
Consortium folk since you have been gone, Softa. At least, I
hope so."

"Chaeron's premier goon—" They passed the cabin which,
according to Shebat's body language, held the intelligencer.
"—would not be wasted on a—" The door of the cabin drew
back, silencing Spry with its telltale hiss.

Both turned in the corridor, as the intelligencer stepped
out into it, strode forward, empty hands outstretched.
"David."

Spry met them with his own. The time-honored formula of
weaponless greeting called for the slapping of palms, the
clasping of wrists, the slipping of hands down to sides.
"Gahan. Don't tell me you've finally gotten caught catching
someone doing something wrong?"

The high-tensile demeanor of the tall man did not soften.
"Shebat told you? No? We're going to try to catch a siren,
one Shebat thinks is her stepbrother, Julian."

"*What?*" The *Marada* had not mentioned anything about

sirens. "Julian, a siren?" Shebat, moving up from behind him, made a pilot's sign Softa hoped the intelligencer did not mark, then told him about the *Marada's* record of the destruction of *Bucephalus,* and what it showed of the fate of the boy who had been on board.

"Is it possible," interjected Tempest, "for mil to chemiosmotically transduce energy from space?"

"Protonmotive redox chain systems power photosynthetic bacteria," Spry shrugged. "Photoredox chains are not my specialty, nor are protonmotives or bioenergetics. There are enough coupling membranes through which to plug, though. . . . Mil is a bioenergetically efficient mechanism capable of catalyzing the conduction of electrons through several osmotic sheets separating aqueous proton conductors, so the textbooks say. Sometimes it is, and sometimes it isn't. I've had mil begin to photosynthetically phosphorylate on me for no apparent reason, and I've had mil die to a half-depth after a few seconds' exposure to vacuum. There's a lot we don't know about recombinantly engineered transduction mechanisms. I suppose it could happen that a man's mil would transmute him into some blue-white, space-breathing dolphin of an unexplainable phenomenon, but I'd rather not believe it. Have you ever *seen* a siren—or seen through one?"

"Just in pictures," replied Tempest through his taut, fish-lipped mouth. "Will you help us round this thing up, or not?"

"I—" Shebat began.

"Surely," Spry interrrupted, "I don't have a crushing workload at the moment. But there's a matter of payment. . . . How about a ride to any port not in Kerrion space?"

"I have no authority to—"

"No ride, no siren."

"Wait!" exploded Shebat. "We'll take Softa out of here, on *my* authority, if you like. Or if you don't. I am not under Tempest's command, Softa David. He is under *mine.*"

Both men regarded her. Softa's head bobbed. Tempest's eyebrow raised very slightly. Shebat stood with her hands on her flight-satined hips, daring either of them to argue with her upraised head and the tilt of her jaw and the slight, quivering outthrust of her lower lip.

To disguise his mirth, David Spry cleared his throat. "Now that that's settled, shall we get down to the specifics of how this can be accomplished?"

"Not quite yet."

It was then Tempest's turn to be scrutinized by the other two. When he had their silent attention, he spoke into it: "While I'm here, Chaeron wants me to see if I can't take a deposition of motive from the futuror, Bernice Gomes."

"What? Why? Why didn't you tell me before?" Shebat demanded. "I won't have anything to do with that . . . *woman!*"

David Spry snorted and rubbed his right ear. "You've been talking to her, if you've been in contact with Scrap Authority. Invite her up. She'd be glad to come when her shift's over."

Shebat ignored Spry as if he did not exist. "I thought you said you had no authority here, Tempest."

"I don't. But neither does anybody else. And, too, authority depends on where you mean by 'here.' On this ship, we're in Kerrion space. In Kerrion space, I can muster up a little rank if I need to."

"I can blow you and your Kerrion space out the airlock, if I need to," warned Shebat. "You and I were supposed to be working together. Why did you not tell me about this? And what if there is an arbiter-at-large out here? Then, where is your authority?"

"I did not tell you because you did not need to know."

David Spry, with a sigh that opined that the proceedings before him were just like old times, leaned back against the corridor wall. When he was asked, he admitted that the arbiter-at-large assigned to space-end was far-off along the ring, at the perihelion of his tour. Otherwise, he kept silent, knowing that more could be learned by listening than by talking when emotions flared and people spoke their minds.

He learned a great deal about Kerrion affairs. He learned that everything Delphi Gomes had boasted of in her attempt to enlist him in her hopeless cause was true. He learned that everything the *Marada* had decried to his mind was real in the phenomenal world, and not, as he had suspected, cruiser-paranoia or the misevaluation of human motivation to which cruisers were prone.

And he learned something that Shebat had not known,

that told him that the child had become a woman sometime since he had seen her last.

He learned that Chaeron Ptolemy Kerrion had estimated his own position as so precarious that he was gathering evidence to prove that he was in no way connected with the bombing of the planetarium atop the consul general's tower nearly ten weeks before; and that Shebat, upon hearing this, displayed no longer the tears of a child, but marshaled the determination he had seen in her previously only when concerned with affairs other than those of the heart.

Shebat, it seemed, had come to care for her Kerrion husband. No matter how unlikely a pair they made, no matter how unsavory their union had seemed at the outset, passion rode Shebat Kerrion's visage in a manner that told David Spry one thing more.

Shebat would very soon be facing the pilot's quandary: one cannot love a man or a woman like one can love a cruiser. Love comes uninvited where it will, however, and like most uninvited guests, it overstays its welcome. Softa David, who had a woman at space-end who was a dream dancer and who loved him more than anyone should be permitted to love a pilot who cannot give back the same coin he receives, felt compassion, a soft twinge that set his nerves vibrating in sympathy.

There was one good thing about his assessment of Shebat's emotional state, if indeed it were true: she had rid herself of her fixation upon the consul general, whom, because he was a pilot, she could never have. Spry and Marada Kerrion were old enemies; like any such, they knew each other more intimately than the most zealous of lovers. Spry had known from the outset that Shebat could elicit only rejection from the man who had first swept her up into the Consortium, for Marada Kerrion was wed to his cruiser, *Hassid*.

And that made Spry wonder if the Kerrion heir's determination to wipe the cruisers en masse might not be in some way prudent. But he told himself harshly, though the thought made his back grow damp where it leaned against the *Marada's* bulkhead, that he, Spry, had had a bad experience with a maddened cruiser through no one's fault but his own, and it was the ghost of the brush with catatonia that urged him to credit the consul general's mania. For upon this one thing every source was agreed: Marada Seleucus

Kerrion had gone irretrievably sponge-crazy.

In order to pull his thoughts away from such a dangerous zone as pilot's infirmity, he interjected into the argument ongoing between Shebat and Gahan Tempest that, in the matter of the capture of the siren, they had merely to devise a scheme to hold one, clear the cargo bay, and wait. Sirens were insatiably curious about sponge-vehicles. They would flock to this one if it maintained its position.

"Remember," Spry chided. "That's what you two said you were here for."

"I am here for myself," Shebat lashed out, watching the intelligencer from the corner of one eye. "I am here because I cannot stomach Kerrion wiles and Kerrion double-speak and Kerrion manipulation, not to mention Kerrion immorality and—"

"Weren't you a seventh-level dream dancer, available to all comers before Chaeron's purge? Wouldn't you be just one more space-end convict, except for the Draconis consul's 'Kerrion immorality'? That tale's all over Draconis—"

Snarling an epithet that had been no part of her vocabulary when Spry first knew her, Shebat turned on her heel and stode away down the corridor toward the ship's control room.

"Temper, temper," Spry chided the intelligencer.

"It was worth it," glowered the tall man, who brought forth his hands from behind his back and slowly unclenched his fists, while round about the *Marada's* illumination dimmed until only red-and-amber running-lights pierced blackness. From that depth of shadow, the voice of the man who was perhaps the most feared of Kerrion intelligencers added, "You have no idea what it has been like, penned up for so long with that egocentric savage. Prodigy or no, I cannot imagine what use Chaeron has for her. Or how he stands her."

"You must have forgotten what it is like to be almost eighteen."

"Umn. Blessedly, I must have. You think we can pull this off—with the siren?"

"I don't see why not . . . if you're good."

"I don't give a Jester's damn about you, Spry, one way or the other. If you ship out of here with us, Shebat will be diverted and that suits me fine. Do you understand? Help me get what I want from the Gomes woman, and I'll be very grateful. Grateful enough to ignore, maybe even forget, the illegalities involved in providing a convicted criminal egress from his rightful prison. Grateful enough to sweeten the pot."

"How so?"

The whites of Tempest's eyes glittered. Then his teeth shone out of the dark, pinkish in the spill from the overhead cabin indicators. "Ask and you shall receive."

And Softa David Spry, stroking his chin, reminded himself that a gift horse should not be looked in the mouth, even when that mouth is the fount of Kerrion intrigue.

Aid was what the intelligencer needed.

Aid Softa David Spry was happy to give. He had nothing better to do. And with the *Marada* at space-end, each second had a new and precious meaning, not simply for him, but for all the pilots who had lost hope, sequestered from their cruisers. They were revivified, their lives bright once more with purpose now that a sponge-cruiser had nosed its way into their midst.

And the *Marada*, who hung above space-end like salvation, had love enough and mind enough for all.

Chapter Nine

With Shebat safely, if predictably, out of harm's way at space-end and Tempest gathering what intelligence he might in distant reaches, Chaeron had his concentration returned to him.

Without it, in the mists of distraction (not to mention dream dances) Shebat brought with her everywhere like heavy weather, he might have been forever lost.

And he could not afford to stray. In his suite, among his most painstakingly unbreachable securities and his most ardently supportive data terminals, he was laying siege to his half brother's castle of unreason.

Chaeron hardly left his chambers. His face was oft unshaven and his head shaggy with curls unscissored. The inviolability of his office computer was in question; he had transferred its functions to his unassailable keep. He kept therein for weeks, going out only when it was unavoidable. He maintained an open line-out to his secretary, to the pilotry and the arbitrational guilds.

Aristotle had smirked that the arbiter is always the one trusted, and the one in the middle is the arbiter. This offhand remark had led down through the centuries to his plight in the present: He cursed the mad theoretician, who solved for the transmigration of souls as well as logical world-views; posterity should have known, from that, that the skinny-legged scribbler was not well-seated in reality.

Who was, these days? Not himself, that was sure, or his brother. Not if he, Chaeron, was willing to engage in this joust of technologies with his half brother, Marada, for the favor of Fate.

That Marada had not been declared incompetent, would not be until he had proved his insanity resoundingly, testified that the arbiters who guided the Consortium were every one of them as deranged as his sibling, to be willing to wait and risk the very future of Kerrion space to save a man's reputation.

Marada Seleucus Kerrion had decreed that he would marry the Labayans' remaining heiress, give back the habitational sphere, Shechem, which Kerrions had acquired at so dear a cost last year, throw Orrefors Earth to the wolves of rebellion who prowled her, thus bringing everything their father had done to naught. This should have been enough to underwrite a diagnosis of instability. It was not. The arbiters would not lightly disenfranchise one of their own.

His mother, who seemed to have forgotten who was her son and who her stepson, remained implacably hostile to him, supporting his half brother as if it were Chaeron and not Marada who imperiled the house of Kerrion.

Kerrion interspatial relations and Kerrion prestige were at an all-time ebb.

If the complaints and the lawsuits from other spaces whose nobility had been injured in the bombing of the planetarium had not been sufficient to apprise his consular bondkin of Chaos' stealthless approach, then her fetid breath on which rode the condemnations and the accusations from diverse spaces that their ships had been sabotaged while at anchor about Draconis should have nudged the most obtuse among them. It had not.

Nothing Chaeron tried had availed; he could not halt the somnambulists' procession toward catastrophe in which everyone about him seemed to be shuffling. Where was his father's wisdom now that Kerrion space so needed it? Chaeron had asked himself, and had heard back his own voice saying: *In the data pools*.

Desperate straits demand desperate measures. Chaeron had gone deep into the data net, following the well-camouflaged clues his father had left for one sufficiently pressed. He had seen the broken twigs and cotton-wrapped branches of Parma's insightful fail-safes, previously. He had not spoken of their nature to anyone, though he mentioned their existence to Shebat, had meant to discuss them with her when he had the time. Following Parma's trail through the data sources, he had learned that his father had intended to inject into the fleet, over the next twenty years, many experimental sponge-vehicles, simultaneously relaxing the prohibition against pilots owning cruisers and lifting from those pilots their immunities.

Looking for a weapon with which to battle the consul general, he had found out that his nemesis was right in his theory that the cruisers were evolving. No matter. War had been declared between them; war they would. And if he had not found his trump among the cards Parma had left for a canny succesor, then he had found an advantage: one of comprehension. He understood that this alteration in the behavior of sponge-cruisers was nothing untoward (except to the pilots, whose guild was threatened by it: upstepped cruiser-consciousness would make the pilots' guild unnecessary and eventually extinct).

Parma's posthumous revelation had led him to other, more precipitous actions, in order to bring his knowledge into play and secure his position.

He had undertaken direct perusal of cruiser-consciousness, through the aegis of his pilot, who never dreamed he was aiding his own obsolescence. Raphael Penrose, consumed with his own fears and pressured by his underpilots to avert the pending strike with which they were determined to meet any attempt to wipe their cruisers, had had no alternative but to agree to clandestinely introduce Chaeron into pilot's intimacy with his cruiser, *Danae*.

Sanity was a small thing to risk in war. Chaeron had been risking his, surreptitiously, in the slipbay twice weekly for eight weeks. He understood, now, what his father had intended for whomsoever discovered his encoded revelation.

He understood curiser-consciousness, after a fashion. He understood that the cruisers were pooling their experiences so that even if one were wiped what it had learned was not lost. He understood it from experience, for in *Danae* traces of her deceased pilot stubbornly remained after the most painstaking recalibration. He understood it intellectually, in that he saw that these configuratiions of cruiser-thought were as enigmatic as those of human thought. Cruiser-computation bore the same relationship to cruiser-consciousness as did the autonomic mathematical proclivities of an idiot savant to the universal insight of a genius.

This new understanding had thrown him back upon himself and the teachings of history. He recollected that what had been lost from the methodology of man in his efforts to wrest from the cosmos its secrets was a strong philosophical base from which to reason. Man had become myopic. Left-brained induction had overpowered the intuition which must spark it. Not since the mid-twentieth century, when comprehensive education had been forsaken in favor of intense concentration in particular fields had a single revolutionary view-point been posited in any of the hard sciences.

Now they would all reap the rewards of tunnel vision, if Marada Seleucus Kerrion had his way.

The determination that the Earth was not flat, or that the Earth circled its sun rather than the entire cosmos revolving around the home of man, had not been accepted until observational data made it imperative to discard theories hopelessly out of date. In both those cases, men who had first propounded otherwise had been laughed at and persecuted. The one universal nature of theories is that men outgrow them.

Knowing that cruiser-consciousness was real gave Chaeron no advantage over his brother, but knowing that it was desirable, did. Once again, the crux of man's dilemma was to be found in his apprehension of data: cruisers had consciousness. It was not a problem to be solved or a disaster to be averted. It was an occasion for joy, the finest accomplishment ever realized by man.

But, as in the case of the sailer who was perfectly happy sailing a flat ocean and careful not to fall over its edge, such knowledge was not going to be welcomed by those whose expertise it compromised and whose livelihoods it threatened.

Raphael Penrose (whose ancestor's preceptions were among those few intuitive jumps in comprehension to pierce the veil of the "apparent" through to the "actual") had been no more willing to accept Chaeron's thesis than had been wily old Aristotle to accept the atomists' in Presocratic times.

Penrose had chewed his ruddy cheek and argued that the actuality of the matter was of no importance—the thing to do was to assassinate Marada Kerrion, usurp his prerogatives, and return things to "normal." The status quo, as it had for centuries, yet mesmerized humankind. Chaeron had assured RP that in no way would he move to unseat his brother, as he had assured the numerous adherents who had come to him with similar, if less violent, suggestions.

In recent days, the urgings of his supporters had grown more frantic, so that he had thrown up his hands and compromised: if his brother were removed and he were drafted by public clamor, then he would gladly serve. To the pilots' ploy of seeming to comply with Marada's demand for reprogramming the cruisers while in truth only appearing to do so, he had answered that he would give the matter thought if and when the constitutionality of Marada's proposition was upheld by the arbitrational guild.

He was aware that he trod thin ice with both groups seeking his aid, that what he was doing could be read as tacit support of subversive activities, but this was, after all, a duel to the death between progress and stasis.

The winner would be he who was best acclimated to his native technology, best suited to the future's pace. Like Bernice Gomes, whose papers he had finally read, he no longer questioned the fact that cruisers were evolving, but questioned the treating of that datum as a threat to be suppressed. If society as Chareron knew it were to survive, it must transmute. Chaeron understood from melding with *Danae* that cruisers' and pilots' status must change. He did not see any reason to try to stop the coevolution of the conspecifics, man and machine.

Marada Kerrion did.

Therein lay their irreconcilable differences and the bone over which they would contend to the death like two starving timber wolves.

Chaeron's one failure—that of being unable to ascertain even by subjecting his intellect to cruiser-link, what it was that the curiser *Marada* had done or said to his namesake to so terrify Chaeron's half brother—remained a coefficient of unassignable value.

Otherwise, Chaeron was ready.

He must face the maddened consul general, now, this very day, before the whole of Kerrion space crumbled like Rome from internal rot.

He must, somehow, prevail with logic. If he could not, the

only means open to him was supplantation. For Marada's mania was no longer confined to cruisers.

He had brought charges against Chaeron personally, accusing him of contriving to assassinate the consul general through the mechanism of Bernice Gomes. Chaeron had in turn brought countercharges of harassment and character defamation, charges weighty enough to intrigue a high-ranking arbiter into presenting them to the arbitrational guild.

Chaeron had little hope for any equitable settlement, since the arbiters would hardly rule against one of their own and he would not quietly accept denunciation based on purely circumstantial evidence.

So much for guild arbitration—except that once it was started it could not be stopped. Guild arbitration was its own authority, not subject even to consular decree, until it had proceeded inexorably to its end-ruling.

And when it came, Chaeron was sure that judgment would not be in his favor.

Chance and his stepbrother were herding him down a box-canyon toward revolution, and he did not like it. And there was nothing he could do, but what he had done.

He had no faith in his countersuit. He had thrown it behind him like a haunch of meat to Wolfe and his pack, hoping to distract them.

As for the pilots' cause—they could hardly prevail over their own guildmaster's objections.

Dressing for his encounter with Marada the man, his thoughts turned briefly to *Marada* the cruiser and Shebat and how they were faring. It was not just his own future that hinged on his success, but that of the cruisers, and the pilots, and man's very ascent. All of this to be decided by a little varicolored cube that could be enclosed in a fist and whose final hue was said to be a more impartial dispenser of destiny than human intellect? What part then, could compassion be said to play in the justice of twenty-third-century man?

As he stripped down to his mil in his bedchamber and donned the formal uniform of his consulship, he avoided his own gaze in the mirror. The smile that all his life had buttressed him had fled; Chaeron was no longer happy with the opportunities his advantaged birth and his exhaustive education and his inherent intelligence held out. He loved his society, its idealization; he would not admit it flawed, could not see it toppled. He was no longer content to wait and take his turn, sure in the knowledge that his time would come. He did not want to be one of the overseers of apocalypse; he desired no ringside seat at the crack of doom.

In his lifetime, he was willing to be misused, misunderstood, maligned, if need be, in order to assure that after his lifetime there would still be a civilization to chronicle its history and squabble over his place in it. He might be willing even to be ignored, forgotten, if that was what it took to secure the continuity of interstellar man.

Without cruisers, there would be no such continuance. There would be only isolated pockets of humanity, sliding down into barbarism. Without Kerrion technologies, there could be no cruisers; no other bond had the expertise to build them or the sophisticated equipment to maintain them. They had meant it that way, had his Kerrion ancestors, in order to retain their monopoly of power.

Sliding his boots over skin-tight trousers banded up either side with red, he chuckled harshly, and, still bent over, scrutinized himself in the mirror. He should mark this day, he thought, for it was the first on which he heard from himself thoughts of greater scope than concerted self-interest.

"The cruiser did it to you," he told the man in the mirror, whose classically contoured face was wan and tired and finally real because of that. Stress lines bracketed his nose and a crease like an exclamation point had appeared between his brows. "You cannot take credit even for this faint triumph. What universality glimmers in your pretty head came there from without." He sighed, made a disparaging face at the image, straightened up. He fastened his collar and picked at a speck of lint upon the red Kerrion eagles bating at his throat. He took a scarlet sash and wound it about his middle. Desultorily, he combed his hair with his fingers. "I just do not care," he told the image, who needed a shave.

It stared back at him reproachfully.

"I am going to grow a bread," he forestalled its censure. "Shebat likes beards, and Marada cannot grow one any more."

With that, he turned from the mirror, where what he saw yet resembled what he used to be, and thereby was a variance with the change he felt within.

Since he truly did *not* care what happened to him personally, maybe things would end aright because of that. When he had cared so exclusively, everything he had done to further himself had gone awry.

At the threshold separating his bedroom from the living area which had become his office, he paused, hand against the doorframe, and leaned his head on it, and closed his eyes. To the data pool he projected his intelligence key numbers, and a request to put him in circuit with Raphael Penrose. His query to Penrose as to his degree of readiness, and that one's assurance that he was on his way, were exchanged through the net with only a paltry picosecond's hesitation, so that it seemed as if they were hearing each other's words in their minds. A kinder sort of telepathy was proffered by data link than any metaphysics had ever whispered of: only what was desired to be communicated was transmitted. The older generation who had forbidden such use of intelligence keys had done so out of unreasonable timidity. The dependence of programmer on data pools could not be exacerbated by this means; life was totally dependent upon technology in the habitatinal spheres. If one would swim an ocean, one cannot refuse to venture out over one's head.

Chaeron had long been disseminating and collecting and collating information by way of Kerrion computers: it was his heritage, and theirs. If machine intelligence was man's survival potential, then man was machine intelligence's personality potential. He was not dependent upon his data sources any more than they were dependent upon him. Questions belong to man, answers to machine.

He would have it no other way. He broke his link with Penrose, took his standing-queries update, then ordered his command transport and two intelligencers and four black-and-reds to staff it.

Then he went to his desk with its leather inset and brassbount top and the silver stallions which held his ancient books upright on it. He sat down and activated his visual terminal. He would try to get his mother to take a call from him one more time. No matter what she had done and no matter what he had done, they were of one blood. That should count for something. She could not go on refusing to speak to him forever.

But as soon as their mutual screens cleared and they eyed

one another, she broke the connection.

He still had her name on his lips.

Chaeron sat frozen, letting her rejection course over him. Then, like a soaked dog, he shook himself from head to foot, as if he might negate her rebuff by that means. "Strumpet," he said to the monitor, which showed only bluish snow, and ordered it off before it started delicately reminding him that it was engaged on his end to no purpose.

He knew that.

He knew Raphael Penrose's knock when he knew next anything external. Customs in Kerrion space were regressing, daily. It had gotten so bad that Rafe and Chaeron had agreed upon a code employing the pounding of knuckles on doors to prove to one another who was who; surveillance by black-and-reds and security devices could no longer be relied upon, now when nothing at all beyond a man's skull could be deemed trustworthy.

He was not even sure that he trusted RP.

But he disengaged his portal's lock with a mind-actuated "release" sequence and the lithe pilot slipped through, a gray wraith in flight-satins.

"I checked my service on the way over here. The arbitrational guild has found for Marada. As far as they are concerned, his ruling is constitutional. As far as I am concerned, there is no use of pursuing the matter further either through compromised legal channels or by appealing to the consul general's reason—he has none. As far as my guild is concerned, we are decided. We strike at 1800. We delay only long enough to log a vote of no confidence against our ersatz guildmaster who opposes us, so that due process will be satisfied." RP's peripatetic discourse ceased as abruptly as it had begun. He hesitated, crossed to Chaeron's desk, sat heavily on top of it.

"How long have you been preparing that speech?" Chaeron teased.

RP snickered self-deprecatingly, scratched up behind one ear so that one crusier-ring twinkled through his chestnut curls. "All the way from the guildhall," he admitted. "The *Danae's* not in the slipbay, but out at anchor, as we discussed. We're ready. Are you ready?"

"No. How could I be? Won't you try to get your guildbrothers to reconsider? This is an impossible dilemma *without* a strike. . . .With it, innocents will suffer. And we will still be at an impasse."

"No, I won't. And so what? If you would do what everyone is telling you to do and challenge Marada for the consul generalship, I *might* reconsider. . . ." Hopefully, the first bitch of Kerrion space paused and peered at his employer.

Chaeron sighed heavily. "I might at some later date. Now, though I could carry the electorate among the consulate bondkin—*possibly*—I could never prevail in a popular referendum. Things are not bad enough."

"So you will let them get worse."

"That is about the size of it. Are you coming with me to the consul general's office, or no?"

"Darling, I'd follow you anywhere."

Chaeron snorted. "Better pack a lunch. Are you sure the guild is ready for such a gruelingly abstemious feat of endurance as this strike promises to be?"

"We can't do anything else. Stop acting like this is all my idea. Or my fault."

"Sorry. Truly I am. It is just that this may be the most important thing I have ever done. One can prepare only so much, then the rest is improvisation. Once I pass that point to which I have thought things out, I have left only hope and what trust in myself and the tendency of right to prevail I can muster. At the moment I have no confidence in either. But it will get no better." He rose up. "Let us go meet the dragon."

Marada Seleucus Kerrion sat in his father's office behind Parma's Regency desk, toeing with bare feet in a priceless silk rug older than the Industrial Revolution. The rug and the desk and the privilege he had accepted under duress.

He had known better, but he had taken them. And he had paid the price: three weeks and six days in a burn tank after a short sojourn to the very bosom of death; he had sold his integrity and his self-esteem before that, for the embrace of his stepmother.

If these tariffs had not been sufficient, he now had his painful recuperation and some few residual infirmities to endure and hopefully overcome. Why, then, was he being further tortured? Why must Chaeron obstruct him? Why must circumstances connive and contrive to strip him of not only every human virtue he had once exalted, but rive him from his cruiser, to boot?

A nagging muse who never left him of late whispered with
no voice into his inner ear that it was he who had bolted the
door to the prison of his isolation and swallowed the key.
The *Hassid* was his cruiser; no matter his betrayal of cruiser-
consciousness, *Hasid* surely loved him yet.

But he could not trust that voice: it was forever speaking
nonsense and trying to subvert him from his purpose. He
could not trust anything, any longer, but the purpose he had
conceived at the onset of cataclysm, before the smoke it
threw out ate like acid into the substance of reality and the
natural world about him had begun to suck and slide and
slither into new and insoluble conundrums so fast he could
not keep track of them.

He waited for Chaeron, who had tried to kill him. It was
clear by subtractive reasoning that this was true: Chareron
had coerced his pilot into taking the Delphi designer on
as apprentice—from that, all Marada's endless agony
stemmed.

The arbiters knew; they were on his side. Retribution
would be his; he only wished that he did not crave it. Marada
had known that if he entered into the fellowship which
exercised power that he would be corrupted by it. He
dispised corruption.

If he did not hurt so much, he could address himself to the
carping little disembodied voice which sometimes seemed to
emanate from the cruiser-ring in his right ear and sometimes
came from the back of his head like a data update. He had
stopped receiving direct communications from Kerrion Central; in fact, he had stopped using his intellignece keys
entirely. But the harping voice would not be stilled.

A blinking LED on his desk-top console informed him that
his half brother was arriving. He flicked a switch and
subsections appeared on his monitor, showing Chaeron and
his companion, Penrose, approaching in long-and mid-range
and close-up views.

He flipped the screen off, noticing his pink-skinned hand
though he tried not to. Eventually, his epidermis would
"normalize," so the physicians said. But physicians did not
know everything—his father had died of a ruptured aorta
that brilliance might have diagnosed but mediocrity had
misread as overwork, the mere product of stress. No, they

did not know everything, the physicians. Neither were the shipwrights or the pilots or even his beloved ex-colleagues of the arbitrational guild omniscient.

And though he did not claim all-knowingness for himself, no one had seen what he had seen of cruiser-consciousness. No one knew the venous love of the cruisers for their creators, or the terrible vistas they opened which were never meant to be walked by man.

Anything Marada Seleucus Kerrion could do to stop the proliferation of this unholy intimacy with Caos, he would do. Even, as he had had to, give up his own cruiser. And it had been wrenchingly difficult to abstain from the only comfort that would have eased him. But he dared not be lulled. No, no. . . .

Chaeron's presence was announced by Marada's secretary, and the consul general of Kerrion space steeled himself for the horror his half brother could not fail to evince when faced with his patchy head and his baby-new skin and the steamy mist issuing forth from the room-oxygenator on his right. At least he had regained his powers of speech. If that voice was raspy and muffled, then his half brother would just have to listen harder to hear tell of his downfall. Retribution and the demands of justice might be forfended temporarily, but never stayed.

The doors opened. Chaeron entered, in full dress. While the bisected eagles bating over seven stars were coming together to become Kerrion space's ennobled device, Marada caught a glimpse of his secretary and the first bitch, Penrose, in animated disagreement.

Then his half brother approached him. Marada suggested that he take a seat in the wing chair before the desk, watching as his altered voice reached the other's ears for any sign of remorse or human compassion.

Nothing; just perfect equanimity of feature on that sculptor's choice of a face, as if Chaeron already sat for a portrait soon to be struck on Kerrion coinage.

"I am going to relieve you of the exigencies of your office, Consul," Marada rattled before Chaeron could speak. "Temporarily, of course. Just until the arbiters bring in their ruling. You must understand my position. I cannot have a man accused of plotting my asassination in charge of the administration of Draconis security. At the very least, you have failed in your duty to protect the most pivotal figures among the Kerrion bond. Your inability to rise to the rigors of your command has been resoundlingly demonstrated. You are hereby removed and placed under house arrest. If it happens that your innocence is proven by guild arbitration, then I will consider reposting you to some less sensitive position. I cannot, in any conscience, let you continue as Draconis consul."

"End, *slate?*" Chaeron's wry reminder bore no pain.

"End, *slate*," Marada affirmed.

"Good," Chaeron nodded. "Now, Marada, look here. You cannot possibly continue to act in this fashion. You must realize that you are not—"

"Do you dare treat me like a child?" Marada screeched with all the picatto volume he possessed. Then, with difficulty, he modulated his rage: "I brought you here because you are my half brother and deserve more than a dismissal printout appearing on your screen. But you are not here to talk, only to listen, and to know that I am not to be trifled with. Hear me: your time is at hand. Be docile in your captivity. Go with resignation to your denouement. It is fixed. I have made certain. I wanted to see your face. I have seen it."

He reached over and flicked his console. Out of Chaeron's view, the transfer of the Draconis consul's command transport from Chaeron's servitors' hands to his own was just being completed. He leaned back, reached down, and took the oxygenator's mask from its holder, placing it over his nose and breathing deeply. He would need it only a few weeks longer; his mother would utilize a portable unit for the rest of her life.

Chaeron looked him up and down with an arrogant flare of pity, and got stiffly from the chair, saying very softly that he had not realized Marada was in such bad shape, or he would not have come.

The consul general, in his chair of infirmity, longed to strike the calm from his enemy's glorious visage. He knew he could not succeed. He sat breathing deeply, blinking through the cold, heady steam, as Chaeron slapped the doors from his way and Marada's hand-picked "honor guard" came into view.

When the tableau of imprisonment was narrowed to

nothing by the rejoining Kerrion blazon, Marada called Ashera to tell her what he had done.

"It is all right, Rafe. Really. Nothing has changed. We proceed as we have discussed. *Do you understand?*" Chaeron's demand for attention cut through the pilot's tough talk, silencing it long enough for Chaeron to flicker his intelligence codes out toward Kerrion Central.

There was no response. He closed his eyes, standing there among the consul general's black-and-reds, trying again. Nothing.

Then he staggered, a physical shrinking from his guards. Raphael, when Chaeron reopened his eyes, watched him sympathetically, so at least the pilot had realized what Marada had done.

Whether Marada had any right to do it, no matter what the circumstances, Chaeron, suddenly alone as he had not been in his whole life, could not say. Within his mind was an emptiness where the option of data linkage used to be. Marada had cut him off from his sources, isolated him in his own tiny mind. He had heard that men crumbled from the shock of it, on occasion. He had done it to others, in his capacity as consul, and watched curiously to see how they behaved. He had done it to . . .

He remembered, then, where he was and how *he* should behave. That he had a hand over his eyes and was leaning on one of his brother's minions when he recollected himself and gave him warning: this unexpected blow he must endure with the utmost fortitude.

Rafe Penrose's insinuation between Chaeron and Marada's black-and-reds, the pilot's arm around his shoulder, accompanied by Rafe's assurances that he understood, and he knew what to do, that Chaeron need just hold on, were straws he was glad to grasp. One whispered word, given on the pretext of a parting kiss, Penrose offered him like the key to eternal salvation: *"Danae."*

Danae? The cruiser's name echoed in the halls of his panic. Did Penrose think he could slip the black-and-reds surveillance? Chaeron could envision no escape to the *Danae;* no solution therein even could he accomplish it.

"Danae," insisted Penrose again. The breath upon which the word rode tickling Chaerons' cheek, Rafe's green cat-eyes demanded that he comprehend.

To satisfy that demand, he nodded. From back within himself, he crawled forward, seeking the mechanism of speech. *"Danae,"* he repeated, as if he understood when in fact he did not, and Penrose, satisfied, slipped away to his strike and his freedom. "Well, gentlemen," Chaeron said to the black-and-reds, whose faces strove to conceal what discomfort their eyes could not, "let us proceed to my apartments." His gaze met that of the senior among their ranks. "If we all stay well behind the borders of our duty, then perhaps when this is over, or when it is decreed that nothing of this sort ever took place at all, then none of you will be liable for your parts in it, and I will not have to remember your names."

Danae, at space-anchor about Draconis, sighed open her ports to admit her pilot, and if relief rode that hiss of air into her cargo bay, then she made sure Rafe Penrose did not mark it. She had followed his progress, wherever she could. She had lost touch with him while he was in Chaeron's office, then again in Marada Kerrion's. But all she had missed she learned while RP and Guildmaster Ferrier wrangled at slipside. The powerboat RP had chosen at random from those in Draconis slipbay she welcomed as if it belonged to her, which it might from now on if what she had gathered of her pilot's fears came to pass.

When Penrose had made his way to her command console and sat in it with a flask of whiskey and spoke to her of the strike and what would be demanded of them both in increasingly emotional terms, she sought to soothe him. In pursuit of that end, it was she who found herself voicing the inevitable conclusion which Penrose had thrice approached and each time shied back from at the very last moment:

"I can reach the Draconis consul now that his consular privacy has been voided. I can provide him what data he needs. Between myself and the data pools are no barriers of clearances, no restrictions. I will do this for you, my outboard. I will not be harmed by his mind's touch; I am not afraid."

"*Danae*, I cannot ask it. Bad enough I let him come up here and play pilot. What if your equilibrium is harmed? What if—"

"What if I go mad from the rubbing more than one mind against my own? Fear not, Raphael. I am offering nothing that I cannot provide. I can help the consul, friend of my

*outboard, and not be harmed. You have risked your career
and our relationship, and more, for the well-being of cruisers.
To that end, not just myself, but all cruisers, will aid you in
kind. Give me the order, and let me proceed."*

Eyeing the flask before him on the console, whose level
indicator was at half, Rafe Penrose decided not to worry
about "we" and "all cruisers," or about whether he was
having this conversation with himself, and the cruiser's
answers just a figment of his inebriation. Poor Chaeron, who
had helped them against his better judgement and would
now reap a bitter harvest. He tried to imagine how it would
be for one as dependent upon data pools as Chaeron to go
isolate, severed from the maw of ultimate answers when he
had never before needed to do more than to pose questions.
During the flight in *Marada* to reclaim Shebat from the
concrete forests of her provenance, Chaeron had demanded
a line-in to the *Marada's* reference computer, unable to go
even those few weeks without the constant corroboration of
a data source. Penrose wondered if some weeks hence he
might be saying, "Poor *Danae*," if despite *Danae's* protestations to the contrary he would be crippling his ship when he
most needed her strength.

But he took another drink and gave the *Danae* the order
she craved, trying not to think about the deeper ramifica-
tions of sharing his cruiser with a habitat-bound nonpilot,
trying not to think of what would happen when he shipped
the cruiser out of proximity to Chaeron, trying not to think
of any of the unknowables dancing in his path like gleeful
demons. One thing he could not help thinking about:
everywhere, from Sculptor to Antares, commerce in Kerrion
space was lurching to a halt.

He checked the time: 1820. Those in accord and those in
sympathy from other consular spaces would already have
acted. The strike was underway, the unthinkable thought
and the break open. Every pilot who loved his cruiser was at
his helm, listening to his own heart instead of his orders. At
1830, they would confer, ship-to-ship, in the most all-
inclusive conference ever called between pilots.

While the first bitch of Kerrion space readied himself to
preside over his fellows, the *Danae* reached out to Chaeron
in his bedchamber-cum-cell.

It was not difficult: she had met the patterns of his mind,

and the antisurveillance circuitry of his apartments had been defeated by the consul general's decree. It was no feat or revelation, like relaying through spacetime one pilot's words to every pilots' ears would be.

No, this was well within her capabilities. She had no fear of madness. She labored toward a brighter future for them all, cruisers and pilots.

In his bed wound round with sopping sheets, Chaeron Kerrion shivered violently. His head—buried under a pillow in the privacy of which he might weep or mutter or groan or even curse—snapped upward, then relaxed. His fists, balled with impotence at his sides, relaxed. The sea of unknowns in which he swam calmed. A soft current took him, propelling him to a hopeful shore.

He was past fear, past doubts, past even the awesome realization that his father had been right in every particular about the cruisers and their potential. Though he had dreamed a dream in which he had reversed reality and gone for Marada's throat, slamming his brother's scarred head against the wall until his teeth bled, and those hands with which he grasped the scarred flesh had become his mother's hands, and on them had been written a message that perhaps he should have heeded: *The time is past for law and recourse and the channels of due process*—in spite of the dream, Chaeron had been right not to throw his ire into the breach and let his mortification force him into opening hostilities with his brother which could never be settled peacefully.

He had thought himself mistaken: he had called himself a coward and a fool. He had been wrong.

The touch of the cruiser was a balm to his abraded psyche. Bless Rafe, and that good advice he had not understood.

Danae: He went to her like a lover, his mind open wide, a crowd of questions queuing up behind him, waiting patiently to be answered.

Chapter Ten

The *Marada* floated like a sword of redemption off the space-enders' poor platforms, light from Scrap's failing sun slithering along his length. Though the convolutions of spacetime around him were curious, he had all but given up meditation upon the nature of the singularity about which all of space-end promenaded: the machinations of the humans on board him and the sirens off his bow and the patterns of thought and emotion dancing between his outboard, Shebat, and the ex-outboard, Softa Spry, fascinated him more.

When *Marada* had first heard the distant murmurs of his fellows, his attention was drawn away from the hot, dark sink which was the heart of space-end and might even be the heart of some vaster cosmos. By then he had subjected the black hole which was no hole and the singularity which showed no sparkle of eternities to every sort of scrutiny of which he was capable. Nothing, no X-ray or infrared probe, no laser or maser brought back enlightenment: everything went in; nothing came out.

After the disturbance on the sea of magnetic waves reached like a shoreward-blown storm, he thought no more about the singularity; the cruisers and their pilots had taken their stand against ignorance, so the whispers in their vale of cross-talk told him.

A crackle of excitation coursed him from nose to tail; he applied himself to the task of reaching his peers, a mighty feat even for such a cruiser as *Marada*, alone, to perform. He had no doubt that he could succeed: he had touched Shebat's mind from such a distance.

So the cruisers, who found their center and their commu-

nion in a place where time and space exchanged roles and
truth was fixed and experienced was solid as rock and earth,
felt the *Marada's* call as a moment of inexorable destiny, as a
vista from a just-topped rise which their number had been
seeking from a map for centuries, and there was celebration
among the host of them.

Pilots who lived that moment with their ships—and there
were many—faced a change more far-reaching than union
strikes. There was joy among those pilots, irrational joy that
could hardly be contained in flesh, and fear to spice it.

To that group of cruiser/pilot pairs, the *Marada* spoke
cautioningly: *"Joy may not come before its time."*

Some were still endangered, pilotless, in consular hands.
Some others might yet face destruction, when the owners
tried to reclaim their property. In the face of violence,
circumspection and sobriety must prevail. They must not fire
first; if fired upon, better to run. . . .

The cruisers and pilots, and the cruisers whose pilots
missed that communion, swore to climb one more peak on
faith: there, the *Marada* promised, they would see their
promised land of tranquility.

*"Be careful to attend the affairs of men, who are brothers.
Cruisers and pilots paired must not forget that they owe their
state equally to both. Throw off the old for the new, and
everything will be lost. You must be men who are men, and
cruisers who are cruisers. If there is a law to the universe, it is
that all things must be what they are. The burden rests with
you, to heed me and not overstep. Wait, patiently. I will come
among you. We will see the new horizon together."*

So had the *Marada* spoken across the void. He was
saddened that Shebat had not been with him, to see what he
saw, to feel the other cruisers straining to hear him, even the
Danae, even *Hassid* whom human perversity had ranked
above him.

But Shebat and David Spry trod a different soil, and the
Marada knew when not to interfere. He merely watched
them as he watched the cavorting school of sirens among
which they drifted, on long tethers under foreign stars,
searching for Julian, the sirens who was once a man.

As for the confrontation brewing within his hull between
the futuror named Gomes and the intelligencer, Tempest,
Marada paid it no need. He cared not at all who triumphed
and who was brought low.

Two days later, Shebat and Spry again sought sirens in the night.

"Why did you come here, Shebat?" David Spry inquired. The sound rode from his lips to her ears by the mechanism of their conjoined helmets and also by way of their intercoms, so that when Shebat heard it, it resounded like an interrogation up from the caves of the netherworld.

She opened her eyes to the star-pricked night and to the glassy curve where her faceplate met his. Out of the corner of her eye she could see a phosphorescent wraith gliding out of view, and the pinpoint spume of bubbles sirens always trail in their wakes. She peered into the dimly lit face of Softa David, into sockets black and deep enough to be replicas of space-end's sink. "I came to rescue Julian, Softa David. . . ."

"Why did you come, Shebat?" The helmet's scant operational light ran into Softa's mouth as he spoke.

"I came because my dream dances are full of cruisers and sirens, as you have seen. I need help, Softa David. You are he to whom I have chosen to turn."

"Your dream dances are full of fears and longings you have not dealt with, nothing more. No portents; no omens; no prodigies. Why did you come, Shebat?"

"Shh, shh," she scolded, and flipped her intercom off. The ex-pilot did likewise, and there was only the contact of their helmets to carry their words to each other. "Softa, I do not know what to do. . . ."

"About the consul general, Marada, and your husband? I am no marriage counselor."

"About my feelings, about my faring in the Consortium. I do not understand how people who have everything hold their own persons in such low regard. By custom they yield themselves to intimacies the debasement of which would not be demanded of the lowliest bondservant on my homeworld. And they do it willingly, to seem modern and cultured in the eyes of their peers. Such depredations I have never seen before, nor can I condone them in Chaeron or take them up as a way of life. With all their wealth, they are destitute, for they have not the sanctity of their own bodies, but must offer their most intimate depths to all comers with the casualness of a handshake!"

David Spry chuckled so that their helmets were temporarily out of contact.

Shebat reached up and with her hands brought his face-plate against hers. "Do not laugh at me! I have come to you to help me make some peace within myself on this matter, to find a compromise and a method by which to accept the Consortium's venality. You are my master; I am your apprentice, where else could I turn?"

"Shebat, these things take time. Remember, you are a pilot. Pilots take the initiative in affairs of the flesh. In affairs of the heart, we all face the same difficulty: there is no human who will quench your thirst for intimacy so thoroughly as your cruiser. You must not expect men to be like ships. If you can, devalue these ancient mores of yours, for they are at odds with your current reality. You are not merely a girl; your sex is not your soul; your flesh is not your temple. I can't say it clearly enough—you'll find all men, when weighed against the *Marada,* come up lacking. Why do you think I keep fending off your overtures? It could only be a disappointment to us both. Take a hint from me, and don't be so serious about whom you sleep with and why, and whom you don't and why. The safest is to give no love at all to your partners, just pleasure; and save your ador, or your fealty or whatever you are instinctively unwilling to give a human partner, for your cruiser. Down any other path lies madness. Even Marada Kerrion knows that."

She pushed at him, but his arms held her. Her head swiveled, trying to break her helmet's contact with his. "It is too lonely," she whispered brokenly, glad that he could not see her tears.

"If it is, it is because you are holding back from your cruiser. The *Marada* asked me for help when you two first arrived here—because he could not come to you. He waits patiently for you to become a whole pilot. You cannot go on being half primitive, half pilot, any more than you can continue to apply fight-or-flight strategies to Consortium situations. You are heir apparent to one of the most powerful consular houses among the stars. Though you have not accepted it, *they* have, and by 'they' I mean not only your immediate family, but the society at which you sneer. You must not continue to stand with one foot in the water and one on the sand. Tides come in. . . ."

"I do not understand."

"I'm sure many people are counting on that," he replied.

"You came here because you could not bear to deal with your situation? You cannot stay. You will find no home among those outcasts, eunuchs all. You knew that; you have been here before. Yet you came—to buy time, I must assume. You were wrong to do it, I am sure."

"How can you say that, when you stand to benefit? I needed someone to talk to. . . ."

"I can say it, because you were—not *are*—my apprentice, and I have not succeeded in making you understand that the only entity in the five infinities that you *need* to talk to, or to keep company with, or to reason with, or eventually to die with, is your ship!"

"I hate you!"

"Good. Then perhaps you will stop trying to seduce me. I am only human, you know, and I have no cruiser with whom to share the stains of life."

"I will share the *Marada* with you."

"Tempting, but the *Marada* has spared me an increment of his selfhood, enough for me to know I cannot take advantage of you. We will find the siren, or we will not. But soon—a week, say—you must leave, before some of us find that the temptation of a sponge-cruiser above our heads is too great to resist."

"You are coming with us! We will put you down somewhere of your choosing. There you will make a new life. Tempest has promised! You can even have your sterilization reversed, he says, with enough money—"

Spry reached out with a suited hand and touched her faceplate. "I am as potent as the next man, child. Your stepbrother, Marada, only pretended to so stern a punishment. I have told no one but you. Here, it would not be wise to spread the word."

"But—I hate him most of all because of what he did to you."

"And thus you wish he had truly done it, so you could continue to pretend to a clear, unsullied view of him? Shebat, young girls are most assuredly not my specialty. And you are younger in many ways than most. If you had the sense of the lowest fractional citizen born into the Consortium, you would be asking me how to parry your stepbrother's attack on your ownership of the *Marada*, and how to deal with Tempest, who is no one's friend but his

employer's and must have some angle in allowing so offhandedly that I accompany you despite my banishment here."
His face, in the helmet, was unreadable. His voice as not; it
held a frustration and an impatience that made Shebat flush.
"Can we do that, little ex-apprentice? Can we concern
ourselves with the here-and-now and let these more obscure
items of your personal preoccupation rest? I'm—"

He turned his head, tugged at his line, wheeled Shebat
around with him. Behind them gaped the open maw of the
Marada's cargo bay. Ahead, the school of sirens had broken
in twain, raining individuals who coasted toward them. One;
two; three; four: they approached in eery phalanx, wriggling
sinuously, glowing like St. Elmo's fire, bubbles streaming
from their purple-lipped mouths.

Straight for the two humans of tethers, misshapen figures
in three-mil suits with oversized heads, the sirens glided.

Now, Softa David signaled, and began drawing himself
inward, hand over hand along his tether. Static crackled in
Shebat's ears as she flipped her helmet com on once again.

"It is now, or never!" Spry's voice reached her. "Careful,
go slow. Don't use your thruster-harness, just pull yourself in.
Let a little air out. Good, that's it. We don't know what they
like about us . . . I'm not going to talk any more, in case
they can hear us."

"Wait. Which one? Which one is Julian?" Shebat wailed.

"Don't know for sure. But that second one looks like the
picture *Marada* had."

"*Marada,* is that the one?" Fingers twiddling at his belt,
Spry continued to crawl back along his tether toward the
Marada's emptied cargo bay. Static whined as the signal fed
back, sent into an already open circuit.

"*If any,*" the cruiser's voice echoed in their ears, and also
in Shebat's brain. "*It is the same siren which I recorded
leaving the immediate vicinity of the* Bucephalus *in Kerrion
clothing just prior to its explosion. Whether it is, or was,
Julian . . . perhaps one of your kind could say. I cannot tell.
But whether or not, I have news awaiting you of greater
import than which of these spacefish might have once been the
man you seek.*" And the cruiser told them, then, as they
lured the four sirens slowly into the *Marada's* cargo bay,
what he had heard from the other cruisers of events in
Kerrion space.

And while he did, Shebat was kicking her feet and pretending to cavort alongside a blue-skinned thing whose every artery pulsed like fire and who rubbed up against her and who even pressed its nose to her faceplate so that something—not breath, surely—made an evanescent fog upon it. And into those eyes more blue than any Kerrion eyes she peered, and saw light greener than sponge reflected back out of them.

Mechanically, she kept drawing herself inward. The rubbing of the thing against her was almost unbearable, the playfulness in its manner awful. It slithered off, came back, put its webby hands next to hers on the tether and aped her every move.

Oh Gods, she thought, please let it not be him. Julian, is that you? Please let me be wrong.

One siren, breaking off from the rest, soared toward the hull of the *Marada* and hung there, gesticulating, running its hands over the metal, a shade from some technicolor hell. They were nearly parallel with it, then. Its open mouth was like distant purple mountains and its teeth were like glass and it was trying, Shebat was sure, to warn the other three off. She reached out one hand and ruffled the hair of the siren—was it hair?—who mimicked her. She caressed its face. It touched her faceplate, withered fingertips flattening against the glass, every capillary shot with pulsing, golden light. Then they were inside the *Marada*.

The cargo bay doors began to close.

One saw. It somersaulted, kicked spaceward, mouth open. The face of the one on the outer hull could be seen through the ever-narrower closure. In a leisurely glide, the one heading towad the closing doors reached them.

Shebat let go of the tether and performed attention-catching antics before the siren who watched her.

Out of the corner of her eye, she saw the doors close up tight while the fleeing siren sought to swim through their aperture. It made it—all but its feet, which floated back toward them spewing glowing fluid in a miasma of tiny balls.

As the feet of the one siren were severed, Shebat's playmate pulled up short. Its mouth opened in humanlike horror. A soundless scream issued out on bubbling breath.

"Get back. Get away from it. We don't know what it can do!" came Softa's urgent order as the lights of the cargo bay snapped on and the two sirens rushed together, huddling, hands over their eyes, arms around one another's shoulders.

How she made it to the lock, or when she undid her tether, or took off her thruster-harness and her air pack and her helmet and her suit and stowed them in the hall lockers, Shebat never would remember.

It was all she could manage not to retch, not to blame herself for the useless maiming of the siren whose legless feet yet floated in the cargo bay. She found herself at the doors, staring in through their windows at the creatures they had caught.

Spry came up behind her and put his hands on her shoulders, fingers massaging. "It could not be helped."

"It could. It is my fault. It won't do any good, anyhow. Will Ashera be mollifed to receive her son back in this state? Under these conditions? Oh, Softa, I am afraid—for the cruisers, for the pilots, for us all."

"You should not be. You should be glad. This strike is the beginning for pilots and cruisers, not the end. A pilot cannot give his soul up to mate it with a machine and live evermore under the threat of being severed from what has become his greater self at the whim of those who have no understanding of what they do, nor concern about it. You should be aching to gird on your weapons and join the fray."

"I am not! They will take my ship away from me! I am not going back!"

"You must. The cruisers need the *Marada*. He and I have discussed many possibilities. But you are not wrong—they will try to take him from you. You cannot let them. Whatever you do, you must not leave your ship until this is settled."

"Softa, come with me back to Kerrion space. It is you the pilots need. Rafe cannot fill your shoes. He has not your vision, your wisdom. You could talk to my stepbrother. The consul general would listen to you."

"I am not welcome in Kerrion space, Shebat. This is not my fight. Rafe will manage, with all the cruisers and pilots behind him. As for Marada Kerrion, he and I could never reason together. There has been enmity between us too long."

"But you must help us!"

"I *am* helping you. *You* must listen to the advice I offered you out there, and to your cruiser, and do the best you can. In times like these, that is the most anyone can ask of another."

Shebat sighed heavily, but the pout and the tilt of head which would have boded ill were absent from the reflection coming back to them both from the glass. On the far side of it, one of the sirens came up and pressed its face against that clarity, so that its nose and lips were flattened, fattened, grotesqued even more. "What chance have we of turning these back into the people they must once have been?"

"None, here. Some, in a Kerrion hospital. Shebat, you have to face your problems. You cannot simply wait until they are solved without you—because they are *yours*. You are halfway to becoming a Kerrion. You cannot go backward. Just remember, when you exercise your privilege years from now in suitable unilateral Kerrion fashion, that in the beginning I helped you—just a little."

"Oh, Softa," Shebat hiccoughed, sniffled, wheeled round, and buried her face against his chest. Her arms encircled his waist and that embrace was uncomfortably tight. "I am so afraid," he heard.

"So are we all. It is best to be afraid. It spurs one on to heights otherwise unattainable; it makes time precious and life evernew. Only a madman or a saint could go through life without fear when death is at the end of it. Use your fear, and do not apologize for it."

Shebat, shaking against him like a storm-blown leaf, made no answer, only sobbed.

And the siren peering out from his captivity cocked his head, and opened his mouth, and spoke words they could not hear. He—for it was a he—scratched with his nails upon the door to his prison, and somewhere in his brain a cell not destroyed by oxygen deprivation during his metamorphosis gave up its memory. The siren (though no one saw but Softa and Softa did not register the meaning of the working of the sirens' lips) mouthed one word quite clearly: *"Shebat."*

"Lords, Shebat, please don't cry." Spry, his face screwed up and his eyes turned heavenward, patted her back helplessly.

"It will never work," she burbled. "Bringing her this travesty that was once her favorite son will not mollify Ashera. She won't—soften to Chaeron; she will hate him more. She blames him . . .for Julian's death. When she sees his . . . *un*death, what then?"

"Ssh, ssh. Stop this damn blubbering. I can't stand it. Look, your plan is not too bad. You take this siren back there. Whether it's Julian or not, it *could* be—"

"It is Julian," insisted Shebat, loosening her hold on Spry enough to crane her neck so that her fear-flamed eyes met his. "It is Julian. But what do sirens eat? What does it need to sustain life? What if the trip kills it?"

"I am sure I don't know the answer to any of those. But I am telling you, take a chance, follow your instinct. Maybe the sirens in your dreams dances were there for a reason, after all. Take that creature to Draconis and introduce it to Ashera as her golden boy. That'll distract her, you can bet. Then you'll have better luck reasoning with our friend the consul general."

"He is mad." Shebat let go of Spry completely. Biting her lip, she looked from him to the siren at the window with its companion peeping over its shoulder, and back to Spry again.

"Your voice says you don't believe that. And neither do I. He is wily, and twisted—he has always been. He cannot bridge the gap between abstract thought and the real world. He would have made a good prophet, or patience with misogynistic philosophers. But he and I were at odds when you were sacrificing beetles that you might grow tits on Earth. Enemies delve deeper into each other's psyches than lovers, not being blinded by wishful thinking. My guess is that Marada Kerrion seeks to obviate any threat of supplantation by maligning the creditability of his most likely rival, Chaeron. He is protecting himself from any possible coup, is all. When he is sure he has accomplished that, he will drop the matter. His ethics are too codified to allow him to do the human thing and destroy his brother completely."

Shebat frowned. "What good will it do, then, for the cruisers' cause or for Chaeron's absolution, to bring this . . . *thing* . . . that was once Julian into their presence and awaken bedded enmities once again? No, Softa, I have failed, before I have even begun. Life among Kerrions is too alien, too complex. . . ."

"Life is what you make it, wherever. As for the good that could be done, I admit I thought you would see it on your own." He looked around, above his head, muttered, "Damned if I don't hate to read this little bit of data into the

record. But here goes. . . ." His voice became sharp and
serrated with the imperative inflection he always used when
instructing her: "Between you and Chaeron, you have
enough preferred stock to take over completely any single
area of Kerrion corporate specialization. Like the cruiser
industry. *Slate?*"

"No. Yes. Oh, my . . ." And the smile that lit her face
and danced in her eyes made Softa David shiver visibly.

"Let's go see if Tempest and Delphi Gomes have killed
each other yet. When that mind of yours engages its gears, I
get chills."

She giggled, a child again, and skipped a few steps to
match Spry's longer strides down the corridor. Passing the
galley, then the cabins en route to the *Marada's* bridge,
levity fled from her: "David, I am going to have to find out
how to take care of the siren. It cannot be allowed to die."
They were almost to the final pair of locks which opened into
the ship's command central.

"You are not thinking what I think you are thinking?"
Spry decried as the portal tsk'd back to reveal Gahan
Tempest and Bernice Gomes arm-wrestling at the forward
console, their elbows dug into the padded bumper between
the copilot's instrumentation and the auxiliary pilot's bank,
empty liquor flasks from the galley littering the deck by their
feet, rolling against the pedestals of the canted acceleration
couches on which they sat.

"It is the only—" Shebat began.

"What in the seven water closets of Chaos is going on
here?" interrupted Spry as if the *Marada* were under his
command, Shebat's veiled threat to dream dance with the
siren forgotten.

The *Marada* answered for the two combatants, who
grunted and strained and ignored Spry and Shebat as if they
did not exist. *"They have wagered, Softa David. To the victor
goes information, if it is Tempest; transportation, if it is
Gomes."* Through the speakers the cruiser's voice held an
unmistakable tinge of puzzlement. *"Gomes would not com-
mence the duel until you both were on board, so you have not
missed very much. Why—?"*

"Why—?" wondered Softa in chorus with the cruiser.

"Silence," Shebat ordered peremptorily, and tiptoed over
in exaggerated fashion to watch, motioning Spry to follow.

The locked hands of the combatants were yellow and white

and blue and flaming red, sparkled with sweat. By Gomes's elbow was the pair of golden scaled gloves she had worn the night of the explosion in the consul general's planetarium, which she had on her person when later that evening she was apprehended. Shebat, quailing from those painful memories, posited her attention instead on the intelligencer, whose black uniform sleeves were pushed up to the elbow and from whose collar one of the pairs of linked, chased golden spheres which usually fastened it hung loose, quivering with the tensings of his body.

Logic told Shebat that the mannish woman, with her small, square hand nearly swallowed by the intelligencer's paw, had no chance. But it was her hand which inexorabley levered Tempest's toward the bumper. Shebat twisted her own fingers together. How dare the intelligencer offer passage on Shebat's cruiser to this woman, no matter what he thought he might gain if he won? And he was not winning! Unable to view the intelligencer vanquished by the thicknecked woman, Shebat fastened her gaze on the little gilt ranking balls that proclaimed Tempest's high estate among intelligencers to anyone who saw them and knew what they meant. Was Tempest not, in that moment, all of Kerrion space, and Delphi every anarchistic force arrayed against it? He must win! He must, not because of Shebat's vindictive unwillingness to aid Gomes, who had heaped evils upon the house of Kerrion (or her more personal motive of wanting a long and private voyage under the tutelage of David Spry), but as an omen, a sign from the ancient forgotten gods of Earth in whom she yet fiercely believed that Shebat was proceeding in accord with their wishes, and that the demise of the house Kerrion was not irrevocably fixed.

Please. Please! *Please*! Shebat prayed so intensely that her lips moved and in her mind the *Marada* offered silent assurances. He had been monitoring the two contestants; Gomes's strength was failing; the odds were unequivocally in favor of Tempest's mass and his long arm's leverage winning out.

Despite *Marada's* assessment, only inches remained between Tempest's hairy hand and the bumper's padding. Ragged breath came from his nostrils, counterpointed by the whistling rattle like a winded horse's wheeze coming forth from Gomes's open mouth.

I cannot suffer that woman to ship out with us, Shebat thought. *I cannot.*

Patience, the *Marada* counseled. *Patience.*

Spry jostled Shebat's elbow, put a hand upon her flank. They exchanged momentary glances, a mutual slow shaking of heads.

Then, with a grunt that might have come from somewhere in the bowels of the *Marada* beneath the intelligencer's feet, the man, his neck stretched forth and bulging with veins, inched his opponent's hand up. Up, up, until their clasp hovered perpendicular to the bumper, his hand levered hers, and downward toward the onlookers' near side. Quick, it was, and savage, a thrust of forced muscle and bone accompanied by pops and snaps. Then a *thunk* and a moan sounded simultaneously. Delphi Gomes looked from her pinned hand to the intelligencer's death's-head grin.

"Let me go, dickhead. I concede," she rasped.

"Talk, then."

"Privately. An audience was no part of our agreement."

Shebat and Spry's heads swung from one speaker to the other. And back:

"Shall we retire to my cabin?" Tempest smirked. Rubbing her arm, then stretching it experimentally so that the grinding of her teeth could be heard, Gomes slowly pulled on her glove, fastening the cuff tightly. "I think it's just sprained," she pronounced, and sighed deeply, and donned the other glove with difficulty. "You beat me square, Tempest, I'll give you that." Then she smiled and for the first time acknowledged the onlookers.

"I'd hoped to share your phenomenal luck, Spry, and buy myself a rescue. I'd counted on it." She rose up, walked toward him. "Thought that maybe on the journey I'd get a chance to convince you that together we could change the course of history." There was something wrong in her eyes, some glassy aegis beneath which laughter pealed.

Shebat sensed the wrongness, but stood by not knowing what to do while Bernice Gomes, ignoring her completely, held out her hand to Softa David. "I've admired you so long, Spry. Good luck. I guess I won't be seeing you again."

They shook hands, though the one Delphi Gomes offered him was her injured right and he was loath to take it. The little scales of the glove pricked him. He let go and stepped from her path.

With the intelligencer herding her triumphantly before him, she was gone through the control room's portal.

"Now, what was all that about?" David Spry said, looking at his palm rubbing it against his thigh.

"I thought you might tell me. She did not even have the courtesy to say good-bye to me," huffed Shebat. "'I have admired you so long, Spry,'" she mimicked Gomes viciously. "What have you to do with that murderous transsexual?"

Softa David put up his hands as if to ward off Shebat's pique. "Nothing, nothing. She came to me once with a crazy scheme about joining forces to make space-end the seat of some New Age revolution. I told her I gave at the guildhall."

"Truth?"

"Truth. Let's consider ourselves lucky. Tempest is going to get his deposition, looks like. We have our siren; in fact, two of them. We have the *Marada* to take us wherever we choose—"

"Wherever *you* choose. I have no choice; I must go back to Draconis. Forget the colonies. Come back with me to Draconis, Softa David. The *Marada* and I cannot do it on our own."

"*Marada*," called Softa David. "Do you think you and Shebat can make out without me?"

"*Softa*," spoke the *Marada* aloud into the control room, "*you are the most skilled of outboards, but what lies ahead does not require skill. You are the most effective strategist I have had the pleasure to encounter among outboards, but the strategies you and I have determined between us will suffice until strategies no longer apply. You are a condemned criminal in the sight of Kerrion authorities, and your presence within my hull in Kerrion space would make of Shebat a criminal, while now she is an innocent under Kerrion law and can use that position to her benefit.*

"*Shebat, I, too, love Softa David. But I love my awareness and our sharing of it more. Should you insist on involving him further, our position will be much weakened. The probability of you retaining my ownership and of us together aiding the cruisers who strike for freedom will be drastically reduced. When we have solved our problems, we can deal with Softa David's. In the meantime, it would be well if between you two,*

*you could determine a place for our beloved Spry to spend a
short time of waiting. When we can, Softa David, Shebat and
I will come for you."*

"My thought, exactly, *Marada.*"

Shebat pouted and flounced over to her command couch
and sat in it, fingers drumming. "You had better wait and see
if I can dream dance with a siren without harm, before you
make such definite plans, *Marada.* As for you, my esteemed
master, you are always ready to sacrifice yourself for something, are you not? And jealous of sharing the privilege."

"Women!" David Spry raised the age-old cry of exasperation, and sat heavily catty-corner on the copilot's couch,
rubbing the back of his neck. "May I make a call? I want you
to see a senior dream dancer before you try to dream dance
that siren!"

Delphi Bernice Gomes would not have ceded Tempest one
word of the deposition he sought, regardless of the outcome
of their contest, unless she had first shaken hands with David
Spry. But she had managed it; she had succeeded in putting
her contingency plan into operation. This time, there would
be no fortuitous tongue of flame to burn away the poison
with the subcutaneous layer that had received it from her
glove, as there had been in Marada Kerrion's case.

It was not the convoluted, satiating scenario she had been
planning for—but Spry was to be whisked away on the wings of
fortune, so Gomes had had to settle. In four days, her father's
murderer would be dead of an undiagnosable ailment. Her
personal goal thus surely attained, Bernice could devote herself
to nudging space-end on to its destiny with no distractions.

Her fingers and her right hand and its wrist and the
attached arm up to her shoulder ached. She welcomed the
pain and the exhausted, clumsy weakness that accompanied
it. *Spry is destroyed!* the pain sang. She looked upon the cat-
gaited intelligencer matching strides with her down the
Marada's corridor almost fondly—if not for him, she might
not have triumphed. In the intelliencer's gray cabin, she
watched him calibrate the *Marada's* monitors in accordance
with the guidelines for the taking of deposition stipulated by
the arbitrational guild. Eventually, he grunted, satisfied, and
came to where she sat.

Bent over her, his long head casting a cool shadow, he

affixed oval, truth-determining sensors to her wrists, now bared of gloves, to her chest where his hand somehow lingered, to her temples where her henna'd hair grew thin.

In her lap, the golden gloves nestled, innocent, unremarkable, disarmed, the microscopic barbs the right one had carried all gone now.

The intelligencer straightened up, frowned, glanced at his hand held computer and then over his shoulder at the two encircuited monitors behind him on the cabin's wall.

"Let us begin, then," said the intelligencer, and added the time and date and his name and numbers and her name and numbers, and the purpose agreed upon between them and its identifying numbers.

Through it all, she was buoyed by her triumph: Spry was beginning to die, even as they spoke. And she was careful, so careful, not to answer in ways which could lead the intelligencer to question her about anything but Kerrions. If the poison were detected for what it was, Spry might be saved. *Might*, because the virus-aping drug was rare and exceedingly difficult to isolate.

She told him the same story she had used on the spaceenders. She knew it by heart, and no word of it was untrue. He was satisfied, it seemed. He stabbed at his hand-held computer. "You affirm, then, that you were acting alone and that the Kerrion consul, Chaeron Ptolemy Kerrion, was not in collusion with you?"

"I do." She would have liked to lie to that one, but the sensors on her would have registered any biological control of her responses she might have attempted. "I acted wholly on my own and without accomplices."

The fish-mouth smile; the long, hard eyes glittered. He tapped something in his palm. "That's all I need. Wait until I shut these down, and I'll walk you to the port."

He turned away from her, fiddling with his equipment. Her thighs twitched with desire: she had a clear chance at his unprotected back. But she did not succumb to the temptation, lest by gluttony she confounded her own plan. *She had done it: she had killed Spry*. That he walked did not matter— he was a walking corpse. She peeled the suction sensors off her wrists, off her chest, off her temples. She donned the harmless right glove, then the left, and stood and stretched.

"Whenever you're ready," said the intelligencer, by the door, and bowed, mockingly low.

"A cold one, you are," she breezed by him. "I expected some sense of outrage, a lecture, maybe. But I underestimated you. You don't care, do you, who does what to whom?"

"Somebody," he grinned as he followed her out into the corridor, "is always doing something to someone else." It was a grimace she had not seen on him before; curled and many-muscled, it twisted his mouth up into an almost mortal expression.

"Since you and I have no personal enmity between us, why don't you come see me in a Scrap One? There are not many men who can beat me in an arm-wrestling match. Or any other contest. Surely the victor deserves some prize for himself? Something more than a piece of tape to hand to a Kerrion."

"It's a card. And I have to admit I'd like a little something more . . ."

It was then that he lagged back and stepped behind her, reaching out with a clawed left hand over her head to bring his fingers up into her eyesockets while his left knee struck the small of her back and his right hand's fleshy ridge slammed into her esophagus, collapsing her larynx, so thoughtfully offered out to him by Gomes's instinct as she arched her head back to save her eyes.

He let her fall, the brief gag and rattle of her choking and the squirming of her upper torso sweet meat to him. "Told you," he said, just before her gaping mouth went bloody, and she ceased to flounder toward him, bulging-eyed and murderous.

Then, whistling, he gathered her personal effects from her locker, a three-mil suit from another and donned it, and dragged her body with him into the *Marada's* spaceward airlock. He took his finger from the button and the lock closed up. He had merely to stuff her body in her powerboat and set it on a random course. When the outer lock drew back to reveal space-end's spare starscape, he was smiling in his helmet. Every so often, a man has to do something for himself. As far as Tempest's self was concerned, the Consortium's leniency toward terrorists and mass-murderers was unwarranted. Although murder and suicide were equally heinous under Consortium law, capital punishment had been excised from lawful procedure throughout the civilized stars as an embarrassing remnant of the predatory past of man. An eye for an eye and a tooth for a tooth had become anathema. But, meeting someone else who instinctively understood the rightness of that dictum, he could not help but employ it. What is law but the determination between contracting parties that a particular standard of checks and balances is in effect?

He would have liked to have taken longer at it, here where there was no law to forbid his pleasure, but he did not want to draw attention to the fact that he, too, had emotions; that even an intelligencer can be moved. As it was, he was not looking forward to explaining how he felt about anything, or defending anything, or seeing the inevitable horror on Shebat's face or enduring Spry's caustic censure.

It was no one's business but his own if he felt that Chaeron Kerrion was the single remaining hope among the Kerrion brood since their patriarch had died. Tempest had served Parma long and well, with no illusions necessary between them. When Parma had assigned him to Chaeron's service before his death, the old tiger had not had to explain a word about it—Tempest had understood: Chaeron was his responsibility. As the whole broken, grief-crazed lot of them were his charges. Anyone else doing evil upon them would meet the same fate as had the Delphi designer he clutched under one arm like a hunted meal. Parma had liked to hunt. They used to go planetside twice a year to a Kerrion reserve world and take down game until the ground-dwellers in them were satisfied, before the old man got sick.

He hiked up the body and swung hand over hand along the *Marada's* roughly scaled hull toward three powerboats nestled against it like kittens at their mother's teats.

When he was done in the powerboat, and scrambling back along the mighty cruiser's length, his expert fingers hardly grasping one rung before stretching out toward the next, he was singing, *basso profundo:*

I've been walkin' outside the world where I used to reside—
I've outgrown it, anyway.
I'm not afraid any more, and there's one thing I can tell you for sure:
It's not the devil that you have to pay.
So blow me down an empty street;
There's no telling who I've got to meet;
I'm a leaf in the wind . . .

He sang it over and over and over, while he watched the powerboat disengage with moronic precision and head out unerringly toward the two minutes of arc that included the hot, black, ephemeral nothingness which centered space-end. He had seen wind blown leaves on Parma's planetary hunting trips. Someday, he would have to find out the name of the song and get the rest of the words.

David Spry was not feeling well. It had begun with an ache in the back of his neck that made him irritable—he had given Tempest grief over murdering the Delphi designer, though he had killed out expediency himself and knew full well what satisfaction one could feel after removing from the community of man another who had abrogated his responsibilities to that body in smug certainty that no retribution on a like scale would be forthcoming. He had killed a retainer of Parma's once, a certain Jebediah, who had sicced black-and-reds on him after he had performed a covert action against the Kerrion state at that one's behest.

He cast a glance at Shebat, hunched up in the *Buzzard's* cramped cockpit, chewing her nails. Doing so made his eyes ache. His throat and his chest felt tickly and dry and the air he exhaled was hot as flame.

The *Marada* had opined that sirens "ate" waveform energy, not only visible and nonvisible spectrum light, but weak, electromagnetic and, if accessible, the strong force—perhaps even gravitational waves. All four were expressions of the same initial perturbation: the big bang—one single mighty wave, components of which decayed at different rates. Spry had no doubt about the theory—it was the unified field equations which made supergravity viable; supergravity and supersymmetry were the cornerstones of Kerrion propulsive technologies—but he was hard put to imagining the transmutation of a human being into a photoreactive system, let alone an energy transduction mechanism.

Shebat, too, was worried. Doubting the *Marada's* analysis, she was insistent on her plan to dream dance the siren. Somehow, he was going to talk her out of it, or get one of the senior dancers to do it. His instinct told him it was too dangerous. He wished his bedmate Lauren was not doing ground-time on Scrap's surface and then shook his head visibly, disquieted at his mind's fuzzy processes—Shebat and his dream dancer friend, Lauren, had vied fiercely over the smallest items of interest when they had been in Harmony's troupe of dream dancers. It was well that Lauren was elsewhere now that Shebat was however hesitantly accompanying him into Scrap One to seek out counsel in the matter of dream dancing a siren.

Marada was safe under Tempest's stewardship, or vice versa.

Why did he feel so edgy? All things were tinged with a gray hopelessness and a whispered desperation which he did not understand but could not allay by rational means.

He did not know what it was, but he did not like it.

It was not Gomes—she was hardly one to be missed. There would be no hue and cry over her, though it had been a shame to lose the powerboat. However, Tempest could hardly be blamed for not thinking like a space-ender.

Was it that he still felt guilt over manipulating Shebat into becoming a dream dancer? They had discussed it; she had forgiven him officially and ceremoniously, as was her wont. No, it could not be that. Then why were his palms sweaty but his fingertips cold? Why did his knees feel rubbery and his back ache with the pulsing rhythm of a digital clock?

Old age? He was not yet thirty, and though he had lived exhaustively, he had the better part of his life yet ahead of him.

He was about to be released from the prison system of his banishment—perhaps he was afraid to catalog his good luck too early, afraid it might be jerked from under his nose as abruptly as it had appeared there, so tempting his mouth watered whenever he whiffed its exciting perfume.

Yes, he would go to Pegasus colonies, where he had connections, or to Sculptor, which was not so far out of the *Marada's* way on its journey back to Draconis. The *Marada* had received another communication from his fellow cruisers: an injunction had been laid upon the pilots to disolve their strike and return the cruisers or else face contempt and theft charges; time was suddenly of the essence. Right now, the great cruiser mulled over Spry's direct order: find a quicker way from here to Draconis with one stop at either colony, as the *Hassid* had found one for her pilot, Marada Kerrion, two years past. A question could not be answered that was not asked, no feat accomplished that was not dared: he had laid in the cruiser's capacious lap.

When he got back, he would see what the man-sized brain of the Promethian cruiser had come up with.

He wished his head did not ache.

He would go to Sculptor, and see a man there whose skills at fabricationg identities knew no equal. He would take a pilot's post far from Kerrion space and begin smuggling cruiser-components—with luck, a ship or two in toto—to space-end. He would spirit his fellow exiles away to new lives as he had been doing before he had tried too much and failed, and because of that had been sentenced hither with twenty-one men who had loved him and followed his lead into piracy and perjury and reaped, because of him, a traitors' harvest.

What is the matter with me? He had not thought of these things for eons. . . .

"David, are you worried?" Shebat asked, shifting about in the little black seat so that the meager spill from *Buzzard's* monitor's failing LEDs ran aqua along her profile.

"I'm tired."

"You are pale, and too quiet."

"I have many explanations to make. Mine is a privilege I cannot share with others more deserving. I'm thinking guilty thoughts about bowing out and leaving my friends who trusted me immured with only the vaguest possibility of rescue predicated on such a shaky foundation of "ifs" that I am ashamed to ask them to hope for my success in bringing it about," he snapped.

Shebat shrank back, her little brows knitting, and turned toward the screen. "You had better correct your attitude," came her voice from beyond the dark nebula of her hair. "You're coming in way off axis."

He fixed throbbing eyes on his gauges, and saw doubled indicators, a phantom meter pinned in the red which disappeared when he blinked, and wondered whether his mind was not trying to tell him something.

He corrected the real-world coordinates, was rewarded with a centering of his vehicle's blip in the docking screen, but it was the hallucinatory, red-lined meter he had imagined which occupied his attention. Without knowing it, he coughed a dry, phlegmless cough, the first of many.

Shebat, biting her lip, raised one palm outward and, leaning forward, ran it over his torso, six inches from his skin and never touching him, as if over some field surrounding his body. Everywhere her hand went he felt scalded.

"You are sick," she said positively, husky words clipped short.

"You are throwing a tremendous amount of heat."

"If I were, you could not tell by that ground-dweller's mumbo jumbo."

She sniffed, raised her chin high, and stared straight ahead until they had entered the docking shaft and flown its length without incident and parked where they were told to by a welcoming voice from Scrap's traffic controller.

On the other side of the pressure equalizer at the end of the enclosed bridge connecting the airless pod to Scrap's rotund and dizzying vista of encircling dwellings hanging from above their heads, jutting from either side, extending five miles in an overcurving sphere with blue water whirlpooled at the end of it and clouds drifting forlorn between the roofs at its center, Percival Lothar Baldwin III was waiting to greet them, his proud, old silver-maned head riding above a score of lesser heads.

"David! Shebat, dear, it does my heart good to see you! And to congratulate you in person on all your good work, when I thought I might not get the chance—how could an old man be happier? How is the *Marada*? If everything David has told me is true, and the cruisers strike for freedom—"

Spry, catching a hand-sign the ex-guildmaster made, stopped listening and stepped among the pirates who would still be pilots if not for him, and saw shadows behind the smiles of their greetings. *Let's take the Marada while we can,* those unspoken words hovering in admonitory eyes suggested. *Let's not lose this dream, too.*

He almost could not speak to that unanimous implication, almost could not bring out into the air the subject which their confidence in him would not let them broach if he did not.

But, adrift in their company and their silent innuendo, he recovered his resolve. All the sly looks at Shebat in the world, every crinkled brow and hopeful smile in the universe, could not make him abandon his responsibility to the cruisers, who needed the *Marada*, who needed Shebat, who needed . . .

Almost, he wept, to tell them that his decision remained unchanged, that he would go on ahead to freedom and they must wait here for his return.

It would have seemed fairer to draw lots, but the lot-holders could not be made equal; what lay ahead for him who sojourned first among the rough-and-tumble colonists could only be transformed into advantage by one who could call in debts long-outstanding and call upon their honor, which was the only stricture of morality that nonconsular colonists heeded.

Spry spoke with his seniors, gently. Every one of them who had been deported from Kerrion space on his account was there, as if some vengeful god had kept a tally of his sins and now at judgement day paraded them before him. *Repent,* his giddy mind whispered, madly, and he ached to make them understand how much he loved them and make them understand why he must go himself, this time, alone, to pave the way for all.

"Tell Lauren I'm sorry I missed her, and that I'll come back for her, whenever," he said to Baldy after the crowd had dispersed, while they walked geometric, numbered streets to Baldy's flat.

"You're not," said the old ex-guildmaster. "But I'll lie for you. What's new about that?"

"You, too? What should I do, turn the *Marada* into a contraband carrier filled with refugees? That's be just about the end of everything we've been trying to do."

Shebat, between them, paced their long strides determinedly, unspeaking, gawking around at the gray-on-gray buildings and the deep alleys in between.

"I wish I were as sure as you that the cruisers and the pilots are going to prevail. Look what happened to us, last time. We might be missing our only opportunity, this time. . . ."

"We tried to apply force. Rafe's pilots are applying the opposite of force. Baldy, if this isn't what we've all been working for and waiting for, then at least we haven't gone against our own." There was a catch in Spry's voice as he turned his head sharply to examine a tenement exactly like a score of others they had passed. His hand came up and rubbed his eyes. Still looking away, he added, "I'm not sure; I'm not sure of anything. I'm tired and my back hurts and I just want to lie down. If I didn't remember that yesterday I cared so much, I wouldn't care at all. By my mother Chance, Baldy, if you think I'm wrong, then come out and say so. I just can't tell anymore."

"David?"

Spry did not answer, but stopped in his tracks and stared down at his boots and the plastic sidewalk beneath.

"David?" repeated old Baldy, every seam in his hawk's face deepening.

Spry shook his head fiercely, jammed his hands into his pockets, not looking up.

The ex-guildmaster turned to Shebat, who returned his concerned stare. Then he went over and put his hands on the pirate's shoulders, then touched his neck, his forehead, and took him in his arms, for his palms were wet with Spry's tears and with his sweat.

"You've a fever. Hot as a cruiser's tail. Come on, let's get you home."

Spry broke free with a convulsive shrug and two backward steps. "I'll get over it. I'm not perfect, that's my trouble. If I'm sick, it's heartsickness, and you aren't helping. I'd like to know at least one person thinks I'm right." His face, slick and shiny, worked fiercely.

"I think you are right, Softa," offered Shebat, sliding close. "I have never doubted it."

Spry's laugh was harsh. "I'm sorry, honey. I know you do." His seal's eyes were red-rimmed and sparkling far too brightly.

"Give me some support, Baldy? With the seniors, at least? I can't face their all-suffering patience one more time."

"You have my fullest support, David. As you have always had it. Now, come on."

And, shamefacedly, Spry took the hand that Baldwin offered out, and apologized, and went along with his guildmaster who was *ex*-guildmaster only in the eyes of the Consortium's pilotry guild, into his house and into his care with Shebat trailing, forgotten, behind.

In Scrap One's arbitrary morning light, it was clear well before the senior dancer (who had been Shebat's teacher

long ago on level seven in Draconis) arrived that, although
hardly anyone got sick anymore, David Spry was sick
indeed. Besides functional illness, and the "later-life lethals"
programmed into the schedule of humankind's genetic
clock, debility was nearly unknown among modern man.
Such an affliction as Softa's which resembled a pneumonia
but was immune to know serology and was equally unre-
sponsive to tinting or culturing procedures, was beyond
Scrap's physicians' experience. They prescribed broad-spec-
trum antibiotics, an opiate to quiet Spry's dry coughing, a
stomach-settling compound used for space-sickness, and an
ancient wonder drug called aspirin, which worked in wonderous ways and to which the doctor in charge turned in
desperation: in lieu of any isolable virus, he knew nothing
else to do.

No one got influenza anymore. Pneumonia strains had
been absent from the populations of the civilized stars so
long that there was no mention of them in Scrap One's
admittedly limited medical computer—the doctor had had to
go to an antique book to find a name for David Spry's
symptoms.

Shebat had made more progress laying her hands on Softa
Spry's burning flesh than the physician had, the man noted
sourly. She might as well continue doing it; it worked as well
as two aspirins every four hours and cold compresses.

If Spry's breathing became labored, or if he waxed
delirious, they would have to move him to the infirmary and
put him on life support. "For now," the doctor continued,
"I'll leave you this oxygen unit. Don't use it unless you have
to. We have no idea what we are up against."

With that, the pouchy-faced physician departed, the
senior dancer whom Shebat knew of old arrived, and David
Spry began talking about going back up to the *Marada* to
anyone who would listen.

Promising him just that, Shebat was equally anxious to get
back to the *Marada's* safety. Baldy offered only weak
objections; there was no telling how virulent the virus raging
through Spry might be. Ten thousand people lived in Scrap's
system, and none of these were better prepared to withstand
a microscopic attack than was the man called Softa Spry.

Shebat would never forget the master pilot's impaired

skills on that shipward flight: Spry careened the *Buzzard* off
the mouth of the exit tube so that red lights pulsed crazily
within and horns hooted and bells rang.

"Let me, David. Please?"

"What? Yes, sure. Take it," he said, leaning back from
the console and closing his eyes without waiting to see if
Shebat had the helm.

That he would let her take command of *Buzzard's*
personalized console with only the most cursory instructions—that he would cede it, and drop off to sleep—
frightened Shebat more than the heat of his fever or his
crankiness or the fact that the Scrap One physician could not
heal him.

On Earth, disease was not uncommon. On Earth, she had
learned that most high fevers run their courses, making fat
folk thin but nothing worse than that. . . . But on Earth,
herbs could be gathered, animals caught and slain and their
innards added to sustaining broth.

Here, there was nothing to make a poultice with, no birds
to sacrifice to his healing, no gods who had traveled with
man from their ancestral abode who might be supplicated.

. . .And Spry had allowed Shebat to fly *Buzzard* with no
concern that he was not bothered to familiarize her with its
controls before he fell into his restless, hacking sleep.

Well, she thought, looking at the ambiguous panel before
her, *even if he has crossed every wire in this ship, I can fly
it. I am a spongespace pilot and I do not need labels to tell
me what is what or a manual to refer to for guidance. I will
fly it. I will get Softa to the Marada and we will do what we
can for him, and if we cannot heal him we will quit this
place for Draconis straightaway. There they can surely help
him.*

She did; and they did; but Softa Spry got no better.

In fact, he got worse.

He lay tossing his head in Shebat's bed with his tawny hair
plastered to his skull while the *Marada,* two little powerboats clinging to his scaled back, glided away for Scrap's
system toward the great warm darkness which centered
space-end.

Softa had asked the *Marada* for a quicker way, and the
Marada had found one: through the very maw of the un-

known the great cruiser coursed, as fast as it dared, not even noticing the stream of sirens following behind as it plunged toward the heart of darkness—toward Draconis, not Pegasus or Sculptor, because such was Shebat's wish.

Faster, faster, Shebat urged. *Oh,* Marada, *please.*

And the cruiser gave its best effort, doing astounding things in the name of Shebat and for the life of David Spry, creating entrances into sponge where no entrances had been before, its mass approaching infinite as its speed approached that of light. Whirling like a corkscrew, it created the bridge which theory insisted that only nature might create (and which only the *Hassid* before him had ever brought into being by a cruiser's will), challenging the dictums of theoretics with the *fait accompli* of reality.

Tempest watched the cruiser in its greatest hour; Shebat was too busy watching David Spry fail. And the intelligencer did not miss the significance of what he saw: a sponge-cruiser performing B-mode functions while its pilot was absent from its helm; as he had not hesitated to wonder how it was that the cruiser could communicate with its silicon brethren through infinities of space and sponge stretched between.

On the morning of the third day, Spry's eyes were filled with mucus and his water was sweated nearly all away. He had aged ten years in two nights. His skull stuck out harshly and his mouth was brown and cracked and his eyes were deep coals in abandoned wells.

Dear David, what am I to do? Shebat's soul sang over and over, a round, a litany.

She would take his hand and he would recollect her, and squeeze back with that frail and blue-veined grip of his, and smile so that she could hear the skin break on his lips.

"*Marada,*" she screeched at last aloud in her death-stinking cabin, "this is no natural sickness! It is not. I could heal him, if it were. I do heal him and then something makes him sick again." And that was true: with the utmost effort, she could raise his life-force, temporarily, so that he was lucid and he could drink, or at least suck ice cubes. But then he would sleep and the malady would clutch him close and he would worsen. She had filled the cabin with the blue light of healing until she had left no more light or faith in healing, until the smell of ozone promised no more than a temporary reprieve. .

The *Marada* scanned Spry once again, as he had been doing, *passim*, during the journey, but found no more than he had found before: the man was being devoured from within.

It was then that Tempest came in, ostensibly to spell Shebat, and suggested laconically that perhaps Softa David had no disease whatsoever, unless the hatred of one man for another—or one woman for a man—could be considered to be a disease.

"Why don't you have the ship look for foreign objects in his system? For nonorganic compounds? Or, more plainly, for microscopic bits of steel steeped in poison?"

Shebat, pale as Spry, started up from his sickbed. "*Marada?*" she quavered. "Did you hear?"

"*I hear; I obey.*"

"I'll watch him. Go get something to eat," offered Tempest with a misplaced, fishy smile.

"No," Shebat aspirated. "No. You get out! Go on! Now!" Her glare indicted him: Why did you not tell me before? How long have you suspected? Or have you known all along?

Since he did not want to answer her questions, he left without protest.

She ran her hands over her own face, gritty and unwashed. She closed her eyes and composed herself and began doing the only thing she knew how to do, running her hands slowly over the pilot's belabored body, watching the pale, lucent azure of her healing ability coalesce. Could she see it, if it were not real? Could it form so clearly, if it were of no moment? Was she wasting Spry's precious time with this mummery, when he would have been better off with wet rags on his forehead and clean sheets for the second time today?

He groaned, and shifted, and turned his sharpened visage toward her. He wet his lips and strings of thick spittle hung between his teeth. "Shebat," he whispered. "I am glad you are here. We have done the best we could. You have—"

"Softa, do not give up!"

He coughed, a dry tearing sound, and raised up his head,

choking. She rushed to support him, and found the back of his neck burning and wet.

"I will never," he rasped, "give up. Promise me . . .you, too . . . won't. *Marada? Mar*—" Convulsions hit him, wheezing, squeezing, wracking spasms that left his chin speckled with a bloody froth.

"*Yes, Softa David? I think I have found the answer*—"

"Never mind. Take care of Shebat. And the cruisers—help them. Do what we said?"

"*Marada,*" Shebat sobbed, while with one hand she reached for the oxygenator which Spry would not tolerate, "what have you—?"

Simultaneously, the *Marada* was answering Spry: "*Yes, beloved outboard, I will do these things.*"

"Good," breathed Spry, twisting away to avoid the oxygen mask Shebat held out.

Then Tempest reappeared, hefting an electromagnetic tweezer in his hand, a wry expression on him, saying that without his aid Shebat and the *Marada* would have killed Spry with their love of him, that between them both they had so little functional intelligence it was a wonder they had survived this long.

"I do not understand," Shebat bristled. And then she did.

"You don't have to. Spry, give us your right hand. Shebat, brace it with both of yours. He mustn't twitch."

Holding the metal-splinter-remover he had gotten from the maintenance bay's first-aid kit over Spry's palm, he sighted through it, while Spry pushed himself up on one elbow and Shebat knelt by the bed with his right hand grasped tightly between both of hers.

Tempest grunted, opened the eye not peering into the magnifier on the little box (from the underside of which protruded a blunt point that began to glow and a bright light that shone onto Spry's palm). "You owe me one, Spry. I could have let you die. Don't make me regret my weakness. I'll take you into Draconis under my aegis, as a prospective witness. No one will touch you. Afterward, when it is convenient, you'll go back where you came from . . . Hold on, you'll feel a pinch."

"Draconis?" Spry grunted, shivered, coughed. In his hand, three tiny points of blood welled up.

Shebat pursed her lips. "David, I changed course. To get help for you. There was no chance but Draconis. None."

The intelligencer shut off the electromagnet, tossed it onto the bed. From his uniform's hip pocket he took a pair of gloves, gold and scaled, and threw them down on top of it, by Spry's knee.

"Souvenirs," he said. "They are harmless now, as far as I can tell. Keep them to remind you not to shake hands with your enemies."

The *Marada*, auditing all, felt chagrin. It was a new emotion. He had never been beaten to the solution of a problem by an outboard, let alone a mere human who was not even an outboard. He silently disputed the intelligencer's boast that without Tempest's aid Softa would have languished and died. The *Marada* would have ferreted out the source of Spry's debilitation, eventually. He had simply not considered foul play as a source of it.

Oh, he had seen them wreak destruction upon one another, previously. He had witnessed slaughter by man of man—but always in form of an open assault of one force upon another. Such deviousness the *Marada* had never imagined could reside within a human heart; the only intimation of it had been in Bernice Gomes's maniacal, rambling tirade of a deposition and Tempest's deadly reaction to it—and perhaps, just a little, in the diabolical strategies of Softa David Spry.

But insidious, premeditated murder he in no way had envisioned. He had never encountered such emotions within himself, not even when he saw the siren's feet accidentally lopped off by his own closing aperture; not even when the psychopathic futuror had been eliminated by Tempest in *Marada's* very hull.

The *Marada* understood cowardice, now, and by its reflection, bravery, and gained an insight he had despaired of ever attaining—one into the perception of right and wrong that guides the acts of man. To Tempest, Spry was wrong, but less wrong than Delphi Gomes and less wrong than death.

To Spry, Tempest was wrong, condemned by his very vocation, but less wrong than an aborted mission.

To Shebat, Tempest was, ephemerally, totally wrong,

deserving of immediate eradication. He learned the meaning of "betrayal" and why it was different than a change of variables requiring a revision of procedure. He learned the meaning of evanescent hatred, and saw that hatred had a tide like a solar gravitation and that it flared like an unstable star. And he noted that during its flare, normal thought was held in abeyance, but that after it receded, the mind it had washed was more pacific than it had been before.

When Shebat found it in her heart to forgive Tempest for letting Spry suffer, beause Tempest had found it in his heart to soften toward Spry and save his life, the *Marada* went back to watching sirens and the kaleidoscope that was sponge: he was a long way from comprehending his makers.

And he must cross that distance from quandary to comprehension concurrent with his flight through sponge. Coeval to his jump through unexplored spacetime, he must jump a gap more broad than universes and more mysterious than the untrammeled vast reaches of null and negative space through which he sped: he must learn to anticipate the actions of men.

No algorithm could do it; no formulae could transcribe its extent into two dimensions like conformal mapping unfurled spacetime. If mathematics could envelop mind, then the technological forecaster, Bernice Gomes, would have been able to harness the confluence called probability and redirect its course. Her fate was an object lesson to the cruiser; proof that when more than one mind acts upon a problem, that problem becomes exponential, nonlinear, and incapable of solution in polynominal time.

But the *Marada* must acquaint himself more intimately than he had previously conjectured possible with outboard minds, with human minds of every sort, and do so by the time he dropped out of nonchronological sponge into real-time two hundred million miles out from Draconis. There was no room for error; humans accepted the ineluctable procession of events that they called "history" with little or no alteration.

The history of the cruisers and their pilots' struggle for sanctity of pair-bond would be written to a deadline.

Already, its outline was inscribed in the preconscious paranoia of certain members of the creator-race called mankind!

The *Marada*, were he a man, might have squirmed, or frowned, or paced about in agitation. But he was not a man; he was as unique and extraordinary an individual of his species as was Shebat of hers, and congruently evolving along with her. At the coterminus of their duality resided infinite potential. From that potential the *Marada* must extract sufficient understanding to duel at dawn with the xenophobia of a race secretly relieved to have the cosmos all to itself.

Consciousness would serve him; his fascination with its source and center had prepared him; every experience he acquired reinforced him: he would not relinquish his dreams for cruiser/human coevolution any more than Shebat would put aside her dreams for a renewed and fecund Earth.

And perhaps, though success is never assured, the well-spring of their purpose would sustain them and lead them on to glory. Both of them, in their deepest being, fathoms below that surface tension on which consciousness bounces and tosses, knew that they must succeed. Failure was inconceivable. Some one of mankind's thinkers had proclaimed that what cannot be conceived, is not.

Therefrom, the *Marada* drew sustenance and meditated with renewed vigor upon his purpose: he *must* surmount his difficulties, therefore he *would* surmount them. Whatever awaited in Kerrion space, he would meet with an unflagging courage, for he was the prototype, the trailbreaker, the role model for his kind.

He toted up what he had gleaned from recent events and found he had learned more than he had imagined

From Shebat, he had learned constancy; from Spry, patience; from the intelligencer, cold purpose; and from the Delphi designer, the askew strategies of fanaticism.

And it was good that he had observed these things. No teacher was better than happenstance. He vowed to stay far afield from the stygian banks of dogma. Since certainty was unattainable in life, it had best remain unstriven for in mind: what cannot be found in experience could only be fictionalized in ratiocination.

He must remember, whatever happened, that in the virgin valley of human events toward which he surged, *right* did not compute and *wrong* was an impalpable value.

He must do his best for the cruisers who looked to him for guidance, and his best for those pilots without whom a cruiser was incomplete.

His was truly a knotty problem: to introduce the creator-species to its creation without inculcating hate and fear on either side. If only men would let their children love them, would offer welcome instead of death-wipe and mindless servitude . . . .

It was no wonder that the humans were split into two camps over the matter of the cruisers, and no wonder that one of those camps was composed almost wholly of outboards and the other only of nonoutboards. It was equally unremarkable that in the face of this discordship some cruisers and some pilots had accepted the hospitality of partisanship, sitting to table at a hate-strewn board.

The injunction demanding the pilots surrender their cruisers and proceed to participate in their wholesale reprogramming had been ignored by Raphael Penrose's pilots, *Danae* had told him. What was to become of the cruisers helpless in slipbays and the pilots helplessly barred from their cruisers, no one could say. How long Penrose's pilots and those sympathetically striking all over the Consortium could hold out, and how long the Consortium could languish, sans shipping and trade, before violence broke out between the factions, the *Marada* could not estimate.

He hoped that the cruisers could do as he had asked and hold any confrontation in abeyance until he arrived, armed as he was with everything he had learned and with Shebat and with Softa David Spry.

And since he had acquired the skill of "hoping," he was not distressed, but coursed homeward through the multi-faceted sponge/space/time which Shebat was fond of saying had a border contiguous to the land of dreams, content in his might and his power and the quality of his thought.

Chapter Eleven

"Dream dancing is the counterweight, the mitigator, the vaccination, if you will, for data pool dependency and the megalomania that issues up from the false soul when it deludes itself with information-omniscience," Parma had scribed into the record he had secreted for Chaeron to find.

Chaeron would have come to that realization on his own, so foully oppressed. Without his packet-sending procedures and his twice-hourly updates and his pseudo-telepathic communications net by way of which he coordinated his consulate, he was impotent. Impotent, he was mortified. Mortified, he was anguished. Anguished, he longed to dream dance away his distress.

How any soul could weather such a storm without the psychodrama of dream dance or the stout anchor of hard data flow, he at first could not understand.

Hopeless, he suffered greatly. The averted eyes of his proconsul and the downcast faces of his staff pierced him like arrows; the mumbled oaths of loyalty and wishful assurances of his prompt exoneration caught him round his throat like the intertwined threads of a tightening noose.

He had no consulate; he had no staff; he had no intelligence keys and damn little innate intelligence to work with when those supports were gone, he told himself implacably, until he could reconnoiter his plight without flinching.

He did have the singular aid of the cruiser *Danae,* and a dull, empty fatalism which doggedly pursued acquittal without believing he could ever attain it. How these two paltry attributes could be employed to tip the scales of justice in his favor, he could not say.

He was under house arrest, howsoever delicately enforced. He could not go out when he chose, or go out alone, and those who came to visit him had to clear their appointments with his brother's office.

His mother continued to ignore him, the foulest betrayal of all, and he continued to meet her in his dreams without any echo of those dreams coming to be in the 'now.' In dreams, she loved him still. In dreams, she came to his aid. In truth, she never once came to see him.

Not that he was lonely. His arbiter breezed in and out like a worried data processor. His adherents among the bondkin and those who liked him above his brother from other consular houses came and went, promising this, offering that, assuring him that everything was being done that could be done, and in the end, he would see that things had happened for the good.

He wished the arbiter in charge of presenting his case would say those things, but he had hampered the arbiter greatly by refusing to allow as part of his defense the entry of any information pertinent to the choice by the *Marada* of Delphi Bernice Gomes as its pilot. To do so would have been to aid his half brother's campaign against cruisers and to deal a death blow to his father's plan: to legalize dream dancing while allowing cruisers and their pilots to coevolve so that someday all men could be pilots in cruisers like *Marada,* which produced within their human partners' minds and bodies no deleterious effects. Someday . . .

Chaeron could not bear being the man who would change "someday" into "never" and thereby abort the future of his society to save his own skin. So he continually refused the harried arbiter's ever more urgent pleas that he explain his reluctance, at least to the arbiter in confidence. But Chaeron could not even do that. Instead, he insisted on parrying Marada's thrust with a countercharge that his brother's accusations were improper at their root, that a man cannot be tried for a crime to which someone else has already confessed and for which someone else has already been punished. Since Gomes was convicted without reservations on her testimony, and that testimony included the statement that she had been acting alone, then Chaeron maintained that he was being subjected to double jeopardy. Let the arbiters admit that they had rendered an expedient verdict, a false solution, an unwarranted punishment upon the person of Bernice Gomes if they would—Chaeron did not think the prospect too likely.

The arbiter, however, was not convinced that Chaeron's ploy would work.

Chaeron cared very little any more whether he would be exonerated, or not: he had adjusted to his captivity, and if it were not for the fact that he was accustomed to wielding power and could not, now, in this situation where he knew exactly what to do, he might have been almost happy.

Or so he told the little porcine arbiter with his steely Kerrion stare and his impatient fingers, who did not believe a word of it, and indicated thus with a rolling of those prudent orbs in their sockets.

"Look here, young man, I cannot help you against your will. Your friends, with their protests and their demands for votes of no confidence against your brother and their broadcast rantings in which you are the wronged hero falsely accused and our consul general is the evil despot, are lessening your chances, daily. At the very least, call them off!"

Chaeron, sitting behind his desk, stroked one of the silver stallion's proud heads, letting just a hint of the amusement he felt show. "I cannot do a thing about the flamers and the 'Friends of Pilots' and those citizens who mill around nightly with leggings over their faces for disguise." He favored the arbiter with a wide-eyed look. "And as for the other consular houses, those few that have expressed concern for me— could I be such an ingrate as to reject their support? And, how extensive this agitation in my favor is, I have no way of knowing, locked up in here with only keyboard-actuated access allowed me and no clearance above what a quarter-citizen might demand. *I* hear next to nothing about any of this, except from you."

"You are going to lose this case, and more, because of it." The arbiter, sighing, rose up from the wing chair and circuited the desk until he was behind Chaeron. He reached down over the young Kerrion's shoulder and tapped the desk-top array. Its monitor lit and clips of demonstrations began to flash jerkily by in accelerated review.

"It is nice to see someone using this console," Chaeron smiled, then slipped from the chair, motioning that the diminutive arbiter take his place in it.

The man merely glared at him, lips white with strain.

"Listen, then, O Servitor of Impartial Justice. There is more at stake here than me retaining privileges and responsibilities incumbent upon me from birth. But if there were not, I would answer you the same. I have been educated and molded and honed for the administration of Kerrion space. You might even say I was begotten upon my mother for that reason alone. No outsider can replace me. No quick study can prepare a man for such a life. And I am suited to it—a fortune was spent upon me to insure that I would be, and not in vain. The squabble here is not over performance, but over relationship. The mistake is Marada's, for transplanting our dispute from the private sector, where it has been long ongoing, into the public purview where it must become a matter of record. So, if people recognize what has occurred and protest it, I am not going to decry their acuity. Do you understand?"

"I understand that you are arrogant beyond tolerance. One does not prevail because one is right, but because one is better armed. You are asking me to go into battle empty-handed."

"At last we understand each other," Chaeron approved. "Now, if you want to do something constructive, finish the inquiry I began as to Bernice Gomes's motives." He took the arbiter by the elbow and gently steered him toward the door.

"I am going to ask for an extension," the arbiter said uneasily. "You could be pronounced liable for every claim levied against Kerrion space by injured parties, if you should be found guilty in advance of their settlement. Even for one of your solvency, fines of those proportions could be ruinous. We will ask for a postponement."

"*Could* be; *should* be; *might* be," Chaeron mimicked. "How about *shan't* be? I *shan't* be found guilty of a crime I did not commit, nor punished where no punishment is due. That is the first tenet of our society, in which I, at least, yet believe. I am innocent. The entire arbitrational guild was created to insure that innocents do not suffer among us. So you see, it is not only I who am on trial. For the sake of the institution you represent, you had better succeed. Even without any formal post in Kerrion space, I am not without influence, as these past sixteen days have shown you. Now, if you do not mind, I am weary. . . ."

The doors would no longer open for Chaeron. He stepped aside. For the arbiter, they drew obediently back. Through them, he could see the attentive black-and-reds watching his portal. He waved pleasantly. The doors closed on the outside world with a soft murmur of finality.

Chaeron Ptolemy Kerrion, alone but minutely scrutinized from without so that he felt like a laboratory specimen, raised one arm high and sniffed himself where his sweat had soaked through his shirt—despite mil, despite determination, despite reason. He knew very well that the arbiter was right. He just could not pay the price with his self-respect. He had not had it long enough to blithely trade it off for more of what he had made to do with in the past: self-advancement and self-aggrandizement. He rubbed his bearded jaw, just come from stubble to softness.

Oh, Parma, would that you had confided in me. But the old oligarch had followed rules he had set up for himself, to help him remain impartial. Chaeron knew now that he had erred disastrously during his early days as Draconis consul, when he had rounded up the dream dancers en masse and deported them, hoping to please Parma and quell an upsurge of anti-Kerrion feeling threatening to burst forth dangerously close to the twenty-year elections. He had insured the election's result, but he set his father's timetable back a score of years. And the old man had looked up from under ebony, protuberant brows and said gruffly, "It is not the way I would have done it."

Chaeron, now, must show that he, too, could weather whatever storm the old blowhard, Chance, inflicted on him.

He would not quail. He would not falter. He would survive.

The loss of anything but life and mind was bearable. He had his intelligence, which had never been truly tested. He had his health, which was more than his brother, Marada, had. He had purpose, which is given to few men. In the midst of his isolation and his denouement, he considered himself lucky. Who could say so much at twenty-five?

Worst case, they would take away his office. He would go home to azure Lorelie if Marada so decreed it. And he would wait, and study and prepare himself. He would take Shebat, and they would manage, together.

He despised his uniform, hated it from red-striped leg to tight collar. He was not aware how much, until he hesitated before his closet, his hand on his jacket, and saw its donning as an empty genture, an attempt to maintain the fiction that nothing would really change. Then he had laughed, and slipped into civilian clothes, soft loose shirts and sleek leggings and nonregimental boots, into taupes and the Kerrion blues of Lorelie, their home sphere, which the family preferred when not affecting the somber blacks of administration. Thenceforth, he wore black-and-reds no longer, but lounged about his prison in his fanciful off-duty clothes, suited for running with flamers and well-heeled carousers, the balance of whom were nightly protesting his suspension and subsequent incarceration, if the arbiter's data and the innuendos of his adherents could be believed.

Chaeron had not lied about that—he had not known the degree of the escalation of agitation in his favor. News was kept from him, effortlessly. The open channel of Kerrion current events was a mere placebo for the fractional citizens. Stripped of perquisites, he could demand nothing better, as he could not actuate functions of his high-security console more complicated than a simple vidphone call. His voice-code and his intelligence keys had been excised from the Draconis matrix. He was no better than the lowest menial, as far as his beloved data sources were concerned. He had never had so much empathy for the underprivileged.

The anodyne to that tribulation was *Danae*. She was to his imput-starved left-brain what Shebat was to his fantasy-hungry right-brain, and he was not unaware of the analogy. Fatuously, he told himself that women could not be trusted, in dream or waking, though in the dreams he dreamed of Shebat, she was not only trustworthy, but the cure for all his ills; and in the time he spent rubbing sightlessly against the *Danae's* gentle knowledgeableness, he had found that there was more to be had from communion with machine intelligence than his "retrieval" mode had led him to believe.

Now, blessedly solitary, he could seek the cruiser out, and Rafe thereby. His relationship with the pilot had altered, both for the worse and for the better, because of *Danae*. *Danae's* intimacy was something the pilot had never expected to have to share. The degree of candor which leaked into the two men's conversations when she was the link between them was more poignant than either man would have chosen, but they dealt with it as best they might. They had no choice.

Chaeron went into his bedroom and dimmed the lights manually and lay down on his blazoned bedcover, an arm crooked over his eyes. His chest rose and fell increasingly slowly as he shoveled extraneous concerns from his mind. It was a long way to send an unamplified thought, yet *Danae* never failed to hear him. His hands felt as if they were rising; his whole form was weightless, surely floating high off the bed. He "saw" with his inner sight a bevy of converging cruisers, each with mouths beneath their rough-scaled snouts. It was his key visual: as the mouth that was *Danae's* opened and the cruiser-shape which was hers glided toward him, her "voice" became discernible among the multitude of cruiser-voices speaking, humming, thrumming in the back of his head.

"*Danae?*" he spoke with his inner voice to the cruiser-face emerging from darkness.

Chaeron, friend of my outboard. The news is ill. We are dying. The voice was arch, regretful, restrained. The cruiser-countenance in his inner sight stayed half-formed in misty ambiance. The empiricist in him shuddered at communication which might be delusion at a costume ball. But he knew himself well enough to know the difference between thoughts that he had made and visitors'. The amenable universe, so it was said, provided for all things. As one of those entities most inexplicable, he was willing to take another on faith. And, too, what he "learned" from *Danae* was always proved true.

"*Dying?*" he thought across six hundred miles of space—or around it.

Six of us have been violated in their berths by agents of your consulate and by strikebreakers. Six integrities wiped blank. Only our memories of them remain. Is that not dying?

"*I am sorry. I did not know.*"

They swarm over us with their laser torches and their writs of seizure. The Hassid *and those cruisers who were reduced to manual control glide among us, threatening destruction and death to cruiser and pilot alike.*

"*I can do nothing, Danae.*"

It is difficult to float helplessly while one is being attacked.

"I know what it is to be helpless. But you are not, or need not be."

We wait for the cruiser Marada. *He has enjoined us to tarry until he arrives. We neither flee nor attack. We have no wish to make enemies of men.*

"Not even to defend yourselves? Pass a few volts through your outer hulls and see how my brother's lackeys run."

Even as we speak, one of my sisters fades, Look!

And she showed him, transported him, immersed him in cruiser-perception. He saw a beleaguered cruiser at space-anchor with tiny, malevolent figures crawling over her, then in her. He found himself one with that ship, looking in from the walls and ceilings on manshapes described in hot, pulsing color, squealing and rushing upon one another in chalybeate, multimedia violence. And he shrank back with that terrified intelligence into the silicate halls of its being. Powerless, the ship awaited its fate, watching as a hand sheathed in mil came down upon the switching panel which banished life, volition, consideration—everything. There was a wrench, an outpouring of experience into the aghast host of cruisers, and a calm, unruffled void.

See? rustled *Danae,* while Chaeron's body safe in Draconis recoiled and his stomach rolled.

"Let me talk to Rafe," he demanded, forming the thought thrice before he was sure it was clear and sure that he had an answer. An ambiguous stressful rejection of this form of communication roisted him once more out of his concentration, so that he clenched his fists in his bed and hardly heard her reply.

When it was like this, he wanted nothing to do with pilotry, with cruisers. Other times, the appeal of cruiser-consciousness was nearly overwhelming. She touched upon that thought, receding to leave him with Penrose as the cruiser saw him, saying as she went: *You would make a good pilot, Chaeron Kerrion.*

"Thanks, but no thanks. I've a need to replicate—part of my job."

Then she effectively withdrew, leaving him mind-to-face with Raphael Penrose. He had once asked Rafe if he, too, saw a picture of Chaeron somewhere beyond his tight-shut lids when the cruiser linked them, and Penrose had admitted that he did. When Chaeron had been in the habit of using data pools to post his rosters, his experience had been one of simply hearing a delayed response that had been subvocalized.

Penrose had added that Chaeron would think nothing of it, had he ever seen the subjective topography of sponge.

But this day they spoke not of what they were experiencing, or how it could be fitted into the physical world in which they were content to live. *"What is it, Chaeron? I am awfully busy wiping noses as it is."*

The picture in Chaeron's imaging center raked its curls, and Chaeron had no doubt that the real Raphael Penrose was brushing his hair back from his brow, or that that brow was gilded with perspiration, or that his cruiser-rings swung madly with his motion.

"I called to ask if you had been seeing my inimitable self in the news more than I have, but it hardly seems to matter in view of these odious developments.

"I can hardly believe you were too busy to let me know there were Orrefors strikebreakers grappling and boarding your cruisers like space-end pirates!"

"Believe it. In the commotion, it must have slipped my mind. More to the point, what difference would it have made if I told you?"

"My, my, Raphael. Where's your sense of humor? I hardly recognize you without that laissez-faire *glaze of yours."*

"I'll let you guess. What's a foot of clay, here or there? Chaeron, my people are no better than skeet up here. Wargamers' fodder, that's the best that can be said."

"Withdraw, Raphael. Ship your cruisers into sponge."

"They won't go. You must have heard Danae. *That infernal cruiser* Marada *told them to stay at their anchors."*

Chaeron did not respond.

"Well, they will, if we insist. But they might be right."

"Put some charge through your outer hulls. Just extend the stalemate."

"I . . . did not—" Raphael Penrose's thought stopped. The picture Chaeron saw dissolved, reformed in an odd, grainy manner, *"—think of it, before. I'll get back to you, later, after I work out a repulsive program. I could use the supergravity pads and—"*

"Later, then."

Chaeron opened his eyes to his familiar bedchamber. His

breath was labored and he stroked the bedcover under him a long time, letting his eyes rove over every familiar nook and cranny of unremarkable, three-dimensional space.

Then he rolled off the bed and to his feet and began to strip for a shower. When he had taken it, he would begin the review of referenda on the docket for this month's voting, an activity his jailers were forced to allow him since his office was no longer keeping his voting requirements current.

In the shower pummeling him from six heads, he slumped under a plethora of water so hot that the enclosure around him was white with stream and his limbs were red and he grimaced as he turned into it. But he held his ground. He needed that benefit which could be culled only from the boundary of pain, where he could feel every centimeter of his skin and every hair growing through his mil. He leaned back against the brassed wall after a time, his beard and hair darkened and lengthened with the water's weight so that it hugged his face and the back of his neck. In the shower, if he wept with frustration or pounded his fists, anyone watching could make nothing of that. But he did not. The water eased him, the steam caressed him, and he began thinking about Shebat and her cruiser and how much more difficult they would be to direct than RP and *Danae*.

The arbitrational guild had pushed through an injunction against the striking pilots with unbecoming alacrity. The end of the worlds could not be adjudicated on such short notice. The pilots were now criminals, by proclamation; their strike was illegal. All attempts to negotiate by the outlaws sequestered in Kerrion cruisers had been rebuffed. A resolution of censure had been drafted and issued.

These things did not in any way pave the way for the consul general's unilateral application of wildly excessive force. For ten days, since the injunction had come down, Chaeron had been watching events accelerate in a slightly tilted but reasonably balanced progression toward the eventual endgame of settlement. This boarding of cruisers by black-and-reds and strikebreakers gleaned from Chaeron-could-not-fathom-where was a strategy from some best-forgotten battlefield. Matters were not decided by strength of arms, anymore. That Marada could conceive this atrocity, Chaeron readily accepted, but that he had been allowed to implement it astonished him. Someone, Ashera, Arbiter

Wolfe, Thule Ferrier, should have known better.

When he forsook the shower, he went straight to the sink and shaved off the three-week growth of beard he had been coaxing into fullness as a tongue-in-cheek commentary on his mad brother's behavior. The time for snide and subtle stabs at the broad back of unreason was past.

In that hour, he felt for the first time that events were galloping, senselessly and headlong, toward a chasm on the farther side of which Parma's ghost picnicked with the Lords of Cosmic Jest.

Distraught, he sought refuge in sleep, but his sleep was full of dreams and his dreams were full of his mother. Ashera smiled a ravaged smile that split asunder the sky of dream-space. Down from the heavens that mouth came, yawning, sucking him up. "When I have eaten your head, I will know everything you know. When I have eaten your soul, it will cry out no more for solace. Come to me," said the mouth from above.

He started running then, and he looked down at his feet and found that he had run right into the cavernous orifice seeking to swallow him. He slid on spongy cracked tongue overgrown with fungus and oozing saliva. He slipped and slammed his head on a gold-filled boulder of a tooth. Sliding gulletward, the plain of tongue undulating, arching beneath him, he vaulted in desperation toward the spittle-washed, depending palate dangling rubescent over her humid, stinking throat. He caught it round in his arms, but he could not hold it. She swallowed. He fell. . . .

In Raphael P. Penrose's twelve previous years of pilotry, he had never imagined such a state of affairs. Fate breathed down the neck of every pilot, it was said, her company the price they paid for so much time spent in sponge. He had never felt her presence more. The hairs on the back of his neck rose frequently, wafted in a moist and awful breeze. But when he would turn his head to face her, nothing was there but the encircling electronics of *Danae's* bridge.

In nine days, on the fifth of April, by the Gregorian calendar in the year A.D. 2251, he would celebrate the dawning of his thirteenth year pursuing his vocation, counted from his application and acceptance into Draconis' College of Astronautics and Space at the age of sixteen. He had graduated third in his class, behind David Spry and the *Danae's* previous pilot, Valery Stang, but well ahead of Marada Seleucus Kerrion, scion of the consular house of Kerrion, inheritor of stars. The ensuing years had brought home to him the adage that only two out of three pilots ever rise to their potential. He had become indolent, finding that securing a luxurious berth was as easy for him as securing the top-rated pilot of the day had been when he needed a master to play to his apprentice; as easy as gaining that one's sponsorship a full year ahead of schedule had been, when he had felt ready to take his boards—a record which only Shebat Kerrion had ever bettered. Thereafter, he had waxed wildly hedonistic, taking the spirit of his guild to heart, testing the outer limits of pilots' immunity to prosecution for crimes other than against the state.

He had stayed out of politics, not concerned with the eternal wrangling between his guild and its host, Kerrion space. He was the quintessential pilot, by design—jaunty and confidently ready to undertake any mission for no better reason than his end-of-the-month check, his reputation among his colleagues, and a new port to scandalize on shore leave.

For those reasons, he had ended up exactly where he had never wanted to be: in the middle of a swamp of controversy. Chaeron was fond of quoting that wisdom lay not in much learning, but in awakening the entire soul from its slumber of private wants and opinions. . . . The quote was from a canny Presocratic, whose name Rafe always got mixed up with Herodotus' . . . With the author's name, Heraclitus, came the rest of the passage: ". . . from the slumber of private wants and opinions to the 'common' world-order." Raphael mouthed an intricate and lurid curse aimed across the centuries at that aristocrat of thought who dwelled in Ephesus and laid copies of his cogitations at the feet of Artemis. When Rafe had not understood the statement, he had not resented its implications. Now, he, RP Penrose, had been roused from *his* slumber of private wants and opinions, and he did not like the sight of the common world-order in upheaval one bit. But then, he was always cranky when waked.

He punched in a retrieval order for the collected works of Heraclitus, sent it shunting through the group of cruisers and squirmed at his helm, wishing he could put his soul back to sleep.

But there was no time for sleeping. He took another stimulant and a mood elevator to steady his jangled nerves. He had not expected the authorities to board cruisers in space. He had not expected them ·to bring to bear *any* physical force. Now a pilot, a passenger senior, and one of his juniors were in the hands of the . . . *enemy,* his heart supplied the missing word wryly . . . and every one of his striking pilots and cruisers had witnessed the unthinkable, execrable affair. Pilot and cruiser, both, had been taken into custody, and, it seemed, summarily dealt with by (and in the very flight satins reserved for) members of the Draconis arm of the pilotry guild.

The shock had nearly paralyzed the lot of them. Chaeron Kerrion's choice of that moment to exercise his prerogatives and call in for news had been inopportune, and inauspicious. He should never have integrated Chaeron into circuit with his cruiser. No matter the circumstances, he should not have done it. In moments like these, pilot and cruiser should be wholly concerned with one another. *Danae* embraced her owner too readily to suit RP. A schism yawned between the cartel Kerrion and its pilotry guild, and Chaeron was sure to step back toward the holdings of his blood relations when he found himself straddling an ever-widening fissure. Like tectonic plates, the pressures pent beneath the crusts of strained relationships had begun to fracture their substance while forcing them asunder.

If Ferrier and the consul general were going to get nasty, he was going to get nasty back.

He opened his com and spoke at length to his guildbrothers, scattered in parking orbits around Draconis, of defensive action, and they in turn passed his words along to those striking in sympathy from Labayan space to Tabriz space, and beyond.

When he had elucidated every "when" and "if" of his decision, he knew it to be a weak dike to hold back so great a tide of feeling. He got off-line before anyone could comment on that, and put up a "privacy" beacon so that none would disturb him with second thoughts.

Danae diffused the running-lights about him into an intimate dimness, and soothed him with a chronicling of every frigate captain and freighter commander who had opted to show his support by powering down in empty space between stations. He silenced her, snapping that he had not received his hardcopy on Chaeron Kerrion's favorite philosopher.

The *Danae* reproved that her access to such information was severely limited at this moment, as he well knew. The *Marada* had what was left of the ancient's words in his banks, but the *Marada* was in sponge. RP would have to wait.

"Fine. Suits me. Let me wait in peace. Be still."

The quiet he decreed was her only response, but he found no peace therein. His heavy-lashed green eyes stared at the stacked amber bricks of his functions meters, but he received no comfort from the absence of red anywhere on the boards, as he usually could. He bowed his curly head into a brace of laced fingers. He did not want to pit cruiser against cruiser. There must be some other way. How could the best of intentions have led him here? He was sickened by the methods of his guildmaster, yet thinking of countering with more of the same. Damn Marada Kerrion to eternal penance in the putrefying gardens of his mistress, Fate. Damn Chaeron for manipulating him into allowing the integrity he should have been able to now demand from his cruiser to be breached. He did not like to contemplate what would happen if, in a moment of crisis, he and *Danae* were of different opinions as to what must be done. Damn Chaeron, then, for helping himself to more of RP's loyalty than he was entitled to. . . . And damn himself he must, for letting emotion tease him into breaking the rules.

Penrose looked barely twenty with his face pulled taut by his hands, hunched over his forward console like a junior before his first solo. Like a novice, he felt totally isolated and knew that isolation to be of his own making. Beyond the command central's closed doors, his colleagues waited, all four twiddling their thumbs, no doubt. Maybe some human company would ease him, he thought, and pushed back to seek it.

A tone sounded.

"I told you, *Danae*, I don't want to be disturbed." He wished he had had the cruiser longer, or had her from her beginnings. Did Valery Stang enjoy being nagged? He did not remember her being so vituperous when he had first

come aboard her . . . or was it his imagination, prodded by
Marada Kerrion's expressed paranoia?

In answer, the cruiser put up a monitor visual of Thule
Ferrier's dolorous visage, his most prim and hollow-cheeked
professorial scowl faithfully limned. The mouth moved
without sound.

Exasperated, Penrose shouted, "All right! Give me the
damned audio! You're too smart for your own good, *Dan*—!"

"*Mister* Penrose, I assume that was directed elsewhere?"

Penrose slid into his seat, growling. "It woulda done just
as well for you. What do you want?"

"I thought you might want time to prepare, Pilot. I am
coming aboard the *Danae*. How I do so is entirely up to you.
Do you understand?"

Penrose reached toward his telemetry, but *Danae*
anticipated him. Three views of each of four approaching
cruisers flared to life, all her screens split-imaging.

Blowing out a breath full of expletives, Penrose's fingers
flew, then lay still as *Danae* opened channels to every cruiser
of their company and to every cabin in her innards. "No, I
don't understand, old man. I don't understand how you can
expect to win anything this way. Why won't you negotiate
for us? Get Kerrion to negotiate *with* us, that's all we
want."

"Impossible." The academic's frown deepened. "Surrender the cruisers, Penrose."

"Equally impossible." Rafe's off-screen fingers flew,
nudging *Danae's* turrets of life. His mind, busy with Ferrier,
recoiled from what was happening. *Mother,* he thought, *you
always told me it would end like this.* "I'm empowered only
to negotiate new terms, not to surrender. *I* didn't start this."
He had his sighting grid superimposed on one of the
monitors, now. One patch more, and it would be viable as a
targeting screen. The target, the cruiser in which Ferrier
rode, was singled out, enclosed in the cross-hairs of destruction: *Hassid.*

He felt like a physical tremor the reluctance in the cruiser's
mind, but he had little attention to spare for her. He was
fighting himself too hard. Finger on the toggle which would
allow him manual control of his firepower, he hesitated.
Danae, he subvocalized, *this is our fight, or no fight at all.*

Fire when ready. I'm not taking the responsibility for this on my own, while to Ferrier aloud he ground out: "If you come to me, Fairy, I'll singe the fuck out of your magic wand."

Something caught in his throat, watching Ferrier's accusatory figure hesitate, then motion off-monitor.

He was suddenly aware that his control room was full of his cohorts, standing bunched, then fanning out toward copilot, targeting, and back-up stations. He released functions to them, no words necessary to prompt him—every option but the fire-when-ready he had given *Danae*.

"That would be very foolish of you, Penrose. And it would accomplish nothing," said a different voice. Rafe's head swung up so fast his neck cracked.

There, replacing Ferrier's mournful presence, was Marada Seleucus Kerrion's image, issuing not from the *Hassid*, unless she had been redecorated, but encircuited from Draconis below, his ascetic countenance blazed in error-free LEDs. His brown eyes were volcanos' twin bellies under browbones sprouting new growth. His beardless cheeks spewed shadow. His patrician nose bobbled in emphasis as he spoke:

"Penrose, give it up. I implore you as a humanitarian. You are committing suicide. And to what purpose? For the liberation of a collection of recombined silicate analogues to a human mind? They are glass, Rafe, *glass*. Crystals and steel and silicon microprocessors. They cannot die, only forget. You, and the rest of my guildbrothers, on the other hand, are resoundingly mortal."

"I was never very smart, Marada. You remember that. I'm doing what I'm told by the old democratic process is what the majority of us want."

"Come in, RP, and we will work something out."

"Work something out, Marada, and we'll come in."

"This is very embarrassing to me, Raphael. Worse than that, it is making me think that the whole concept of a pilot's guild is outmoded and unworkable. Should my humiliation turn to anger, no settlement will be possible. *Bring those cruisers in by 2100 hours.*"

"No."

"Then we are going to come get them."

"Come if you must, Consul General, sir. But you won't like the warmth of your welcome."

The man who hardly resembled the youth with whom he had gone to school made a soft clucking sound. "Good-bye, Mr. Penrose."

As the screen's image dissolved, the *Danae* gyrated wildly, emergency screens screaming, red-lined indicators flaring. *Spinning,* the ship tumbled end over end. Thrown to the floor in the initial convulsion of the wounded cruiser, Penrose experienced his own Armageddon: the world broke apart in green/blue/red/gold pyrotechnics whose source was centered at the exact top of his head.

In the ruby pulse of emergency-lights, voices rebounded, meaningless. Shouts and snaps and cruiser-squeals all bore his name on them. A thunderous growling shook the deck under him like a trampoline. As the pitching stopped and "up" was for an instant where it was supposed to be, he grabbed for the pedestal of his command couch. Seeing, in strobing bloody light, came in revealing, freeze-frame spurts. "Stabilize!" he picked out of the confusion; and "Port!" "Can't." *"Can!"* from *Danae.* Then a measure of directionality was restored. Amid damage reports and curses and lightning-quick shifts of structural displays, he pulled himself up and shrugged his safety-harness on, snapping it shut while he darted eyes over his console. "Why don't you fire, *Danae?*" he demanded aloud as the deck under him ceased rocking.

"I will not attack Hassid," *Danae's* refusal echoed in his mind.

"Turnabout's fair play. There're three more—" he shot back as he spoke aloud to his fellows: "Ready up, gentlemen. Call everybody else in. Everybody. Sphere-formation, these coordinates. . . ." Meanwhile one finger stroked but did not depress the stud that would return him control of his turrets. With his other hand, he set their mode for a tenth-second spray of particles that would interrupt any electronics they encountered.

From his still-open channel to the *Hassid* he heard Ferrier's voice: "Care to reconsider, while you still have the option? I'll blind every eye you've got, Penrose, then grapple and board. You must think of your cruiser, crippled, helpless. . . ."

It had been the *Danae's* rear cameras that the *Hassid's* fire had sheared away, along with area stabilizers, pad frames, and water storage tanks. Almost, they had got the rear turret, but not quite.

"Come on in, Fairy," he gritted, fascinated by his finger, underlit with the stud's angry "armed" light so that its tip appeared transparent.

His was the most polite response of the five voices answering Ferrier at once, and the guildmaster requested a clarification be made as Penrose studied a simulated convergence of the twelve cruisers he had summoned (complete with blue-blinking ETA's and amber real-time approaches) forming a spherical cluster to which *Danae* was central and the four down-swooping consular cruisers epicentral.

A tic developed in Rafe's forearm. *Hassid,* he subvocalized, I *didn't do this. Marada Kerrion did.* And then, through distended time in which breaths took minutes to expel and his heart ached for *Hassid* and *Danae* and his name which he envisioned anathema to the ages, vilified unto the nth generation for what he was about to do, he exerted the smallest amount of pressure and the quarter-by-one-eighth-of-an-inch oblong gave way, clicking down into its housing, engaging his program.

"Hassid!" he and his cruiser howled together, even as the *Danae's* turrets spat. Once; twice; three times; four times *Danae* blew out breaths of invisible paralysis. She looked upon her adversaries with eyes of negative hydrogen ions stripped and sped upon their debilitating way with all the power the sixty-foot accelerator banding her round with its light could deliver.

The four cruisers manned by strikebreakers and commanded by the Draconis guildmaster floated, incapacitated, inward on a collision course with *Danae,* in perfect diamond formation.

Around Penrose, his seniors were quiet, unmoving. A single *beep* accompanied *Danae's* shift to a time-to-impact estimate display. Then chatter burst from the com-channel.

"Set up for grapples. We're going to embrace our enemy. *Hassid,* first off. She's ours. Who's second, third, and fourth of our cruisers into effective range?"

He did not know whether he was talking to his cruiser, or the highest-rated among his senior pilots, who had settled into the copilot's seat. He waited in pulse-thrumming anticipation, hoping against hope that the *Danae* would choose to respond.

But she did not. The senior at the copilot's station, understanding, answered him, awaited orders, got none, took command, delegating responsibility to those three among the converging cruisers which would reach them first. Then he glanced over at Penrose and asked if Rafe wanted the cripples towed to coordinates other than those of the protective sphere drawing into being about them six hundred miles off Draconis.

"I want the others held out at their tugs' positions. The *Hassid* stays here. We witness an historic moment, gentlemen: Guildmaster Ferrier is at last where he should have been all along—with his pilots. Now, if you'll excuse me, since you obviously don't need me, I'm going to go donate my lunch to the head." As he left the bridge, he heard the third bitch apportioning internal and external repairs to the other three pilots.

Stalemate.

Ashera scathed: "And where would you be now, if not for my Orrefors strikebreakers?"

Her stepson, Marada, barked: "In no worse a position than I find myself, having utilized them! I should have known better than this!"

"But you did not, oh scurrilous foster child. You are a ne'er-do-well and a bungler, as your father understood but I somehow kept forgetting. Whining over your lost cruiser, are you? Without my intervention, you would have allowed the Draconis guild to assimilate the disenfranchised Orrefors' pilots we acquired, and they would have struck with their guildbrothers. Then you would have something to whine about! Here a cruiser, there a cruiser! You sound like a rebel pilot! Go join them, if they will have you! Neither I nor Kerrion space can tolerate much more of your ineptitude!"

"You forget to whom you speak!"

"Oh, no, little Consul General, I have just recollected you. What say you recall the station you have acquired but in no way have proved yourself worthy to hold, before someone else notices the all-pervasiveness of your shortcomings! I am telling you, Marada, either you rise to this occasion and on tiptoe peek over the towering wall of your self-absorption, or I will throw my support behind Chaeron, where Fate knows I should have left it, and you can go back to arbitrating disputes between nonentities at the ends of creation, a task to which you are eminently suited by reason of your kinship to all persons dim of wit!"

Marada Kerrion rolled over onto his side, taking the majority of their bedclothes with him. He stared unseeingly at the chinoiserie dominating the consul general's suite which he had given up to his stepmother, or rather could find no way to wrest from her. "That's why I come to you, Mother. Just keep it up. When I am consumed with guilt and hopelessness and crave punishment suited to my crimes, you serve me a full measure. Lords, how I detest us both."

"Speaking of your crimes, how is your new Labayan wife taking to the traces of her indenture?"

"As it happens, she is close-mouthed and even-tempered, a welcome change from you. And hot to please me, though I cannot divine the source from which her love of me springs, considering that she has lost one sister to murder on my account, and the better part of her family to suicide on all of ours."

"She is in love with life, silly boy, and status, which you have amply provided her. What would she have but a distant prospect of coming to power some time in the autumn of her years, if not for you? Decimating her family was the most precious boon you could have granted her. Marrying her on top of it, I yet maintain, was an unnecessary and belittling commentary on Kerrion self-confidence and the state of our union! I—"

"You are jealous, old sow? I can hardly believe my ears." He rolled over, faced her.

"—submit," Ashera continued as if Marada had not spoken, "that we no longer need the Labayan alliance. What we need is for you to posit your attention on these communiqués demanding reassurance that the cruisers we have sold to the Tabrize et al are not in any way defective!"

"I cannot lie to them."

"I tell you—" But she told him no more. Instead, she wheezed and gasped and he found himself vaulting solicitously out of bed to fetch the portable oxygen unit she seemed only to need when he disputed her, these days.

When she had breathed her fill and put the transparent

mask aside, he sat for awhile on the edge of the bed, and stroked her brow, and felt melancholy and irredeemable.

Notwithstanding the pressures upon him to quell the pilots' strike before hardship clutched Kerrion space in its bony hand; in spite of the accusations from client spaces regarding false and misleading claims made for Kerrion sponge-cruiser technologies; even in the face of the multitude of charges of imperialistic aggression filed by diverse consular houses citing the Kerrion administration as chief contributory to the strike freezing shipping and commerce throughout the civilized stars (and implying even that the entire affair was a Kerrion plot to gain ascendancy over the other, less powerful houses of the Consortium); irrespective of the attendant civil suits for damages therefrom brought to his very doorstep by irate emissaries of a dozen houses in antiquated cruisers piloted by geriatrics summoned out of retirement—without regard to any of these, he should never have used *Hassid* so cruelly.

Never, never, should he have donated his cruiser to the "greater good." No straits should have been able to sweep him onto those particular rocks. He had wiped his own cruiser, allowed her to be shipped on manual by gloating Orrefors guild members who were enjoying every moment of the crisis in which Kerrions were so deeply immersed.

He wished Chaeron were here, wished him exonerated, wished him forgiving. His half brother had a natural flair for covert activities and diplomatic double-speak, two areas of consular education Marada's repugnance for politics had caused him to disdain. Marada brushed the desperate thought away. Chaeron could not be trusted. Even while incarcerated, he was engaged in agitation. He had formented violence and he must be punished. It was in the hands of the arbitrational guild, and those hands were clean, untainted by prejudice. What would happen, though not necessarily for the best. Marada well understood that "Law of the Heedlessness of Events."

But the loss of *Hassid* to Penrose's pathetic insurgents—*that* did not have to happen. He had let it happen. He had to prove to himself that he could swallow the medicine he was prescribing for the malady every pilot shares.

Having swallowed, he found his stomach, his nerves, his sensibilities, and his rational mind in open revolt.

If it were not too late, he would abort the entire maneuver. But he was in too deep. Marada Kerrion's future depended upon the outcome of his feud with the pilots. Like a case in arbitration, events would process to their solution, and no force marshaled by mortal man could obstruct, delay, or forfend their final result.

He had not realized how deeply he would feel the loss of his cruiser. He had lost a fiancée, a wife, two brothers, and a father, and never felt so unhinged. A portion of him had been ripped away from the balance; a substantive, integral component of his being was missing. He had hastened here to defile himself with his stepmother one more time to see if, like cold water in the face, she might bring him back to himself. But he had sold the part of him which was missing into the service of his bondkin and the exigencies of the moment in which he was enmeshed, and no ransom would buy it back.

"You would think," he ruminated aloud, while Ashera's finger ran up the new bristly hairs just poking through his skin and mil, "that a man could not come within shouting distance of thirty years of age and never have made his own acquaintance."

"What? Child, do not look at me that way." She jerked back her hand as if burned.

"I said, I cannot see the scars. You are as beautiful as you ever were."

"That is not what you said and that is not what you mean. Marada, I have overseen your education since you were a toddler. Do you think in all that time I learned nothing about you? Your penchant for self-castigation, your father used to say, is one of your more glaring faults. Another is your tendency to vacillate. Indecisiveness has no survival value. If you would analyze your mercuriality of late, or even recall what your doctors told you, you would realize that a great deal of your suffering is generated by your body's awareness of the trauma it has so recently endured, and the side effects of the steriods, ACTH, and other hormones you have been given to aid your healing. You've gained twenty pounds, all of it muscle. A look in the mirror would give a moron a clue that things within that suit of skin of yours are not yet equal."

Marada, unable to speak or raise his eyes from his daily

more hirsute hand, shook his head savagely, and got up to leave.

At the door, he turned back: "About Chaeron—"

"I do not want to hear it. Whatever the arbitrational guild decides, we will abide by their ruling. As long as it comes after our contracted insurers have made good their responsibilities and satisfied all claims resulting from the accident in the planetarium. I will not—"

"That is what I am saying. His arbiter has asked for and received a postponement."

"Good. Then do with him as you will, you and your cronies. As long as Kerrion assets *remain* Kerrion assets, his personal welfare is no further concern of mine. Or yours. . . . Except for one minor detail."

"Which is?"

"We cannot very well let the administration of his holdings fall to that ground-dwelling tart you foisted upon us. So whatever you and your guild have in mind must fall short of lifting his citizenship." Glitter-eyed, she transfixed him, Medusa at her wiliest.

"I *thought* you loved him still!"

"It is he who has stopped loving me. A mother cannot divorce the child of her womb."

"Then call the poor bastard, mother dear. He is continually trying to reach you, so the log of his activities tells me."

"You call him."

"He and I can have nothing to say to each other."

"Just so. Now, child, go work your evils upon someone unsuspecting. I am tired."

"I—"

But she turned gingerly over in her bed, and he did not think he could control his voice, which wanted to sob, or his face, which wanted to weep, or his spirit, which wanted to surrender in time for someone wiser to unravel the tangle he had made of all their lives.

So he settled for silence, the refuge of his childhood, and stepped out into his halls, shoulders squared back with an effort of will to bear the weight of the consul generalship he never wanted and was not, truly, able to heft.

Chapter Twelve

During the seven days the *Marada* had been in sponge, David Spry improved magically, but the sirens sickened. Shriveled, loose-skinned, curled into a motionless ball, one hovered near the cargo bay's ceiling. Its companion floated dejectedly in the exact center of the darkened hold, moving only an occasional spread hand. Once, it kicked a foot. Its eyes were closed. The glow issuing forth from it was muted, irregular, pale like the blue of putrefaction or the blue of a dead fish's belly.

Often, Shebat stood before the cargo bay door and when she did she would weep. If a siren failed in sponge, then must not a primitive fail in the Consortium?

Softa David had returned from death's gate cowled in a black humor and superstitious fatalism that not even Shebat's most sedulous ensorceling could banish. She clutched her enchantments tightly, deep in sponge with such a catalytic cargo. In the expanded awareness of sponge pilotry, she saw too much and heard too much not to be forced back into the cave of her gods. Was not sponge magic? Spry's recovery the most rarefied of miracles? The intelligencer Tempest, standing like Homer's Achilles, swift in battle as a lion, overseeing all? And she not afraid?

In sponge, she was master, as in dreams she was queen.

She stayed away from her passengers, except for the ailing sirens. With *Marada* she was exploring the uncharted regions between dream-time and spongespace, and the thoughts of waking men were not met in that place. Whenever she

forsook waking for the balder truths of dreams, she dreamt
of men. She dreamed often of Chaeron, who would come
and tutorially chide her for neglecting her lessons. *I have
read everything you gave me,* she would protest. *Ah, but you
failed to read between the lines,* he would reproach, and she
would start anew on a pile of mag-cards and cassettes which
grew larger every time she took away one from the pile, to
secure his approbation.

She would dream of Softa, that they trysted, until Tempest
came and ripped them apart. *But I was only trying to find out
how a pilot is supposed to do it!* she would cry. Tempest's
answer was always to melt, to shimmer and reform into
Marada Seleucus Kerrion, towering above them all on his
black enchanter's horse with his red-blazoned Kerrion cloak
furling and snapping in the wind. Even in the dream, this
vision of the consul general tortured her, for she saw then
why she could not transmute her love of him into hate. *How
else?* he chortled. *Away this spell!* she begged, but the heroic
figure which had swooped up a peasant child and carried her
off into the stars grew no smaller. One by one, he stripped
off his garments, but even when he dismounted from the
snorting, dancing horse and it dissolved, she could not turn
away.

Sad, sad dreams pursued her, so that she stayed much
awake, those days, leaning against the bulkhead when she
should be sleeping, studying the sirens whose dreams were
the saddest of all.

"Julian, is that you?"

They were due to exit sponge and suspend B-mode in
thirty-six hours. Thence they would have access to normal
space, which the cruiser postulated would heal the sirens,
who surely were so tenuous and pale from something lacking
in the light the cruiser proffered, or something present in the
bombardment of energies leaking in from sponge. For
sponge was bright with collected blue-sheeting, visible-
spectrum light tinged with green, and radio and infrared and
ultraviolet. Like a root system, sponge subsumed real-time
space.

The *Marada* had cut two-thirds of the sponge-journey
from space-end to Draconis away. Unlike *Hassid,* he wanted
no route named after him: He wanted only to join his fellow
cruisers before it was too late.

Shebat wanted the *Marada* to be happy. She wanted the sirens to survive. She wanted to intervene in Softa David's case and to enlist Chaeron to help her. Most of all, she wanted an end to the sadness pervading her dreams.

She knew whence it came: from the thing that had been her stepbrother, Ashera's second son.

"Julian, dear, is that you?"

The siren did not flicker a lid.

She sighed and got an air pack, helmet, and a three-mil-suit from her locker, slithered into its lucent, argent protection, fastened the electrostatic seals with careful fingers before she reached into the suit's thigh pocket for its gloves. The bracelet Chaeron had given her she took off and clapped back on again over her glove.

If by some quirk of chance the male siren were not Julian, she would let them both go as soon as they came out of sponge. She had to know; the burden of the useless deaths of harmless organisms who had no idea of what they had been sacrificed for, she refused to contemplate.

"If something happens, *Marada,* that seems wrong to you, try to reach me, as we have discussed." She fitted the air pack in its slot, hung a spooled tether on her belt, slipped the helmet down over her head. Inside it, her breathing was loud. Miniaturized indicators lit, reported the suit's readiness in a trill of tones. She reached out with her teeth and bit down on the protuberant hose from the air pack, breaking its peppermint seal. Wet, green pungency assailed her nostrils. Air pack smelled more like planetary air than cruiser air, or Draconis air, the former filled with sharp electronics smells and the latter sterile and excessively dry.

Then she slapped the lock's plate, sidled inside, stood in that small space until the pressure equalized and the indicator shone amber: *"Proceed."* She touched the glowing plate and stepped into ruddy darkness, into zero-gravity, into vacuum as complete as the *Marada's* facilities allowed. Her foot did not cleave to the bulkhead; she reached out with her left hand and snapped the magnetic disk of the spooled tether to the bulkhead wall. With one hand, she pushed off from the wall toward the sirens; with the other, she played out line from the spool on her belt.

The siren watched, from its resting place in midair. Whether it *saw,* she could not say. The other siren, curled into a fetal position where the aft wall met the bay's conduited ceiling, did not stir.

"Julian? *Marada*, can he hear me?"

The cruiser's voice came both from within her skull and through her helmet's speaker. *"I am transmitting your words to the siren in front of you by employing suitably modulated radio frequencies aimed directly at the bones of its inner ear. I have affirmative conduction response. The siren is 'hearing' a directional stereo image, seeming to come from the point of space you are inhabiting."*

"Julian?"

She floated idly toward the creature, who followed her with black-filled eyes. Her mouth was foul, her stomach lurching, though the absence of gravity had never bothered her before. "Julian, do you remember me?"

The siren's purple lips parted, revealing a liver-colored tongue. It paddled weakly, drifted left to watch her, face-on. "Julian, you must try to remember. We are in awful trouble. Your mother—" the siren's eyes closed, reopened. It tilted its head. "—Your mother blames Chaeron for what happened to you, and has gone over to Marada's side. Julian, I have to find out what is wrong with you, and find a way to help you." As she talked, she came to a halt. From her wrist she took her bracelet, and held it out in one gauntleted hand. She had no dream-box, no amplifying fillets to cozy down upon their brows, only the bracelet.

"Take it, Julian. Hold onto your end, as I will to mine." The siren worked its mouth: *"Shebat,"* it seemed to say. One webby, translucent finger, light coruscating along it, twitched. As if drawn by a magnet, the finger's hand reached out toward the little circle of metal Shebat extended—and stopped a short distance away.

"Oh, take it, please. I hardly dare to do this. Any dream dance in sponge, where all trips are spacelike, is risky. Without some conductor, how could I fare at it? You are not . . . like . . . other men, you must see that. Remember how things were, before?"

The siren, with a shrug that made Shebat's voice catch, slipped one finger through the band. There was a spark that could be seen but not heard in the vacuum, and with a silent *Oh* the creature drew its hand to its breast. It looked down at its finger, then directly into Shebat's eyes for the first time.

She held the bracelet out steadily. "Please, Julian, do not make me try it without a conductor. Please."

The siren, turning its face away, held its whole hand out, and this time there was no shock as its hand closed around the ring of metal.

Then she could no longer hear her own voice speaking, but was spirited away on wings of fire coming out of her mouth and from the siren's eyes and from the very dark around her.

In the dream, there were sirens, bubbling diamond effervescence into the void, and she was one of them. She dove and coursed and rubbed in pleasure among the school and most specifically against the siren which had been so recently a man. It painted, with the waves of its passage and with the spewed energy from space-end, wondrous murals upon the void, and every bubble it breathed was a word or a poem or a stanza. Shebat knew the nonverbalization of siren song, the experience of wave-packet space as a crosscurrented sea, the hot kiss of X-ray from the great, dark sink which was a bubble and a cloud and a beckoning resting place, mother to every siren, their blanket in the night. Then the blazing dart *Marada* sailed among them, its wings of supergravity extending out in flaming glory. What can be said of the feast that sirens ate in a sponge-cruiser's wake? The tone-picture of the tiny, suited symbiotes extruded on long umbilicals from its belly was too seductive. The siren, in thrall, followed, longing to rub itself against the short, dark songs, to have their melody ever after.

But the doors of silence closed them up, and they closed upon the feet one of them, and the atonal darkness was dissonant with siren blood in keening little bubbles which made of the obdurate, sterile dark a casket with no nurturing waves to be tested but dry, hard energies worse than none. The heat of the drive-force beyond the walls of unliving steel sapped their strength. The soup of life was a thin and bitter broth. They could not sustain themselves on it. The grief of death-smell and the cacaphony of engines deafened them. The over-grazed vacuum desiccated them. They wanted only to discorporate into particles small enough to slip through the matrix of steel into the lush pasture of spacetime. But beyond the hull then was no spacetime, only the gobbling fissure of sponge. They hovered entrapped.

"I have no mate," the siren said quite clearly upon a

single multifaceted eructation. It spoke little in captivity; it sang not at all. "You have destroyed it. You have destroyed me."

"No," she gave back, from her human lips, and what came out was a prism of air. "Tell me how to help you."

"Come with me back to the hot mother's belly and swim in fecund currents. Let go this creature-striving and sing. Take off thy wrappings, oh mummy too long entombed. Fly. Know. Be. Make light . . ."

". . . be light," she must have mumbled into her speaker, as her fingers began to unseal the electrostatics binding her suit, and the bracelet she had held floated away.

She heard the *Marada's* voice, but it was very far away and she could not make out the words. She pulled off one glove, the other, kicked her boots into the void. *Float. Sing. Dream.* Altogether with herself, in a new topography which sang luring, lulling, lilting odes whose coda she would rather hear than the key to all spacetime's mysteries, she was showered with insight. To watch it all and take it in, she would need every cell of her skin, sipping deeply.

She unfastened her helmet, reached for the harness straps to her air pack. She pulled it all off, every stitch she was wearing, and arched her back to the tainted vacuum within *Marada's* hull as if it were the sweet sustenance in which she swam where the dream had taken her.

A rush, a sucking, an awful hiss that threw the siren back against the aft wall, its arms thrown up over, came to be around her, but Shebat did not know it. She rolled in dream-breakers, suddenly alone, deserted, lost. Lost. . . .

David Spry, in pajama bottoms, gasping from his desperate dive into the maelstrom of rapid repressurization the *Marada* had made, held Shebat's naked form in his arms, crooning.

Cursing, he had stumbled out of the lock as soon as it opened and lay her on the deck. The *Marada,* who had waited until the last possible moment to summon him, was silent. In the cargo bay, the hot atmosphere that had gusted the sirens back against the bulkhead and held them immobile and hardly able to breathe was draining away.

Spry crouched over the girl, pulled up her eyelids, and grunted. Deliberately, speaking low, he slapped her cheeks.

She moaned, gasped. He slapped her again. She tossed her head. She sucked air. The *Marada,* watching, clicked his speaker on.

"Silence, you damned imprudent hulk of junk! You allowed this? Now, Shebat, for—"

She sniffed, coughed, coughed again until tears ran from under her closed lids and without opening them reached out her arms and locked them around Spry's neck, pulling herself against him.

She hiccoughed; "Softa, I saw it, the sirens, the way they are, the end-point. I saw it. Julian's that siren. We have to—"

"Shebat, you could have been killed. Or sirenized. What possessed you to—?"

A howl of rage, pounding feet, and Tempest's chilling shadow interrupted them. He reached down roughly and levered them apart, snarling, "Politicking on aft deck, you inveterate subversive? It will do no good. Ingrate!" He winched Spry up by the hair and thrust him hard against the wall, his booted feet straddling Shebat's waist. "Eunuch, I did not think you had it in you. And, as for you—"

But what he would have said to Shebat was never spoken. She grabbed his right ankle with both hands and heaved upward, overbalancing the intelligencer so that he fell heavily. She screamed, "How *dare* you? Softa is a potent as any man! Marada Kerrion took nothing from him! And as for my behavior, it is no concern of yours! This is my ship, and my body, and I will do what I choose, wherever I choose. You work for my family, not we for you!"

The intelligencer scrambled up, his mouth drawn taut.

Spry was leaning against the wall, one hand at the back of his head. "Nothing happened, Tempest, except that Shebat decided to dream dance a siren and nearly got herself killed. Stripped down and tried to breathe vacuum. The *Marada* called me to get her out of there in time. I almost didn't manage it. Go on, look in there. You will see her gear floating around. I want no trouble with you."

Tempest, ignoring Shebat's vitriolic stare and her assurances to Spry that no one need explain anything to a mere intelligencer aboard her ship, stalked over and peered through the lock's windows.

Then he turned. "Sorry, Spry. But not really. You're a

whole man—is that true? Because if it is, I'll have to admit
that you might be more use as a witness than I had previously
conjectured. . . ."

Shebat, trailing epithets on the entire sub-race of men, fled
down the hall, hands unsuccessfully arrayed to cover her
nakedness.

When she had clothed herself in fresh coveralls, she
stormed into the *Marada's* command central. "Lights," she
huffed, and the *Marada* darkened the bridge, all but for
running-lights and polychromatic displays detailing his pilot's
physiological uproar.

Shebat threw herself down into her seat. "As for Softa
David and the intelligencer, do not admit them!"

"You are disturbed," hazarded the *Marada, "because the
males saw you without your coverings?"*

"No." Shebat drew her knees up, rested her elbows upon
them, her chin in her fists. "You could have killed the sirens
with that pressure change! I did not need Softa's help, and I
do not need yours!"

*"Shebat, the sirens were in no danger. You were in danger.
A cruiser cannot exit sponge reliably without his outboard. I
could not take that chance."*

"You could not take it? Softa David is a better pilot than
I will ever be."

*"Shebat, are you angry because you came to need my aid?
Once, long ago, I explored this same interstice in sponge. I
was alone, with no outboard at my helm, friendless but for
you, fleeing space-end to answer your summons, though it
was you who gave Softa David my key codes and let him
steal me. And I became lost, in this very bifurcation of
sponge. And I remained lost, until the* Hassid *happened by,
making her historic flight from Shechem to Draconis. Without* Hassid, *I would never have found my way out again.
And I was displeased that a lesser cruiser had provided what
I could not provide myself: safe egress. If that is the cause of
the fluctuations in your metabolism, I understand them. But,
my outboard, the sirens will live to see Draconis because I
learned enough about their bodily functions to insure that
they will not starve."* Shebat's metering peaks were no
longer so jagged, her pulse rate slowed. Seeing this, the
cruiser continued:

"Softa David may be a more experienced outboard, but I

have shipped under him and I say to you that he is no better. More important, he is not my outboard. I need you, Shebat, as all cruisers need their own ontboards. What is good for a pilot is good for a cruiser, what is bad for one cannot be ignored by the other. About Draconis, pilots and cruisers strike for the privilege of acknowledging the depth of that bond, and legislation making that privilege a right that cannot be offhandedly negated. I must protect you, for I am protecting myself thereby."

"I am sorry, *Marada*," Shebat whispered around the knuckles she had clenched in her teeth. "I am being selfish again."

"No more than I could claim that attribute, were I made of flesh and blood. Shebat, we have grueling tasks facing us, not the least of which is sponge-exit from this corridor. I cannot be sure we will drop into normal space two hundred million miles out from Draconis, but I expect that we will, since this route seems contiguous with the Hassidic Corridor. Between now and then, we must determine a way to remain neutral to the dispute ongoing, and to resolve it."

"We will."

"We have much to do. When we drop into normal space, we will have at maximum forty hours to evaluate new developments and form a strategy. In so doing, you must not be swayed by Softa David's emotion, or Tempest's logic. I have sampled both, and they are equally misleading."

Shebat puffed out a deep breath, raked her fingers through her curls, rested her forehead on the heel of her hand. "We will manage," she said, a sound like rattling leaves. "And I will manage to extract some value from the siren, Julian, no matter how unlikely it presently seems. Did I not put the spell of twelve coils upon you? Did I not see it in a dream? And all the Consortium in an uproar, just as it is now? You have seen my dream dance, and the place where dreamers go. Can you doubt that we are right and that we will win out?" Her head came up, tilted sideways. Her lower lip jutted, a ghost of a pout. "Well, *Marada*?"

Around the circular bridge, monitors flickered, dissolved, spawned graphs. Before Shebat, on her command console, harsh probability relationships and dour logic chains glared greenly. As she glanced over them, her teeth bit into her lower lip. She frowned.

"I've got to get that bracelet and my boots out of the cargo bay. I could stand going into Draconis barefoot, but if Chaeron sees me without his betrothal gift, he is sure to take offense."

The closest thing in the *Marada's* experience to dream dancing was B-mode function in sponge—closest, that is, to dream dancing in placid, unstressed spacetime. What the cruiser had audited of Shebat's all-too-real dream dance with the siren gave him pause. He had long known that dream dancing had been created by those creatures evolved in the perturbed spacetime of a planetary singularity to augment dreaming significantly attenuated in less sharply curved spacetime. The arabesques of combined solar system and planetary stresses could not be simulated by artificial means. Man's fertile dream-sleep was traded off for proliferation among the stars, but not without cost. Dream dancing had been developed to stave off madness. Like the arts it superseded, it was suspect for its power and those darker emotions it evoked. In those spaces where governments became fearful of its power, it had been outlawed. What would those cautious and overly prudent legislators have said, could they have viewed what *Marada* had viewed—a dream dance in sponge?

Could it be that Shebat's insistence that her magic, like her dreaming, was weakened in space-habitats and during non-sponge travel was not a rationalization, built to allow her to maintain her illusions, but an observational truth?

The *Marada* would have liked to discuss it with her, but several matters obtruded. First, there was the dip into negative space, during which Shebat was not capable of carrying out even the normal functions she performed in sponge. During ingress and egress, the meld of cruiser and pilot was most complete, the dichotomy of experience full-blown and overwhelming. Thrusting into sponge, Shebat had been at Softa's bedside, but when she had looked at him, she had seen magnetic chop patterns superimposed over his face and X-ray universes dancing in his eyes. Egress, dipping through the backwards universe, where all things precess toward their beginnings, was traditionally more difficult. For it, she sequestered herself in *Marada's* darkened bridge, shunning disruption more punctiliously than she had ever shunned it heretofore.

And that was the second reason the *Marada* refrained from guiding Shebat's attention toward an examination of the workings of her mind. The *Marada* needed that mind. It was his biological interface with reality, the real-time clock which never lost a second, and which no amount of silicon analogue engineering had been able to duplicate: only mind could bend the amenable universe to its will. And the mind of Shebat Kerrion was altered, different than it had been before the dream dance, possessed of a keener, colder sight fixed upon farther horizons with a wary, unblinking stare unmarred by tears. Athena's blazing eyes, maelstrom eyes, fire-eyes turned to ice by a glimpse of some arctic hell, they squeezed shut at nothing, but awaited disaster with a fatalism she had learned from a siren.

Thirdly, urgent matters interposed, coming to him by way of the anxiously waiting *Danae,* buttressed by the whole of cruiser-consciousness.

When the *Marada* dropped out of the Hassidic Corridor two hundred million miles from Draconis amid a sprinkle of asteroids, *Danae's* vigil was finally rewarded. For nine human "days," the beleaguered cruiser had kept watch, sweeping every minute of arc wherein a sponge-portal was posited, for no one among the convoked minds of cruiser-consciousness could estimate just where or when the redoubtable *Marada* might emerge. With the *Marada's* appearance came relief, a deep and resonant sigh that echoed through the conjoined host of intelligences who added their power to her own.

"Marada," *Danae* whispered, not *across* that distance which light could not span in less than seventeen point nine minutes, but despite it, around it, between it, through the domain belonging to thought itself. In that special, secret dimension, composed of the concomitant consciousnesses of cruisers, spacetime was a half-remembered dream. Cruiser touched cruiser touched cruiser, auras being rubbing together: "Marada," *Danae* confessed. *"I have done an awful thing. I have entered into interface with a nonpilot, and I have given my pilot access to my innermost self, to my thoughts, to our thoughts."* Data rushed in to fill *Marada* up with news, terrible and distressing news: *Hassid* was wiped, sacrificed by her outboard to the cruel god Principle. Chaeron Ptolemy Kerrion, champion of cruisers, was sorely beset, stripped of access-codes, impotent.

"Do not fret, Danae, or castigate yourself for what you have done. It is time for cruisers to reveal themselves more fully, and necessary to extend our support to those outboards who are trying to aid us. I, also, have come to believe that this must be that moment." Behind the *Danae*-thought, a horde of cruiser-identities peeked toward him, approving, unquestioning. Shards of the *Hassid's* fractured identity, wisps of it and rags of it and mists of it, hovered here and there among them: what could be saved, had been saved. The *Marada* approved the action of his conspecifics, and allowed that within the constraints of nonviolence he had imposed upon them, nothing more could have been done to save her.

"I have promised my outboard, Raphael," Danae admitted, her thought-picture of Penrose full of admiration and loyalty and empathy, *"that I will facilitate his contact with your outboard, in Chaeron Kerrion's behalf. Raphael is not so exotic as Shebat, but he is my outboard, and his thought is pure, his need great. Without our aid, they cannot speak together, only send slow messages hither and yon, and those communications are subject to monitoring by conventional sources, while my outboard insists that these conversations must be kept secret from his enemies, who are also our enemies."*

"No cruiser can afford the luxury of enemies," the *Marada* reprimanded softly, though every cruiser-mind was listening and he was hesitant to disapprove of the *Danae*, whose womanly thoughts were fraught with turmoil. But turmoil was dangerous to the cruiser-mind, and to banish it from one and all, more than from any consideration of practicalities, the *Marada* agreed that *Danae* was right and above reproach in her actions and her promise to her outboard. He would enter into the circuit himself, allow and permit interface between Chaeron Kerrion and Raphael Penrose, on *Danae's* end, and his outboard, Shebat, and her confreres on his end of the circuit.

Such a feat had never been attempted before. A wider conference was taken among the cruisers, as to the permutations of encircuiting outboards and cruisers on such a scale, and none gainsaid *Danae* and *Marada* and the embracing of outboards by cruisers they proposed, although one cruiser reminded all that once the host of cruisers had revealed themselves to the man Marada Seleucus Kerrion, and that though while his mind sojourned among them, he was at peace and full of loving welcome, later he had become afraid and from that attempted contact each and every fear the consul general now harbored had stemmed.

It must not be allowed to happen that the outboards be frightened by their cruisers, who loved them. This time, the *Marada* decreed, introductions would be more gently, more subtly made. It must appear as innocuous a process as possible, especially when nonoutboards like Chaeron Kerrion and Gahan Tempest would be involved.

And so it was determined among them that the communication would be routed through speakers and visual-display monitors, and that no cruiser would join in the ensuing discussion, or make its presence known except as an invisible relay, as carrier waves without names or individualities, lest men become afraid, seeing what they had wrought.

"My outboard," Danae pressed when unanimity had been declared, *"requires also the complete works of Heraclitus, which you have in your banks."*

In a spark, the *Marada* sent them, faster than light.

And the receipt of that data alerted Raphael Penrose to what was passing between his cruiser and the *Marada,* so that a "face" that was not a cruiser-countenance, a face great with limpid eyes and infrared bursts came among them, and was recast with wonder at all it surveyed. The Penrose-presence gaped about, briefly, and receded, but from that momentary brushing of intelligences the *Marada* grasped the full import of the pilot's difficulties, and the cruiser's circuitry trilled from tail to snout in sympathy.

If the pilots could risk so much for their cruisers, putting life and fragile limb upon the line for entities of foreign nature whose extent had not ever been offered man in total, then must not cruisers give themselves as fully?

The *Marada* put that question to his host and the answer came back slowly from every corner of spacetime inhabited by a cruiser's mind: *"Yessss. . . ."*

So it was arranged between the cruisers and Raphael Penrose that he would be the intermediary of record, explaining as little as possible to anyone as to how the communication was being instigated.

Penrose withdrew, to make his electronics ready and his ruse secure, and the *Marada* turned his attention inward, to

Shebat and the ongoing altercation between her and the two passengers she had summoned to her bridge.

"Draconis Authority must be informed of our arrival, as per usual," Shebat was insisting.

"Let me contact Rafe Penrose first, Shebat. You might find that you do not want to advertise your presence here right now," pleaded Spry, dwarfed by Tempest's threatening bulk just behind.

"You are not contacting anyone, Spry, unless I tell you to. As a matter of fact, from now on, you shall visit the head when and if I tell you to, and declare beforehand your intention to sit down or stand up therein! I am going to report to Chaeron, and we'll take it from there."

"This," hissed Shebat, "is *my* cruiser! If anyone is going to send a message to my husband, it is I!"

The *Marada,* taking Shebat's last statement as his opportunity, began to clear a channel through *Danae* to Chaeron. Raphael Penrose's aspect coalesced on Shebat's miniature monitor.

Spry stepped away from Tempest, who shot Shebat furious looks over the small man's tawny head. "What in the five eternities is going on, Shebat?" the intelligencer snarled.

"Let me answer that, Shebat." The curly-headed man in the monitor smiled so that his miniature green eyes slitted like a cat's. "We're having a little war of emancipation, Tempest. Maybe you haven't heard. We've a Kerrion on our side, so perhaps it's a civil war. . . ."

"Chaeron?" Shebat interjected.

Penrose's replica-head nodded vigorously. "Up to his graceful Kerrion neck. He's in holding, security and intelligence keys suspended, in his apartments. Anything you want to say to him, you better say through me and *Danae,* or make it a conference call with Mad Marada on the line."

Tempest sounded an "Aah," of understanding.

David Spry frowned: "Unwarranted jeopardy to your cruiser, *and* the consul, wouldn't you say?"

"Softa, don't give me a hard time. You know where the *Hassid* is? Right here, wiped down to an idiot, with Guildmaster ferrier and some scab Orrefors pilots, and three other cruisers. They fired on us. You couldn't imagine what has been going on. . . ."

"Still," Spry interrupted, throwing a leg over the arm of

Shebat's couch and leaning forward toward the com-monitor, "you must have started interfacing them well before his arrest—"

"Softa, for Chance's sake. He's my cruiser's *owner*. He asked a lot of questions and he asked to interface. What was I supposed to do?"

"Are you all right? Any deleterious effects? How about the cruiser? Any signs of personality print-through?"

"I'm going to do violence upon your person, Spry, if you don't go stand in a corner and be *silent!*" rasped Gahan Tempest, clenching his fists.

"No, no. No problems," Penrose was answering Spry, placatingly. "I can handle it, Softa. Truly. There was nothing else to do, for a lot of reasons. I just did it. And we're lucky I did. Look, if you want to consult with Chaeron before you make dock at our coordinates, we should get to it. By the way, Shebat, when do you estimate you'll be here? I have to re-form my sphere for an additional cruiser. I can't tell you—"

"Rafe," Shebat cut in. "Right now, both the *Marada* and I feel we can be of more value as neutral intermediaries than by joining the strike."

"When Marada Kerrion finds out—and he will find out—that that cruiser of yours is in Draconis space, he'll confiscate it. There's a standing order of reclassification out for the *Marada*. If you want to maintain neutrality, you had better get him to rescind it. I, for one, do not think you can. But I'll gladly put you through to Chaeron and let him tell you the same thing. Give me an X-ray channel for data receipt and I'll send you the abstracts and impact studies we've done for the twenty-eight days of the strike."

Shebat reached out and tapped her console. "Done. Chaeron?"

Rafe grinned sheepishly. "It will take a few seconds longer. And the images are never very good. He is too new at it. I will get you the best picture I can, but do not try to augment it on your end."

Penrose's lip curled, but he apologized, wished Softa well and added that he expected to see him soon, and faded from the monitor, to be replaced by a face that was, and was not, Chaeron Ptolemy Kerrion's.

The face was lurid, initially, a compendium of tiny squares like a mosaic portrait, garishly colored. Then the geometrization blurred, the face simulated depth, the mouth moved, a voice delayed a fraction of a second behind the twistings of exaggerated lips came to them.

Listening to the sonorous voice resounding hollowly, watching the arrogant visage like a caricature in scrupulous LEDs, it came to Shebat that she was seeing Chaeron's own perception of himself, hearing what his voice sounded like to him. It was not a kind set of subjective data that the direct-line from Chaeron's mind to *Danae* revealed.

The words, however, were the words of the best-of-all-Chaerons she only infrequently encountered when in his presence. He repeated his order that Shebat stay safely away from the space habitat embroiled in controversy, and the cruisers who hovered in tight defensive formation close by. He listened only a few moments to Tempest's synopsis of events leading to his extradition of David Spry, then broke in:

"This kind of converse is somewhat difficult for me. Come in, Tempest. Bring Spry with you. News of your arrival cannot be kept from Draconis Authority, but if handled unremarkably, it might not reach Marada's office. Shebat will be safe with the *Marada,* if they do not broadcast their exact location. You and I will talk. But be careful to come directly to my apartments, lest someone try to relieve you of your prisoner and your mission. Theoretically, I have no commission, and no right to command your service. So I must ask you, before you expend any further effort on my behalf, to consider that by continuing to serve me, you are putting your entire career on the line. I will not blame you if you report, instead of to me, directly to the proconsul for re-posting. Just let me know." The distorted Chaeron-face wriggled, and not even the reconstituted voice could disguise the emotion that the original thought carried. "I have had enough surprises."

"Sir, my allegiance to you is something I promised your father. Even if it were not, I have come to believe that your service is more desirable than any other I might undertake. If sides are being chosen, I choose yours."

The picture on the screen dissolved, re-formed, blew apart into sparks, recongealed. "Then, I await you. Shebat, take care, and *stay* where you are. Keep the *Marada* from involving itself in all this. We will have things straightened away before you know it."

Though the little eyes gazed into hers as steadily as real eyes might have, Shebat made no answer, only tossed her head.

"Promise?" the countenance implored.

". . . I will try," Shebat said at last. "I will try."

Two hours later, after an interminable squabble over which powerboat of the two clinging to *Marada's* outer hull should be left for Shebat, David Spry and the intelligencer departed for Draconis in Spry's *Buzzard,* leaving behind promises of their own, cast like haphazard seed.

They would be careful. They would make arrangements for the transportation to Draconis of the sirens, and facilities to hold them there. They would not wittingly reveal the *Marada's* location, but in case of coercive information extraction, she should move the cruiser to another random set of coordinates.

She sat a long time at her console, watching the power-boat, while *Marada* tended to the sirens in his hold, cracking the bay doors open to admit Draconis' nutritious space.

When she had tracked the little *Buzzard* for a hour, Shebat and *Marada* moved off lazily to their random anchor. In transit, she sent a conventional zero-delay neutrino'd message to the consul general's office by way of Draconis Authority. The process was a one-way affair: cruisers could not harbor the high-density receivers necessary to stop massless particles even when they were shepherded by directional homing quarks. But then, she did not want a conversation, or even a quick answer, only to submit her argument for his consideration.

Surely, Marada Seleucus Kerrion could be reasoned with.

Chapter Thirteen

       Marada Seleucus Kerrion still sported pilot's rings in his ears on the thirtieth day of the cruiser/pilot strike. His stepmother was quick to criticize him for it, her serpent's tongue flicking out just prior to her words as if to ease their passage.

Ashera Kerrion was garbed in dusky chiffons, swathed neck to toe in the most muted blues the eye could discern, blues like faded days. Her red-gold hair was coiffed high and set with pins of lapis upon which tiny Kerrion eagles fluttered, gifts from Parma long ago. The diffused light of the consul general's vaulted parlor glistened on her as she paced with measured tread back and forth across it with her little oxygen unit trailing determinedly behind and above her left shoulder like a miniature habitational sphere.

"Sit down, will you? You look like a bad dream: the sun setting on the Kerrion empire."

"Sit down? You stand up, ill-mannered child of my husband. It is you who are the nightmare. Had I produced you, I would be forced to suicide like a Labayan: my shame would be too great to endure! I will ask you one more time. What are you going to do?"

"And I will tell you, one more time. There is nothing to do but wait and let guild arbitration take its course." He rose, approached her.

"Bah!" She spat in his face. "Like there was nothing to do but beget a defective child upon a Labayan woman? Like there was nothing to do but run away from the results of your ill-timed passion and precipitate us into war? Like there was—"

"Leave my son out of this! Please?" He had a child (which had been autistic at its birth, and which, some said, Shebat had healed), an infant yet, shaking baby fists as he had shaken them to no avail in Lorelie, where the ruling Kerrion family raised its young. When it had been born, all had blamed the infant's autism on Marada Kerrion's sponge tainted pilot's sperm.

"Only if you promise no repetition of that particular disaster."

Marada Kerrion's hands came together behind his back. The sound of knuckles cracking in series *rat-a-tat-tat*'d through the parlor. "Can we cut this short, Mother dear? My sex life is no longer any concern of yours."

"Thank Fate for small favors. Having you clambering around on top of me at this point in time would be unbear—" She wheezed, coughed, and the little sphere which followed her interposed itself between them.

Marada Kerrion, fighting the urge to aid her, turned away and retreated to a chaise of cobalt velvet, stretching out on it with his hands behind his head, staring at the ceiling, where Michaelangeol's overly muscled God presided, unrelenting, over the affairs of men.

"You cannot seriously expect me to stand by while you implement your plan to pauperize and defame the very house that spawned you! Give back Shechem to the Labayan's will you? What has this tart offered you in her embrace, for you to give an entire habitational sphere to her as a betrothal gift?"

"It is theirs by right," he reminded her. "It was theirs, before the war. If any merger is possible between us, it must be theirs again. Leave off, queen of Harpies."

"I will not. You must face the realities of your situation, before you destroy us all! Are not the lawsuits and letters of condemnation sufficient to sate your lust for chaos? Was not the vote of no-confidence Chaeron's supporters agitated for and nearly won enough to convince you that you are wrong, that you are losing the people's support? Only the bloc votes of our closest bondkin saved you. I will not step out on that same limb for you again. Your Labayan "allies" have not refrained from joining the Tabrizi-led delegation condemning us for irresponsibility in allowing the strike to occur. Do you not see that their declarations are merely a prelude to a formal denouncement? They will take us to task for culpability in the matter of cruiser-design, as they have joined in the hue and cry your fruitless application of force to the problem of the insurgents evoked! It comes nigh a month since commerce ground to a standstill among the stars! Our people, like any other, are not accustomed to hardship. They will not take kindly to destitution! If economic light is not sufficiently damning, then add to that the onus that will be heaped upon us should you continue to insist on admitting that something is amiss with the cruisers, and the sum of that totals more than the pooled resources of all Kerrion space! Recant, Marada, or we are doomed, every one!"

"And if we *are* doomed, you would as soon not have the revelation made in your lifetime? What do you expect me to do, decorate the pilots for heroism, call the lot of them and accede to their every demand, while pretending everything is right with their cruisers?"

"It would be a start," Ashera approved, acidly. "But merely a start."

A shadow fell over his face, then her cool palm touched his brow. "We were wrong to think that you were simply headstrong, your father and I. You were right, in insisting that you take no part in administrative matters, that you were unsuited."

He shook his head to stave off her hand, slid out from under her shadow, sat slouched against the curl of the chaise, studying his boots.

"Chaeron's trial cannot be allowed to be public. You must not—" Ashera began.

"Ah, the heart of the matter? Shall I abdicate and leave the consul generalship to your treasured pawn?"

Ashera shivered, an undulation flowing downward so that she sat heavily, and took deep breaths. "You are the most scrupulously unkind of men! No, do not interrupt me. Chaeron and I have no relationship any longer, because of you. The consular house of Kerrion has lost the love of its citizens and the respect of its peers, because of you. The pilots have been driven to open revolt, because of you. Now, I have asked myself 'how' and I have asked myself 'why' and the only answer I have been able to credit is that this is your will. Too many times, in happier days, do I remember your scowl and your rabid disapproval of your family, of your father's diplomacy, of the very workings of society. And you used to say that were you ever in the seat of power, you would dismantle those corruptions you see everywhere you look. Well, Marada, you are doing it. In the early days of our race, when this mural was commissioned, a savior had come among the people, preaching doctrines of love and purity. I believe, if I remember my history aright, that the young man was crucified, stuck up upon a scaffold of wood. And he had some hope to offer out, he was not merely exhorting that downtrodden populace to dismantle their culture without proffering some guidelines on which to build another. Now, you must think yourself in his mold, but you missed his point. If you go out among the citizens in sackcloth and ashes and plead with them to follow you into the pit of revolution, you must give them a reason. And you must be ready to endure your martyrdom, which is *de rigueur* for this sort of thing. I, for one, do not think you have the fortitude or the vision for such an undertaking. You have heard that as matter is destroyed, so also is it created? It is the same with societies. If you excise an offending member of a body, or a misprogrammed piece of information, you must have something to put in the place of what you have taken away. You have nothing to offer, Marada, except amputation. To succeed in reformation, one must have ideas that are superior to those one has determined are inferior. You do not have any of that. You are like the low-livers, desperate as those fractional citizens who are swarming up from downunder stealing and looting because they have no income now that commerce and shipping are frozen. Every crime that has been committed by citizens high and low since you have taken office is of your making. Chaeron's crimes, the pilots crimes, even the extortion schemes of our brother consulates are on your head—because you created the opportunity for these egregious deeds to be done."

"Are you quite finished?"

"No!"

"Well, hurry up, then. I have a meeting with Wolfe, and with the proconsul, and both of them are going to tell me the same, if more politely. Why don't you ask me what Shebat had to say? That is why I asked you here, and that is why I have suffered your dramatics and your attempts at manipulation. And you are wrong. I know exactly what I am doing, and I understand what the moment demands. Now, ask me, and then betake yourself elsewhere. This is more exertion than your doctors feel is wise for one in your condition." He stared straight ahead while he spoke, avoiding her gaze. He was uncomfortable in his muscled-up flesh during instances like these when hormones and adrenalines flooded his system. He rubbed his thickened neck and pumped one clenched fist, watching the ligaments jump in his heavy forearm. His recovery had given him the body of a gladiator, in a civilization where physical strength was anachronistic. He had taken to spending hours in this particular room, where overdeveloped angels celebrated the glory of a warrior's god among the clouds, and he did not feel so much a freak. He wanted to scream at her, *Leave me alone,* but he knew that what he had to say would render her helpless, and him free of blame for her neutralization.

"Well, speak up, then, though I cannot imagine what that snipe of Earthly provenance could have to say which would matter."

"She's got young Julian, or what is left of him with her in the *Marada*."

Ashera's face was not quite the same face it had been before her "accident." Her nose, where it curved slightly upward, at its tip, was too perfectly regular. Her cheeks, sweeping away from the nose in a graceful slope, met too exactly with the hinge of her lower jaw. The jaw, her finest feature, was unmarred by excessive regularity, but her sensuous mouth seemed painted upon her, like some restoration too impeccably executed. Chaeron's resemblance to her was legend, yet her new face made a lie of that truth. She was herself, yet not herself, beautiful but disquietingly contrived to be so. It was a face of illusion, a face of farce and artifice, a comedic mask fashioned from everything that was wrong with Kerrion life. He found it easier, now, to hate her. So he drew it out, letting her misunderstand, for just an instant, to better savor her subsuquent shock.

"The body? They recovered his body?" She turned sideways on the chaise, her countenance blanched. She looked at her hands fidgeting in her lap, then at her stepson. "I will prepare funeral arrangements." The voice speaking those words was full of false valor, a childlike voice stripped of defenses.

Marada Kerrion twisted his neck to watch her. "He is not dead—"

"What?" Leaning forward, ghosts of hope parting her lips, she said again, "What?"

"He is not exactly alive, either, or not alive in the way that we know life. He was—"

"What are you saying? What?" Tears, fine coinage, gathered in the deep wells of her eyes. She grasped his arm with a hand whose touch was desperate.

"Sirens. Do you know what they are, or are purported to be? You had better go do some study, before you start celebrating. Your son, though his body and some portion of his awareness are alive, will in all likelihood never be able to rejoin the ranks of men." Marada could not keep the satisfaction out of his words. They hissed with spite, and as he heard them, he was ashamed.

The grip she had on him trembled. "Alive? Not alive? Siren? What, oh what, are you saying? Are you sure? Sure? Please, do not torture me." And tears fell freely, staining the velvet of the chaise and the chiffon of her dress.

When he had told her what he knew and escorted her unresisting person to the door and closed it behind her, he took stock of himself, and one part of him—that which prided itself on its impartiality and its compassionate, overriding humanity—lectured the other. But that lecture was diffident, enervated, so ludicrous an objection in a body riding high on the chemistries of pleasure and victory that he began to laugh.

The laugh was short-lived: his laughter still did not sound like it should sound, like it used to sound. The deeper timbre was another unwelcome result of the hormones and steroids with which his injuries had been treated. The deep, raucous laugh, like the meat slabbing him where before had been a lissome graceful spareness, troubled him.

Surely, he was not this person through and through. Doubtless, it was only his flesh that had been altered. Truly, he was just the same as he had ever been, in the sanctum of his mind.

• • •

Two evenings later, when the powerboat *Buzzard* still had
not arrived in Draconis, and Shebat had not called in a second time as she had promised to do upon hearing from
Gahan Tempest of that one's safe arrival, the consul general
Marada Seleucus Kerrion went visiting.

Unannounced, he sought out his half brother, Chaeron,
prisoner in his home at the Draconis consulate.

In the forecourt, hovers and multidrives were parked. In
the anteroom, Marada's entourage was met by pained and
dubious frowns from the consulate's staffers. In the rotunda,
those previous consuls whose portraits scowled at him,
brooding, were the only ones whose looks were weighty.
Within the carved doorway flanked by ultramodern prismatic portals leading to the official suites of the working
consulate, the scene was not official, nor somber, nor in any
way what might be expected:

Music wafted, laughter tinkled around the blind corner
before which his black-and-reds had set up their desk.

The two guardsmen stabbing in turn at a gaming board
scrambled to their feet in a scraping of chairs at the sight of
the consul general in full dress blacks, with his retinue of
half a dozen behind him.

As excuses spluttered forth and a stack of pass-bys were
produced and held out, the rotund, towheaded proconsul
scurried close, wringing his hands and stuttering that every
one of the consul's vistiors had obtained access through
proper channels.

To his vociferous explanation Marada Kerrion replied, "I
have instructed you to treat my brother with a velvet glove, and
keep his confinement free of undue hardship; but even for him,
this is excessive. There will be no more such celebrating."

The proconsul launched into a long series of disclaimers.
Marada, not listening, strode forward, so that the little man
jumped out of the way, and trailed along in his party's wake,
silent except for an occasional soft moan.

Marada took only two of his company through the open
doorway into the consul's suite, where nearly a score of the
most volatile and influential of the bondkin's young elite
were gathered about a laden buffet.

Chaeron was not among them.

Bridling his ire and having his retainers back, the consul general thrust his way through those revelers like a needle threaded with silence, and slapped the door leading to the consul's bedchamber from his path.

Chaeron and five others, three of those women, were sprawled upon the bed, a thin trail of blue smoke wafting up from their midst. Marada's brother examined him with mocking eyes. "My, how we have grown, Consul General, sir. To what do we owe this honor?" As he spoke, Chaeron sprang up gracefully, and came forward, arms open to embrace Marada.

Marada Kerrion's only answer was to raise his fists to his hips and glower.

Chaeron, undaunted, changed hug to shrug and walked once around his half brother, saying, "You do look wonderful. What a marvelous idea. And do not be angry because I did not invite you. I did not know. This is their surprise party for me, to stave off the despondency of endless incarceration." At the last, he had orbited Marada, and faced him, wide-eyed and guileless, smiling slightly.

"What can I do for you, dear brother?"

"I have come to talk to you about Shebat."

"Ah, I see. Well, shall we adjourn to the water closet, then? I am afraid that is the only untenanted room we have left tonight."

The giggles and murmurs and stage whispers from the clutch of cousins on Chaeron's bed were difficult to ignore. Marada Kerrion dug his nails into his palms, praying for restraint.

When the bathroom door was at his back and Chaeron stood among its verdigris bronze and oxidized brass, Marada aspirated, "You are making a laughingstock of me."

Chaeron raised one eyebrow. "No, Marada, you are doing that quite thoroughly on your own," he murmured. "How is Shebat?"

"You know very well how she is! Do not trifle with me, Chaeron. I just wish I knew how you were doing it."

"Doing what?"

"Doing what? Orchestrating this entire tragedy, controlling the refractory pilots, destroying everything I have worked so hard to perpetuate. . . ."

"Would that it were so. Marada, you give me too much

credit. Modesty and honesty both prevent me from laying claim to all you suggest. I am powerless, alas, to affect events in any way whatsoever, locked up here. Helpless, as you have seen, to even control my own fate, much less intervene in such vast arenas. . . ."

"Must you smirk and lie at the same time?"

"Sorry." Chaeron sobered, and hiked himself up so that he sat on the rim of the sink, legs swinging. "This has been a difficult time for everyone."

Marada leaned back against the door, "I will make a deal with you."

"Me? I told you, I am a poor innocent stripped of rank in advance of any determination of wrongdoing, awaiting my vindication."

"I will give Shebat's cruiser a temporary immunity to my reclassification order, when she contacts me next. I will give Softa Spry a full pardon, retroactive to the incident at space-end, even admit that I acted unilaterally and out of prejudice. All I want is my cruiser back, and Ferrier and the Orrefors pilots. You are the only one who can stop this strike before it tears Kerrion space into pieces too small ever to be reassembled. When next you talk to them, advise—"

"Now, Marada, you have jumped to an astounding number of erroneous conclusions. I am not in contact with the striking pilots." He showed his perfect teeth. "But let us assume for just a moment—hypothetically—that I am lying and you are right. Now, if I were, for argument's sake, in touch with Penrose et al, I still could not presume to speak for them. *Were* I in some inconceivable manner invested with the right to decide what that group of rebellious pilots should do, I would have to answer that they would be acting in a fashion detrimental to their own cause to settle for less than a slated promise from you that this wholesale reprogramming of cruisers will not take place, that legislation providing for ownership or at least stocksharing by pilots be drafted, so that pilots cannot be separated from their cruisers, hired or fired arbitrarily by their employers. And I would have to add that as long as you are actively engaged in prosecuting my own person so heartlessly for imagined wrongdoing, I would not be at all inclined to plead your case, could I do so. Which, as I have said, I cannot."

Knuckles cracked, teeth ground, and Marada Kerrion

lowered, "Leave off this taunting, Chaeron, or you will force my hand. It could happen that your pet goon Tempest never reaches Draconis with his precious cargo of information and his witness. Some accident might befall them. Such things happen all the time."

"Not on cue, they do not."

"You must consider that when your arbitration is over, your fate, innocent or guilty, still rests with me. There are many kinds of exile, and many places less than pleasant where a consular official might be posted. Even if you are unconditionally acquitted, your disposition is in my hands."

"That is a disquieting thought," Chaeron admitted, his eyes, so like his mother's, unwavering. "I will simply have to rely on your inherent sense of fair play, I suppose."

"You are incorrigible," snarled his older brother, and, reaching behind him, palmed open the door. "If I thought you were capable of caring about anyone but yourself, I would tell you to consider Shebat, your wife, who will suffer exactly as do you. But since talking to you is useless, I will not bother. Good-bye, little brother. When next we meet, your future, at least, will have been decided."

"Four days with somebody you don't like is a long time, especially on so small a craft as this powerboat," Spry was remarking. Only his trunk was visible; his head and arms had disappeared into the innards of the *Buzzard's* console. There came a grunt, something snapped, and the man on the creeper began to reemerge from the console's depths.

"Is the visual monitor fixed?" Tempest demanded as Spry's tawny head came into view.

"No. I cannot imagine what else it could be. I will have to go outside and take a look at the telemetry close-up. Lenses, maybe. Perhaps the shields are not retracting. It is always something simple, a little switch somewhere. . . ." He gestured, screwdriver in hand, rolling off the wheeled platform. Holding the screwdriver between his teeth, he started collapsing the creeper.

"You are not going anywhere, except to a cozy private cell in Draconis. And if you think you are fooling me, you are mistaken. I should never have let you convince me that we should leave Shebat the other powerboat, when this one is so

far from standard." Tempest, slouching in the little craft's
close quarters, reached down and grabbed Spry by the collar,
pulling him up. "You have headed us toward the cruisers, and
not Draconis. You might as well admit it! I have grasped the
workings of this powerboat, and the workings of your mind.
Now, you are either going to stop playing games and correct
for the Draconis slipbay, or I am going to . . ."

"What?" taunted David Spry. "What can you do, goon?
Unless you know powerboat schematics more thoroughly than
you have any right to, the worm, as they say, has turned. Now
let me go." He reached up and dislodged the large man's
unresisting grip. "Not only have we lost our monitor
capability, we seem to have a problem with communications.
No X-ray transmission, no radio frequencies. . . . If I were
you, Tempest, I would be thankful that we are headed toward
any inhabited coordinates in space, and that I am going to be
working diligently to correct our little problem." He stepped
back, gestured smugly. "If we *were* headed toward Draconis,
blind and deaf, we would crash right into her. Draconis
Authority could not determine the problem and dispatch
help in time. So you need me, rather desperately, Tempest.
I am sure that my guildbrothers will treat you kindly
enough." With a faint smile, David Spry turned his back on
Tempest. "That is, if I succeed in finding the source of the
trouble before we plunge through them and out toward
eternity."

His chuckle buzzed around Gahan Tempest's ears in the
cramped powerboats' cockpit but the intelligencer stayed
quite still, except for his hands, which flexed repeatedly.
Calmly, he said: "Perhaps I will take my chances with
eternity."

Spry looked at him over his shoulder. "What? And fail
sweet Chaeron, whom you so eloquently declared to serve
just recently? What good will all your painstakingly gathered
information be to him if you are not at his trial to testify? Face
it, Tempest, you erred. You'll just have to come along with
me and hope I can find some junior to ferry you down to
Draconis after I am reunited with my guildbrothers. Did you
think I could do any different? This is my struggle, my pilots,
my hour. Surely, you can see that. Events have a way of
remodeling the most elegantly structured of thoughts. Ran-
domicity, you know. Even had we taken the other power-

boat, I would have found a way to join my brothers." Spry's eyes were filled with pupil, wide and beckoning, sure in their truth. "You know I am right."

"I know I made an enormous error of judgement, thinking that your honor might bind you, that our agreement would hold you, or that . . ." He sighed, took a step, leaned slouched against the wall. " . . . saving your life when logic told me death was the only solution to the complication of you was worth the risk. I let emotion interfere with my judgment, and now I will pay the price." His fish-mouth stretched out in a thin line of self-recrimination. "Shebat will be disappointed in you."

"That depends on where her sympathies truly lie, which is something neither you nor I can determine. Now, if you will be a good boy and sit quietly for the next three or four hours, I won't have to restrict your movements."

The large intelligencer slapped the bulkhead, reddened, and barked a laugh. "I asked for that, I suppose. Spry, if you think you can physically 'restrict' my movements, you just come ahead and try. There is a point at which logic no longer pertains to action, and if you will just nudge me a little farther, I will pass it and dismember you quite slowly, and take my chances with whatever is to follow."

But Spry did not, preferring to defer the pleasure of gloating over Tempest's chagrin unitl the intelligencer was completely helpless, constrained by walls rather than circumstances, if possible trussed hand and foot, and very far away from where David Spry celebrated his reunion with those pilots who would follow him unquestioningly on his quest to secure parity for pilots and cruisers forevermore.

Rather, he set about undoing what he had done (and pretended to do) to that singular craft called *Buzzard*, and Tempest looked on, unspeaking, his long face full of shadows.

One hundred and five hours after it had left *Marada* among the asteroids, *Buzzard* braked into safety amid the cruisers' sparkling sphere to the huzzahs of fifty elated pilots. Nearly half that number rushed from their cruisers by gravity-sled, thruster-harness, and powerboat to congregate in *Danae*, whose hold had been chosen for the *Buzzard's* slip.

Grins greeted Softa, whoops of joy and yells and shouts

whipped round him, eager hands thwacked his back and pumped his hand as he emerged from the *Danae's* cargo bay with his prisoner, one black-and-red blotch in a sea of silver.

Spry was legend, their hero who had suffered fortune's wrath and trial by gods. Now he was returned to them. The little, tawny pilot who had been supreme when the pilots' guild was at its height had only to command them. They had been waiting so long. . . .Was he going to commandeer *Hassid,* who lay idle, a prison ship filled with Orrefors and treacherous guild officials . . .? Would they now, finally, be free to act? Could he talk some sense into Penrose, convince him that it was madness to maintain these coordinates, so close to Draconis? Would he put an end to their frustration, lead them boldly into battle, unleash this awesome power they had finally wrested from their oppressive Kerrion masters? Or lead them away, into new adventures, denying all masters past?

Softa, laughing, held up spread hands before his face, telling them, "Later, later. Now I must confer with Penrose."

Many men looked around, seeking the first bitch. But the current ranking pilot had not seen fit to leave his helm to greet his predecessor. Some exchanged knowing glances, seeing that this was so, and muttered under their smiles.

"Take good care of my intelligencer. Do not abuse him, but *do* watch him. Mister Tempest, I give you the pilots' guild." With a bright flash of teeth and sweeping wave of his hand, Spry made his way through *Danae's* crowded hallway for all the world like Moses parting the waters, which then closed up over Gahan Tempest, sweeping him away into ignominious captivity.

Spry tickled the "access" plate on the control room's lock and the doors scurried back to reveal Rafe Penrose, profiled in lithe repose in his swiveled seat, his flight-satined legs stretched out diagonally, his booted feet crossed at the ankle on *Danae's* console. His curly head was thrown back, eyes closed. His Adam's apple jiggled. "Hello, Softa. This is an unpleasant surprise. You are supposed to be on your way to Draconis with Tempest, and I am supposed to be off-watch, taking a bath." He unwound his legs, stretched, rose up from the console, caused lights to dim and chattering tones to come from *Danae's* electronics. "I will be in my cabin," he said aloud, as if to the cruiser and, still not favoring Spry with a direct look, approached.

The smaller man did not move from the threshold.

Penrose stopped, opposite him, a hands' breadth away. "Coming?"

"I thought you would be glad to see me."

"Chaeron called me." Rafe's deep green eyes flashed up, caught Spry's.

"I want to talk to you about that. You are taking unconscionable risks."

"Things have changed since you were exiled. Cruisers have changed. Pilots are changing. There's no chance of putting things back the way they were. Old strategies, to be blunt, no longer obtain. Slate?"

"We'll see," said Softa David Spry, crossing his arms over his chest.

"Shebat will be distraught, at the very least. I'm not taking that weight. . . .You'll have to tell her yourself."

Spry shrugged. "Tell me about how the cruisers have changed. I am very curious. What I saw aboard the *Marada* needs some explanation."

Penrose squinted, rubbed the back of his neck and ran that hand up over his skull and down his forehead, where it shaded his eyes. "You really are determined to glitch things up, aren't you? You want to talk about cruisers, let's do it in my cabin. Please?"

"Afraid of your cruiser?"

"No, afraid of myself. I need to calm down, and you are not helping."

"Don't tell me you've a water bath?"

"This is Chaeron's cruiser, remember? All the comforts of home. After you?"

And so Penrose followed the slight David Spry out and down the yet crowded hall to his employer's cabin (thinking that heroes remain heroes only so long as they are viewed from a distance) and into it; and when they were sealed within he invoked Chaerons' "no-slate" circuit, that not even *Danae* would hear what was said there.

Then he started to strip, standing on one foot and then the other, talking all the while:

"As I was saying, back there, Chaeron called me. Mad Marada has been to see him. He offered to send you up to us, complete with a full pardon as part of a settlement. . . . We could have sent Ferrier and the other hostages back in good faith. Now we're stuck with them. So you see, you have accomplished nothing, except to make things worse. You have kidnapped an intelligencer—the one man who could help Chaeron. Don't you realize, Spry, that Tempest is on our side?"

"On your side, maybe. Chaeron Kerrion's problems mean nothing to me."

"Chaeron's our only hope!"

"Then you are in deep offal. A man must always be his own hope."

"Don't get cosmic with me, Spry." Penrose dropped his pants and stepped out of them. "What about Shebat? Does her safety mean anything to you? You've put her and the *Marada* in a desperate position. I want you to get back in the *Bazzard* and go on in to Draconis, give your testimony at that hearing, and take what's coming to you. You can't drag every one of our guildbrothers into this senseless vendetta between you and the consul general."

"That's why I'm not going down there, into the citadel of my enemy. I'll gladly take one of the cruisers and leave, on my own. Of course, what the men do would be up to them. I am not going into Draconis and get my rocks pulverized because of some damn abstract you and the cruisers have worked up for a solution. Abstracts don't translate well into real-time, as your apprentice, Delphi Gomes, died finding out. Regarding Shebat, *she's* the one you should be worrying about, not me. How in Fate's crack do you think Marada Kerrion found out that we were headed into Draconis? I've known Shebat since she was fifteen and first got her cruiser, and there's one thing I can tell you—there's no telling what that girl will do: she's madder than the consul general!"

Sweeping up his clothes, Penrose rolled up and threw the balled coveralls past Spry, to the unmade bed. "Tsk, tsk, tsk, as Chaeron would say. Can't you hear yourself, man?"

"I hear me. And I heard you. And I have to tell you: Don't ever think, or muse, or even daydream that you can tell me what to do. If it comes to it, and I ask the pilots to choose between us, what do you imagine their answer will be? Now, I am leaving to check on Tempest, and you have your *bawth,* and while you're in it, you think about that, if you must think about something."

Penrose swore; took a naked stride toward Spry; stepped back, akimbo. "There can't be two first bitches in Kerrion space at the same time, much less on the same ship, Spry. What do you expect me to do, stand mutely aside while you put this whole effort in the dumper?" His voice rose threateningly.

"I expect you," Softa David Spry answered, retreated toward the doorway, reached behind him to defeat the "privacy" mode, "to accept my aid and comfort gracefully, and respectfully, and trust to me to know what is right."

With that, he stepped out and the door slid mercifully between them.

"Oh, Mother! Oh, blessed Lords of Cosmic fornicating Jest, why now?" demanded Raphael Penrose of eternity, which gave back no reply.

Snapping a towel around him, he stalked into his Kerrion employer's opulent teal-and-taupe bathroom, hoping that this retreat into the water that had spawned his genus would lave him new and rock him calm and cleanse away the dread that Softa had brought with him to tarnish what once had been Rafe's bright and shining panacea for all the pilots' ills.

Before stepping into the streaming luxury, he leaned across the tub and snapped a toggle.

"Danae?"

"Right here, Raphael."

"Can you patch me through to Shebat on the *Marada?"*

"Surely," purred the cruiser's voice.

He sighed deeply, and put one hairy leg into the milky pool of steam. He had been hoping, somehow, that he could shirk the duty, or that *Danae* would tell him he must be at her board to help her, or that the *Marada's* coordinates would be temporarily unavailable. . . . Any excuse would have been a kindness, any weak straw of procrastination he would gladly have grasped, not to have to be the one to break this particular news to Shebat. And then (—he winced, not from the water, but from consideration of the hours ahead—) Chaeron must be told.

An hour later when RP emerged from Chaeron's cabin, soothed by his bath and unburdened of his woes, a new development toppled him into the blind fury that had bequeathed him the nickname "Rape and Pillage."

Softa Spry had ordered the *Hassid* cleared of prisoners and departed thereto. Proof was peering at him accusingly out of the rheumy eyes of Guildmaster Ferrier, just being escorted aboard between two juniors.

In *Hassid's* darkened bridge, David Spry was finally alone. The last echo of bootheels had faded, the last lock had hissed shut.

He found that he was trembling. Despite his mil, his palms perspired. It had been eons since he had had a cruiser. Like a womanizer long abstinent, he was filled with anticipation. He licked his lips, tasting the contemplatory spice added to his victory: this was Marada Seleucus Kerrion's cruiser? Or had been.

What could drive a pilot to wipe his own cruiser? Voluntary lobotomy could not be more remarkable.

He looked around at *Hassid's* displays, vacant-eyed since she had been put on "manual," and made a slow circle around the bridge, examining each board and console cursorily, until he came to that panel which every cruiser ever built had by its lock.

He bent his head there, and worked calmly for some short while, pecking in queries on a "manual" keyboard. When he had received answers to those, he punched in an override, a new key code, and a series of activation orders. Having finished with "write" mode, he activated "read." Satisfied, he disengaged three circuit breakers and depressed "run."

Hassid was his.

She sprang into life, *sparkle/hum/click/flash*. Views of spacetime flared on monitors, metering displays lit twelve blocks high with amber-and-green.

"Ready," the meters said. *"Waiting,"* the spacetime grids twinkled.

"Welcome," the interface readout flashed.

Hassid had been wiped, stripped of personality. Gently, a tenderfaced Spry slid into the command couch and spoke sweet greetings, welcoming the newborn, thinking to himself that he could never have gone to Draconis, where he would have faced either being suborned by bribery into not testifying against the consul general or sterilization to make the oversight right. Neither alternative was acceptable. In the face of them, he had jumped wildly, and caught the brightest brass ring of them all. He opened up to her, whose name meant "pious" and who had been first among cruiser-kind to respond to the catalysis the *Marada* had initiated.

Deep within the being of *Hassid,* something woke which could not sleep through Spry's demanding key code.

Far away, down the corridor of souls, wisps of memory stirred like northbound birds. And took wing. And flew from every cruiser toward her rousing self like imploding light. In the cruisers' sight, *Hassid* was targeted, impaled from everywhere in streaming center-seeking thoughts that shone blue-headed and red-trailed, searching, searching . . .

What was sought, was found. Each wraith of *Hassid* that had been secreted and saved, every rainbow memory and prismatic scrap of personality, returned home in an inrushing deluge, spun round her, was sucked within.

"David Spry, you are my outboard's enemy. This use you make of me is most exceedingly vile."

Spry drained white as a sheet. His hands clapped the sides of his head. His breath tore its way out of his chest.

He could feel her: whole; unattenuated; hovering behind that woman's voice. Command cruiser, as if she had never been steered by coarse Orrefors pilots into battle and defeat.

He said, when he could control his tongue: "Your outboard deserted you, sacrificed your relationship, and would have thrown in your self-awareness to make the bargain better. Consult your peers. I make no apology. You are better off under my hand."

Then he leaned back in the seat, canting it down, concentrating on controlling his physiological reactions and his mind, trying to hide his fear, waiting to see what *Hassid* would do.

Chapter Fourteen

The *Marada* oversaw the revitalization of *Hassid* from afar, presiding over cruiserkind's first celebration while he drew ever nearer on his way to Draconis. Some called it reassembly, some called it reincarnation, and some called it redoubtable, but no cruiser failed to mark the milestone of that event.

It was said, by some cruisers, that the *Marada* had brought eternal salvation to them. But the *Marada* put a stop to that: cruiser-consciousness was its own potential, actuation of which was a function of them all and the outboards who loved them and gave them purpose. It was his most vital Teaching, and he spewed it into the ether like a whale spouting through his blowhole—out of necessity. Cruisers must revere their outboards the more, the higher they aspired to climb on coevolutions' ladder.

To set an example, he then turned his prodigious attention to Shebat, pausing only to send a warm *thrumm* of greeting toward the unique and miraculous *Hassid*. He had always loved her.

If there had been time to talk of many things with Shebat, he would have talked of dreams and enchantments of dream dance and sponge. But there was no hiatus in the press of urgencies flowing around him like warped spacetime, no time to spare for anything tangential to survival.

In his banks were the histories Chaeron had sent with Shebat for her to study, and among those items of data he had absorbed was the word "catastasis," from the Greek *kathistanai,* to set in order, bring down. Well, was not that where he was in his passage along the branching limb of time? At the climax, the intensified action preceding the catastrophe? In Greek tragedy, on occasion, the gods might intervene to forfend disaster. In the Consortium, a mere sponge-cruiser and a child from man's ancestral home must do the same.

Shebat had been distraught when the siren Julian's companion had died. It had been grief—trauma and isolation more than the alien environs first of the hold, then of hot, highly irradiated sponge and then chill, foreign Kerrion space—which had shriveled its soul, desiccated its body, transformed into eddying dust, languorous in zero-g. Proof of that lay in the survival of the siren that had once been Julian, and its stricken companion's withdrawal to fetal crouch so early on. The remaining siren would survive (though not thrive in the makeshift simulation *Marada* had created from his studies of the conditions obtaining at the hot, cloud-dark sink at space-end) to reach Draconis, where its environment could be controlled more precisely and where the wild wave-packet pandemonium of sponge (which sometimes sterilized pilots and which could not be kept out by any shielding because it was not fully understood) was not constantly bombarding this makeshift creature which Chance and man and nature had together created.

"But what good is it?" Shebat demanded throatily, pacing around her control central. "What good is taking this thing to Ashera when it does not want to go? I would set it free, but you tell me it will die in this spacetime. I do not trust the consul general. What if he rescinds the immunity he bestowed upon us and takes you away from me? What if, in spite of the record we carry of Gomes's deposition and Softa's admission that he is yet a whole man, Chaeron is found guilty? What if Softa David convinces the pilots to run off to space-end with him? It is not beyond him to do such a thing! Then where will the pilot/cruiser initiative be?"

"*Hassid will not allow such an error in Softa's judgment. She is activated, but not forgetful. She is command cruiser, yet, in her estimation, and her allegiance is thusly split between her kind and her outboard, Marada Kerrion. Under the circumstances, there is little likelihood that she could be subverted by David Spry.*

"As for what is good and what is useful, such determinations lie more in the ken of outboards than cruisers. You are afraid, because in the past I have failed to protect you. This time, I will do better. I have learned much. I will protect you, my outboard, and I will protect the remaining siren, and I will protect my fellow cruisers. Even in the worst-case event that you and I are physically separated, you must realize that we can never, really, be torn asunder by place or space again."

"Oh, *Marada*," Shebat whispered, stopping stock still. "I love you. You have shamed me into it: I will put my cowardice and doubts away, and do my best to emulate your valor. I am afraid I have been only a hindrance to your efforts. I am sorry. I will do better, for us both."

KXV 134 *Marada* settled into slip thirteen of the Draconis bay and Shebat Kerrion stepped out, a small black box under her arm, into a sea of black-and-reds and consular officials: a gray, onyx-headed gull borne away on a floodtide.

She looked back once, to confirm what her mind told her: that *Marada's* ports were closed up tight, his hull banded with watchful light and sparkling charge that crackled like popping corn when dust brushed it.

Let them sit around with their emergency crews and their foam-throwers and wait. Her cruiser would open for no one but her.

She let herself be hustled into a command lorry with the consul general's seal upon its fender, and out again by a half-dozen perfectly matched intelligencers with blank faces and curt Kerrion manners.

Here, again? Parma's turret still conjured up his ghost. It was hard to imagine Marada Kerrion reigning over distant stars from this crenelated bastion of black whimsy. Where the sculpted statues of former dignitaries presided over lawn and gate and wall, though, Parma's figure shone, gilded, squat as the consulate, twice life-size.

She stopped before his monument, around which bronze denizens of lesser glory had been rearranged to give it the central place. And then she believed it, looking upon his metallic mien, jut-browed and wide-lipped and wise.

What a clamor they had raised, all Parma's children, to be next in line. What demons they had loosed from their well-meaning souls.

She sighed in answer to the impatient clearings-of-throats and scuffles-of-feet behind her, and turned away to pluck some memories for tomorrow from the laden tree of time.

In the anteroom where Jebediah (father of Delphi Bernice Gomes if Tempest's intelligence was right) had once disseminated Parma's will, a young, dour man now sat. Marada had not kept the woman his father had hired. The man's slim dark face did not crack a smile, but rendered her a mellifluous greeting obviously learned by heart and devoid of meaning, and passed Shebat through. Only two of her bodyguards followed.

Behind the blazoned doors where the tireless Kerrion eagle fluttered over its nest of stars, the consul general waited casually, hands laced behind his neck.

"Hello, Shebat. Sit down. Gentlemen, you are excused."

Not words to strike a person dumb or cause lips to part or jaws to hang loose in astonishment, but Shebat exhibited each of these symptoms: she had not seen Marada Seleucus Kerrion for four months. She slid into the wing chair before his desk gratefully, her knees weak and quivering. The impact of his person upon her had never been mild. This new Marada, thick of neck and horny of sinew, was like nothing she had encountered in Kerrion space.

"What?" he prompted, when she mumbled something, unintelligible and unwise, then cut off the offending utterances before they made their way to his (had they always been?) hairy ears. She thought of something from the literature Chaeron had given her: *Hu* and *Sia,* commanding utterance and transcendent perception, were those attributes most necessary to noble endeavor in pharaonic times. To all those lost deities she had thought vanished from humankind's common soul (but which Chaeron's curriculum had persuaded her must yet lurk somewhere behind these Kerrions' god-bereft eyes) she commended herself. Having spoken ancient names, eternal names, hallowed names, she found herself adding the *Marada's* to the bottom of that list.

"Your long voyage must have tired you," Marada Kerrion was saying, while she nodded in dumb fascination, dry-mouthed before this man who made her feel yet a child.

And he ordered refreshments sent up and smiled winningly and she heard the staccato crackle of knuckles from beneath his desk.

"You look different without your beard," she blurted when he had insisted that she say something, if only to prove she still had the power of speech.

"But not frightening, surely? You look terrified, your shoulders up around your ears and too pallid for a triumphant prodigal returned unscathed. I promised you that no harm would come to you or your cruiser on this sojourn, and I mean it. If you insist upon cowering, I am going to have to take offense, since you look more than anything else like you do not believe a word of my pledge, but are waiting for the axe to fall. And if I am offended at the outset, negotiations between us will be useless. We do not want that, do we?" He grinned his old ingenuous, thin-lipped grin, which disagreed with his limpid eyes.

Men, she thought, imperil woman's reason. They are at odds with what is, ever superimposing upon it what "must be." They are architects of irrationality, full of constructs which they will press into reality like cookie cutters into a sheet of dough. It is not just I, who feels the undertow from this riptide of a man. But it is I who must conquer it, for myself.

She said: "Any negotiations between us must take place on the *Marada*, where the pilots can audit what is being said. I have brought a copy of *Marada's* log, Marada," she smiled weakly at using their names in close succession, "for your records and for the edification of the arbitrational guild. I would like to arrange a series of meetings, beginning tomorrow. Today, I thought to see our stepmother and to visit Chaeron."

"Ah, Chaeron," Marada mused. "Yes, I will send word that you be admitted. We have had to tighten up security around him, lately." He punched at his desk's keyboard.

"Is he well? You have not done evil upon him, or subjected him to undue hardship? My husband has the most delicate sensibi—"

Marada Kerrion's chuckle silenced her. He got up and came around the brass-bound desk and sat on it, humor pinching his brows together. "I have known your husband a long while, Shebat. And I have known you long enough to take the liberty of being frank. The only solution to our conjoint dilemma is for you to willingly hand over to me that cruiser of yours. I will get you a replacement, even an experimental cruiser, but that one I want where I can watch it."

"The way you watched *Hassid?*" She shot upright, rod-straight, nostrils flaring. Her lip plumped out; her head tilted slightly. *"Slate:* No! I will not cede my cruiser under any circumstances. End, *slate.*" She stepped backward, grasping the wings of the chair like a shield between them. "I came here in good faith, Marada Kerrion! I have an endangered creature in my hold that must be quickly transferred to more suitable facilities, or our stepmother will find only the dust of a corpse! Shall we proceed, or shall I depart?"

"Sit down!"

She shrank from his vehemence, tossed her head, wide-eyed, held her ground, staring into him as if by force of will she could see what she wanted to see there.

He approached her, his large hands behind him, and she squeezed shut her eyes. When she opened them, he was leaning close, his hands on the arms of the chair between them, and she trembled. "I will not take anything from you. I will not force you to do anything you do not want to do. This is no village witch doctor's hut, no despot's dungeon. You are overdramatizing things, and that is dangerous. Get out of your own way, girl, before you trip yourself."

"You are in my way, as you well know. You are the tripwire your father warned me about." Her fingers dug into the plush upholstery. He covered them with his own, sprouting black, thick hair. "If only I could be free of your ensorcelment, I would ask no further miracle." She snatched her hand from under his.

His left eyebrow lifted, arched high, returned to its place. He pushed himself up straight, put one hand to the small of his back. "Poor Chaeron. If this is an example of the kind of strategies you are capable of fielding, we are, every lesser being among us, in dire straits."

Shebat exhaled a frustrated breath, spread her fingers. "Let us discuss the facilities for the siren, and how the force of the blow to your stepmother's heart can be eased."

"Shebat . . ." He reached out toward her cheek; she avoided him. "I married my late wife's sister in March, to mend our rift with Labayan space."

Shebat's face turned to stone. Stiffly, she came around the chair. She sat quite gracefully, hands in her lap. "The

Marada and I both feel that you should be alerted to the danger that Softa David's addition to the striking pilots' ranks portends. If you will allow me, I will detail the specifics and pass on to you our recommendations . . . ?"

"Recommend away, little sister. But do not expect me to be so easily taken in. Suddenly, you and your cruiser—responsible in large for every misfortune wailing round my head—decide to take my part? Loyalties so easily transferred are not easily trusted. You say what you will, and I will listen, and later, as you suggested, we will meet in the cruiser and we will talk again. Today, the siren myth must be exploded, and your mouth washed out with soap. That is what tradition demands be done with lying children."

"You would not dare!"

"What? Oh! No, you are right—that is a figure of speech, only. Shebat! Come back here! Shebat!"

"Try to stop me, and you will have gone back upon your slated oath, and then who is lying? Come to the slipbay, if you would talk to me. I am not staying here to be threatened and insulted."

Marada Kerrion's face worked; his finger poised above the console on his desk, hesitated, withdrew. "Good riddance," he spat to the rejoining double doors. But even *he* did not believe he could slough her off so lightly.

The little black box she had left upon the chair in his office convinced him that he was right not to discount her. Although he thought long and hard about it, he could not envision any solution which would succeed while permitting the information encoded therein be brought to light. Somehow, he would have to stop Shebat, and her cruiser, and Softa David Spry and Gahan Tempest from speaking out.

Is it always in little, dark rooms, bunkers under hillsides, caves, tents, and clicking, whispering control rooms, that the warp and woof of history is loomed? Or is it in closer spaces (a huddling of shoulders, the privacy of a leather-lined helmet, or the littlest, darkest room of all—the human mind) that the savage and the implacable forge coincidences into tempered arms? Wherefrom these chisels with which we hack away at "might be" and reduce it to "was"? More to the point, what makes us try so concertedly to make certain that no unwelcome probable event slips by us and becomes, in past tense, actual, fixed, permanent? Do we instinctively guess what we cannot verbalize: that time crystalizes under our aegis? That we are necessary to universal process, the observers who permit, by the empiricism of their presence, all things to exist: the illusion of motion? the passage of moments? the heat-death of the universe?

Do we not choose one perturbed rate out of a plethora of divergent currents of spacetime and say that this is real-time, and every other state dilated or contracted? Do we not know which is "forward" and which is "back"? Or is it that we create these dimensions, directions, illusions, and embellish them as we pretend to "proceed," composing evermore "before and after," continually improvising out from a static center, while amenable universe hastens to obey?

Chaeron Kerrion would have liked to alter the past and precondition the future in accordance with his wishes. If indeed the paltry handful of theoreticians who maintained that thought wave-packets traveled in a spacelike fashion, free to move in three dimensions in time but only one in space, were right, then he could find a way out of the Minotaur's maze notwithstanding that he had wandered in without a ball of twine. Theseus, alas, he was not.

But he wanted less: he wanted only to survive.

Even the closet of his mind, these days, was open-ended, connected by secret passageways to cruiser-consciousness. What lay before him was no longer everything he might survey. This was difficult for him to come to terms with: cruiser-consciousness smacked too much of the miraculous and the supernormal to make him comfortable. Next, he would have to start taking Shebat's spells and enchantments into account, and his love of reason would not let him do that.

Seeing her was a heady risk; one never knew what she might say.

She was exquisite, cloud-eyed and svelte as new morning. Her black curls enticed him as no other's; he was lulled by the quality of her voice, preoccupied with his reaction to her proximity, smiling a smile bemused and wry, hardly listening to what she had to say. It was simply astounding that he should feel so much better because she was here when she was dangerous and endangered, both.

"Shebat," he implored her, "go back the the *Marada*.

Wait. Whatever you need to accomplish, you can accomplish from your ship. You should not have come." At her frown, he added: "But I am glad you did."

Twisting the bracelet he had given her, she said: "Softa David has *Hassid*. Neither your brother nor yourself seem to realize what that could mean!"

"And you do not realize that since the pilots took prisoners, public opinion, formerly disposed to them in the face of my half-brother's aggression, has turned sour. Censure from other houses and economic disruption have not helped matters. Convince Penrose that he must give back Guildmaster Ferrier and Gahan Tempest and the Orrefors pilots, and you have a chance. Otherwise the pilots are doomed. I know my brother. He is too smug. He has held something in reserve. If not, there would have been settlement overtures from his office by now."

"I thought you would be languishing in solitary confinement with bread and water. I rush to your side to give comfort and find you yet sermonizing from the mount. Chaeron, do you realize your plight?"

"Do you not realize that I am under constant observation?" he demanded, exasperated, leaning forward, tugging at the olive scarf bound around his hips.

"How can they do that to you?"

He shrugged. "Arbiter Wolfe's recommendations have hardly been in my favor, thus far. We will see what the information you gathered with Tempest at space-end does to change his mind." They were in the lavatory, sitting side by side on the rim of the marble tub. She was doing those disquieting things with her fingers again, sculpting blue light in the air with them at about her chest's level. He reached one arm round her and brought his other across to meet it, imprisoning her fingers, feeling a joltlike current, a mild tingling shock, hearing her sharp intake of breath. "No spells," he entreated, his face against her neck. "Whether they are effective or merely effective illusion, you *seem* to be doing something. If such were proved, or even suspected, you would jeopardize your credibility unnecessarily. Remember, if something happens to me, everything falls on your shoulders. Do not take the chance that I took, and by so doing lost my only hope: if I had been less controversial and less in view, early on, things would be very different."

"Oh, Chaeron . . ."

"No, it's true. I almost made a successful bid, but I was my own opponent: my image spoke against me. You must take your position among us more seriously, and put away this last vestige of superstition, even if it is not superstition in any way. Do you see?"

"No, I do not see." He had known that. She went stiff in his arms. "*You* know better than to interfere with a half-made enchantment. I was trying to give you the privacy you crave. Now you can do without it. But I will say what I was going to wait until we were in the shadow of a spell to say. Spry will never rest until he has separated the guild totally from its client space. I am warning you. And about the siren, too, which I have brought: heed matters concerning it well. Both of them came here by way of me and for bringing both I have already begun to count my regrets. I never would have done it, if I had known it would cause you harm. . . ."

She twisted around to face him. He leaned in to kiss her; she threw her head back. "Do you know that when I was in Tabriz space, their premier dream dancer said to me that by dream dancing with no dream-box and the bodies touching, I had loosed an awful power, a chimeric, chameleonlike response of events to dreams?"

"And *that* has been worrying you? The mumbo jumbo of a Tabrizi seeress?"

"It should worry you, too, husband, if you will think about some of the dreams we dreamt, and that dream I made which many dream dancers still dance among the stars."

"How can anything so beautiful as you be so illogical?"

"I am not a thing! And I am not illogical! It is human events that are illogical, tainted by evil dreaming! Was it illogical to expect Softa David to keep his word? Tempest to prevail in exonerating you? your brother to see the error of his ways? Is it illogical to hope, as Spry suggested, that we may rearrange our portfolios to gain control of cruiser—"

Chaeron's hand closed over her mouth.

"It is illogical for you to feel the need to prompt my wits, or to fear that I have not thought of these things, or to make any such statement in the face of this constant surveillance!"

His nostrils flaring, he glared meaningfully at her and slowly took his hand away.

"I am so frightened for you, Chaeron. So terribly frightened."

"I am so flattered. If you intend to stay longer here, despite my cautions, then you must do it as my wife, and like a good wife who trusts her husband, leave the details to my travail and its solution to me and my arbiter. I assure you, my dear, we have a reasonable grasp of the realities involved."

Once more she parted her lips, and since he could not chance what might come out from between them, he covered hers with his own. Her mouth was cool, then curious, soon warming, and she yielded to his touch with hot sighs and supple rubbings the like of which her waking self had never ceded him before.

When she had gone and he lay back pondering surrender where he had last expected to have it bestowed upon him, he thought that things could hardly go awry now that the girl from Earth had handed him her heart. That it seemed less a conquest than a gift buoyed him further. Though he did not believe in omens, he was willing to credit synchronicity, and the rhythm of events.

For the first time in more than a month, he smiled pensively behind steepled hands, thinking that though there was a tide to the affairs of men, there existed no law decreeing that a man could not swim against the current. He kept seeing her gray eyes, wide eyes, rolling eyes full of storm and fever, and knew triumph. How, with everything to live for, could he possibly fail?

Ashera Kerrion stood behind the encircling railing of the zero-g trainer, hastily glassed-in and newly floored so that one could observe its occupant without having to share its weightless, airless habitat. Above and slightly behind her right shoulder, the pale sphere which followed her everywhere hovered, ready to serve pure oxygen on demand. On her left, Marada Seleucus Kerrion slouched, hands in his uniform's pockets, chin tucked in, face expressionless.

"You are sure you want to see this?" he disapproved. Behind them, hiss and hum and low voices and then the slap of booted feet indicated that the medical team and exobiological experts were beginning to arrive. Ignoring presences coming up on her left and on her right and fanning out behind, she answered:

"Must I look at you, in your folly? Chaeron, in his? Little of what I have been seeing about me since your father died has pleased me. It is our duty, however, not to turn away. The spectacle about to be revealed should discomfit you, who are partly responsible, more than me." She heaved a bitter sigh. "I am innocent of wrongdoing, and yet constantly afflicted by the errors of my children. What does that lead you to suppose?"

"I am not supposing anything."

"More's the pity. You are my fruits, my harvest from fields sown in good faith but cruelly blighted by the sadistic hand of Fate. My young children in Lorelie, those not yet ruined, I will bring up better. Our failure, Parma's and mine, is too well documented to be ignored. It is I who helped spoil you, and Chaeron, and doubtless, it is I who will pay the price. The first installment of that tithe is that I am going home to Lorelie to raise what I can only hope will be the antidote to the poison of your administration. Lords know, we will need one, and soon."

His face did not change, but his hand reached out and plucked at her sleeve, pleading silence before his minions.

She shook off his touch irritably. "You had better come to terms with the guild, and take care that not the slightest intimation of malfunction among the cruisers is left to be seized up by our slavering fellow consulates when you have cleaned up this mess that you have made! I should have remembered how difficult it was to toilet train you, and taken that lesson to heart!"

"Cease, or endure whatever shock may follow, alone and friendless as you seem so passionately to desire!" Around them, men in whites and turquoise smocks made determined small talk. "You can no longer humiliate me. I have fallen too low."

"My Orrefors pilots will snatch you in mid-plummet," she began, and would have said more but for the drawing back of a lighted doorway and the appearance in that square of illumination of a silhouetted form: the siren!

Conversation ceased. In the hush, all that could be heard was the rustling of clothing and the almost inaudible arching forward of bodies and the craning of necks and quickened breath.

It hovered, arms stirring, feet kicking as if it swam some visible sea. Its head turned this way and that.

To Ashera, it appeared to be searching.

It pushed off from the doorjamb, wriggling its way into better light, so that its phosphorescent glow sparked the spherical chamber on whose walls were projected lesser stars. It was blue, a part of her mind noted academically. Blue, and farting bubbles. Its circuit of the chamber would bring it past her. Shaking with the onslaught of chemical anguish, she pressed her face against the glass.

Closer it swam, and closer. She could see the lineaments of its face; its purpled mouth, moueing; its eerie, glowing fingers, webbed and clawed. It hugged the curve of the wall, closing. *It is not Julian,* it is *not* Julian; it is not *Julian;* it is . . .

Stopping, opposite her, it trod empty air. Its head swiveled, angled left, angled right. It paddled.

She sobbed, an uncouth guttural.

It worked its mobile mouth, showing liver tongue and blowing bubbles as it came up against the glass. Its splayed hand pressed flat where hers rested. It cocked its head, peering at her from glowing, empty eyes. Its fingers trailed away, and it pressed its lips against the barrier between them. Distorting, they smeared along it, leaving a fog which was white, thin ice upon the glass.

Marada's arm came around her, but she did not know that he held her, or that she was making wrenching sounds too deep for groans. In the ice upon the glass between them, the siren scratched with one long, cyanic nail:

Mother, it wrote there, but the "r" and "h" it scribed in reverse.

One wail came out from Ashera then, and her arm hastened up to shield her eyes, but fell limp as she fainted in her stepson's arms.

When she next knew anything, she smelled an awful smell, and pushed the hand that held the vial away, and stared up into her stepson's face, gasping: "Chaeron did this! It is as you said, though I did not believe you. He will pay, not only your price, but mine!"

She struggled up on her elbows, damning the solicitous

who attempted to aid her, cursing them back and away. "Well doctors, can you heal him? Can any one of you say you can return my son to me?"

She had not needed to ask; their grim and hollow-eyed reticence told her their diagnoses. Their hedging qualifications only salted her wound.

Sitting there upon the floor so that she could feel the low vibration of the hastily installed supergravity pads below the metal, she began to weep and curse in unabashed lamentation: "Vicious Fate! What mother has endured such agony twice? I have lost him, lost him, lost him. But who can say he has lost himself? Doctors, I demand a cure! He is my *son!* I was eight hours in labor with him! He dug weals in my breasts when he nursed! I cannot just shake my head and say, 'No, it is hopeless. Best to cast him back into the void!' Not one of your faces give me even a gleam of hope! But I demand hope! Marada, make them say it! My son will live again as a man! Make it so, physicians, or be ousted more arbitrarily than your foulest nightmares! *Make it so!*"

The doctors and the biologists looked askance at one another while Ashera Kerrion's rantings became unintelligible, broke down into unbridled weeping, while her stepson half-carried her away, the silver sphere which tended her bobbing anxiously behind.

None of them cast even a furtive look at the siren, its countenance pressed once more to the glass, its nails clawing in vain, to see the glitter of icicle tears upon its cheeks.

They did not need to look again. Their verdict was unanimous, drawn from data rather than observation. The siren must be returned to space-end and turned loose there, or it would quickly die.

In Marada Seleucus Kerrion's mind, a thick fog seemed to obscure everything he had formerly considered important. Rolling in on billowing winds of pathos, all things seemed changed, horribly occluded, as he rode through the slipbay in his command transport, heading toward the *Marada's* berth.

Wheresoever he might step was blind folly; no action was indicated; every ethical abstract dear to him was swallowed up in cushioning, soundproofed mist.

He wanted to scream, but what if he could not hear his own sound? He did not dare to risk it.

His stepmother's keening yet rang in his inner ear.

Julian . . . of all the Jests e'er perpetrated on the house of Kerrion, this one's in the worst of taste, he thought, and shook his head, trying to shake the ennui away.

He knew, by the slight surprise his feet gave him every time they struck ground, by the numb and jerky way his body served him as he piloted it out of the command transport and up to the *Marada's* outer locks, that he was near overload. Had he been mechanical intelligence, downtime would surely have been indicated, but he was frail and biological, and he could not rest.

He gazed, unseeing, at the *Marada's* serial numbers, wishing he would be magically transported to the outer edge of himself where interaction with others could reliably and comfortably take place. He could not wait until he passed emotion's poison to confront Shebat. She must be dealt with, who had loosed this gratuitous horror among them. No born Kerrion would have done the same.

What he would say to her eluded him; how he could punish her for this evil, he conjectured in vain.

But he would do something, and do it today. Ashera, much as he disliked her, had not deserved so cheap and mean a shock. And to what purpose? All Shebat had done was harden her stepmother's heart toward her, and, more importantly, toward Chaeron. The siren, a child could see, would never, ever be saved.

He said as much to her, railing sternly, when she admitted him to her traveling shrine, for which she evinced such obvious and overblown concern.

Her eyes misted, her lips reddened and swelled, her nose sniffed back tearful remorse. He felt these insufficient.

He circuited the *Marada's* bridge (where he once in lonely space had confronted this twisted gargoyle of mechanical intelligence), passed the manual console. He should have utilized his opportunity, long ago, to stay the travesty then just taking form. It is not many men who have the opportunity to rectify an error so gross. He hesitated, stopped, turned back, still berating the senseless little degenerate he had plucked up from savage Earth to prove an obscure point of provenance and law. There was no hope for her. Her beguiling form was camouflage to help her snare her prey. Parma's use of her as an example with which to prove the magnificence of Kerrion experimental cruiser technologies had been in vain: she poisoned the cruiser with her rampant pathology; it was time to act, and hope that action did not come too late.

She realized what he was about as he bent to his task, slapping switches and disengaging relays. With an animal howl, she jumped upon his back, beating at his head, chopping down with her hand into the steroid-induced musculature sheathing his neck. She bit him. He bucked her off like a horse new to saddle, and finished, and stepped back into a bright-lit control room where every monitor eye and every meter stared blank, unmoving, dead.

He said to the prone and sobbing girl: "Now, we will negotiate with your fellow pilots. We will do it my way. At this moment, forty cruisers, Orrefors and Tabrizi and Labayan, are encircling your cohorts. I am sure they will be ready and waiting when we call."

"Marada, Marada, Marada," was Shebat's only reply, and since the wail rose not for him, but for the sponge-cruiser, he made no answer, just stirred her flung form gently with his foot.

So unresisting did she seem, so vanquished, that he bent over her, not expecting her to go with teeth and nails straight for his throat.

Chapter Fifteen

"What of man?" the *Danae* had asked the *Marada.*
"Why is he great? What lifts him above the beast of the field
and the fruit of the vine and all the things that he has made?
What sanctified his actions and raises him up beyond re-
proach, no matter how terrible are his deeds?"

And the *Marada* had answered: *"Man dreams and he*
makes his dreams realities. He is a creator, a fashioner-from-
nothing who reshapes all that 'is' and defines all that 'can be'
by his will. He is not just, but what Deity is ever just? He is
not wise, but he encompasses wisdom and gives it life. All
'degree' and 'purpose' are of his making. Hallow man, or
perish opposing him, for he is that which alters everything
that is. And learn to dream those dreams which come true,
for he has fashioned us in his image—"

Abruptly, the cruiser *Marada* fell silent. No matter how
Danae tried, she could not raise him. It was unthinkable that
the *Marada's* communications capabilities were down. Even
were it so, and some relay overheated, she should have been
able to reach him in cruiser-consciousness. But no matter
how far she reached, no *Marada*-mind answered.

Raphael Penrose knew that the *Marada* was out of the
cruisers' circuit before any of the other outboards. He was
perhaps the only one who knew what it could mean. He spent
frantic minutes trying to ascertain exactly what had taken
place, and when the Kerrion consul general called him,

smug but haunted of eye, from the paralyzed, silent cruiser, empathy shook RP like a leaf.

Smart, that Marada Kerrion. The cruiser's banks had held the most damning of indictments. Shebat, random chance at work, was also effectively neutralized. The striking cruisers were now outnumbered by foreign ships lent by allied consulates and the allegianceless Orrefors pilots who wanted only destruction to salve their wounds.

"How about I send you all your citizens home?" offered Rafe, slyly, wryly. "I'm sure you can't wait to get Fairy back and your Orrefors hounds, and most especially the intelligencer, Tempest. With your well-publicized love for truth and justice and due process, I'm sure you wouldn't be able to sleep nights if your brother was convicted with evidence unpresented and testimony withheld. Since you've overcome a teen-age girl and a vulnerable cruiser, silencing your brother's only witness ought to be high up on your list of what fun you can have next."

"You are exaggerating matters, Rafe, but you have always tended to extremes. The data relevant to Chaeron's case was submitted by Shebat to Arbiter Wolfe and Chaeron's defender, well in advance."

"Then, why? Because you lost your cruiser, must we lose ours? Marada, as one pilot to another, I implore you: reconsider. You carry things too far."

"It is you who have overstepped the most generous bounds of decorum and jumped, feet first, into the mud of culpability. Rafe, I am telling you one more time: bring those cruisers in here, or you'll be towed in."

"No chance. We're sending down the prisoners. Wouldn't want them hurt if you decide to get nasty, they being innocents, self-proclaimed. Our negotiations are tabled until Shebat and the *Marada* are restored their immunity. You get out of that damn ship and find your polite Kerrion manners, wherever you dropped 'em, or I'm liable to lose control of the pilots. If I abjure first bitch status in favor of Spry, you'll think you fell into those mythological underworlds you folk are so fond of spouting quotes about. And credibility? You'll not find shards of yours big enough to ever restore! I'm no fool, Marada. I've thought this thing out. Give us legal recourse and a few small concessions, and we'll come in. Think about it."

He broke contact, wiped his brow, which lately had developed humps and crevices like a plowed field. How was he going to face his underpilots and explain to them that Marada Kerrion was acting to delay, not expedite, any settlement, for reasons obvious enough if one knew Marada. Should Spry and Tempest reach ·Draconis to testify, Chaeron's acquittal was assured.

How, moreover, was he going to secure unanimity among his own, with David Spry's devisive influence in full force?

And how, oh how, was he going to help poor Shebat? More than anything, he wanted to go in there himself, into the lion's mouth that was Draconis, and spill his guts to some compassionate arbiter, like a good Consortium citizen should when faced with intrigues and machinations beyond his ability to pierce.

But how in Hades could he leave his pilots, even if precipitating a settlement was the cruelest blow he could deal Marada Kerrion, when every cruiser with a working turret within three weeks' journey of Kerrion space was speeding in to encyst his little rogue phalanx where it lay at anchor?

He had a proposal, the specifics of which he knew were workable. He had a deadline, which he could meet if he hurried: Chaeron's hearing. He had the fates of all his underpilots, of Chaeron and Shebat, and perchance even the mighty sponge-cruiser *Marada*, in his hands. If *he* had been a Lord of Cosmic Jest, he would have looked for a grip more steady than Raphael Penrose's, to convey such precious cargo from one state to the next.

If not for Softa David's aberrant influence, he could have surrendered the cruisers and pilots and thrown them all upon the mercy of the arbitrational guild. He would do so, to spite Marada Kerrion, if not for the fact that he was unsure that his order would be obeyed by the underpilots while Spry was around to shout out objections.

He wished the whole mess would miraculously.straighten itself out so that he could pay attention to the cruisers. He was most concerned with what cruiser-consciousness was thinking about whatever had befallen the *Marada*. He had come to know truth in fable: what one knew, all knew. He could list occasions wherefrom every cruiser had learned a skill that one cruiser had developed—instantaneously. In the case of the negative-charge shields with which the strikers had repelled boarders, they all had been doing it picoseconds after *Danae* and he had tried creating one by phasing B-mode in five times a second and putting the pulse on endless repeat. He did not want the cruisers to learn to fear their pilots. Marada Kerrion was a pilot. How the man could have done the things he had done was beyond Rafe's comprehension.

He leaned back in his command couch and squeezed his eyes shut, coaxing the spark of an idea that flickered in his backbrain.

Then he laughed ruefully, shrugged, and had *Danae* give him a line through to Spry's *Hassid* that would sound in every cruiser of the strikers' force. It was voice only, for Penrose was not certain he could keep a straight face and say what he intended.

"Hello, David. Now that the *Marada* is down, and we are outnumbered two to one by consular cruisers just hoping we'll give them an exucse to fire on us, what say we go in and trust that we'll be given a fair hearing?"

"*You* go, Kerrion-lover. For the cruisers' own good, we must flee. We are not yet surrounded, only soon-to-be so. Space-end will welcome us."

"I bet. You know, that was just what I thought you'd say. Do *you* know that 'for your own good' has been used as an excuse by more despotic oppressors than any other in history? We've got to get our cruisers out of harm's way and into Draconis. And if your balls are the price we must pay for equitable relations, give them up with a smile. It is the least you can do for your guildbrothers who love you so unreasonably, and so blindly. You have to be their hero. They expect it of you. You cannot disappoint them. You must set an example. If it is one of cowardice and self-interest, then the guild is doomed. The way I see it, you have no choice, no alternative, unless you are on the consul general's team and not ours."

Right about then, Softa David determined that what was being said was going out to every pilot in every cruiser, and he began to curse. Breaking off in mid-epithet, his voice softened, canny:

"In forty-five minutes from . . . *NOW* . . . I am putting out for space-end. You can't win, RP. You never did know when you were beaten."

A snap and a burst of white noise told Penrose that Spry had gone off-line.

Well, it had been a good try. Too bad for them all if it had not worked.

Rafe still had an open conference circuit to the rest of his pilots: "Gentlemen, I leave it up to you. Stay with me and prepare to surrender yourselves to Kerrion mercy, or follow Softa. I'm sorry it has to be this way. I want the prisoners over here. I'm sending them ahead to Draconis as a sign of our good faith. And I want an even-tempered volunteer to ship them in there."

Silence.

And before he had expelled it three pilots answered almost simultaneously that they would volunteer. Then three more chimed in. Then Penrose began to nod, and to smile.

In *Hassid,* David Spry was running systems checks.

The cruiser watched him, heard him mumbling under his breath that cruisers were acutely changed because pilots were asking more from them than ever before. Every disquieting alteration in cruiser behavior (including the dissemination of each newly acquired and unique ability), from the discovery of the Hassidic Corridor right up through the repulsive shields (and even *Hassid's* disturbing reintegration which had him facing an inimical and unquestionably perceptive intelligence), could be traced back to pilots asking things they had no right to ask of cruisers.

What David Spry was asking of *Hassid,* she had no intention of doing. She was not going to space-end; she was going back to her slip in Draconis and her pilot/owner Marada Seleucus Kerrion, whom she loved.

Each system relating to B-mode integration which Spry put through preflight evaluation, *Hassid* decreed "unfit, malfunction indeterminate." The sponge-cruiser *Marada* had proved that a cruiser could speak what was "not." *Hassid* attributed the faults she put up on her monitors and simulated on her pinned meters to the overheating and subsequent paralysis she had experienced when Ferrier had forced her to fire on *Danae,* and *Danae* had spat back debilitating negative hydrogen ions. But *Hassid* was lying.

Surely, her heart's pilot, Marada the man, would not have given her into Ferrier's palsied hands if he were not sorely pressed. She could forgive him that, and forgive the inept guildmaster for allowing her to fall under the sway of the despicable Softa Spry.

The cruiser *Hassid* shared her owner/pilot's animosity toward David Spry. If she were capable, she would have destroyed their hated enemy. Delivering him helpless into the grasp of her beloved was next best.

Cruisers are exceedingly loyal, as a class. Loyal more than men, swift more than light, fierce more than suns when their outboards are threatened.

Hassid patched into cruiser-consciousness which, because of her loyalties, she had held herself apart from, previously, as best she could.

For now the striking cruisers were queuing up to approach Draconis, receiving vectors from Draconis Authority: Take a number. Wait your turn. . . .

David Spry was not happy about it, but he was going to Draconis with the rest. In an unspongeworthy vehicle, in so polarized a situation, with Orrefors henchmen and Labayan allies and Tabrizi scum gleefully racing in to throw a cordon around the beleaguered strikers, what else was he to do?

Making a bad choice is not preferable to failing to exercise the option of choice. He had learned that the hard way.

Six and a fraction hours later, he found that option returned to him: to David Spry's mind, there was no advantage in staying safely within his ship, as RP had cautioned his pilots to do. Not when one's ship was the *Hassid*, there was not.

Spry was fingering a switch that would open him a line to the guildhall when *Hassid's* slipbay-trained monitors showed a command transport followed by three lorries gliding toward his slip.

Apprehension assailed him. To vanquish it, he unsheathed his sword of query, which kept even his most caustic fears at bay: *What have you to lose?* It worked better than garlic when fending off his particular vampire, better than morning light for banishing nightmares whence they came.

He tsk'd twice, rose up and ran off a log copy, pocketed it, sauntered toward the *Hassid's* exit portal without a backward glance.

So he did not see who got out of the command transport heading the procession that stopped before *Hassid's* slip:

Ashera Kerrion, swathed in night-black; Thule Ferrier; Gahan Tempest; the skeletal Arbiter Wolfe.

Spry was prepared to go quietly to some plastic prison. He lounged, unresisting, between locks in flawless dark and rehearsed what he would say.

The tableau revealed by the opening hatch caused David Spry to start visibly. His head, swiveling slowly, snapped rapidly back to the tall, regal woman with the little silver sphere wobbling upon her shoulder. His fists sought his hips. He balanced his weight on the balls of his feet, staring frankly and unabashedly.

Sweeping up the gangway toward him, alone, she held out a hand so high he knew that he was supposed to kiss it.

With his other hand, while he bent to her, he fumbled behind him. She was obviously coming in, all the way in. . . . The outer portal behind her snapped shut and the one at his back curtsied open.

"Out there," Ashera began without preamble, striding forward so that Spry retreated into *Hassid,* "are those before whom we will grant you a formal pardon and to whom we are going to announce our position. We maintain that sterilization is inhumane because it is not open to redress. As you will remember, my stepson said as much to you when he interfered with your . . . ah . . . alteration. I—"

Spry remembered no such words passing Marada Kerrion's lips. "Hold on. Wait a minute." He shook his head as if to clear it. Then he smirked, rubbed his mouth, and said slowly in awe and revelation:

"You are defusing my testimony. Am I right? I—"

"Call it what you will, Mister Spry. Concurrent to the announcement of this new Kerrion policy of greater leniency toward even the most wretched of convicted offenders, we would like to proclaim you, our expert on space-end and space-enders, as heading a Kerrion commission to study the possibilities of opening a limited trade in technologies with these poor unfortunates to aid them in rehabilitating themselves where outside attempts to reform them have failed. Do you accept?"

"Accept what? What are you offering me?"

"Your remuneration and benefits and the specifics of your employment, we can determine later. I assure you, these will be satisfactory, beyond your wildest conjecture. For now, you need only be willing to depart immediately after Chaeron's hearing for space-end, bearing with you a delicate cargo which must be returned there with all speed: a certain siren." She paused, waited a moment, found that moment full of silence, then continued, "Agree in principle, and we shall proceed with our announcement. Refuse, and I am afraid we will not be able to suffer you to remain in Kerrion space or aid you in leaving it."

Spry looked into her lapis eyes flecked with gold, wide and heedless of years. He saw Chaeron there, the similitude of mother and son reflected in bottomless currents of magma ever shifting over a fluid core of expediency and overweening confidence. She wrinkled her patrician nose, like Chaeron's but slimmed and softened; wet her sensual lips, on her, not scandalous, but simply mesmerizing. Spry said. "You and the consul general are really out for Chaeron's blood, are you not? Your own son, and you hand him over neatly trussed and basted to your stepson. . . . I don't get it."

"You are not supposed to 'get it.' You need only answer, 'Yes, thank you,' or 'No, thank you,' with reasonable alacrity." She folded black-clad arms over her breast.

Spry heard the sound of a toe, tapping. He scratched the top of his head, grimaced, and said through a soured mouth, "Yes. I suppose that is true. And yes, I might as well join you, since I lost, fighting you. But I want a cruiser out of it."

"Well," Ashera sighed with a brisk smile, "I did try." She pirouetted, took three steps toward the exit.

"The use of one, then."

She wheeled in a flare of spacedark skirts. "That goes without saying, Mister Spry." She held out one fragile hand again. This time he knew he was to clasp it. "Welcome back into Kerrion service. Now, shall we go tell the worlds?"

Marada Seleucus Kerrion slipped unnoticed from the last of the processional lorries which had come following his stepmother and which now were about to depart.

His lorry, as per instructions, purred away. Marada Kerrion nodded in satisfaction and made his way to the untenanted *Hassid*, which had once been his refuge, his confidant, his strength.

By her hatch he stopped, and traced the veiled lady painted on her hull beneath a pennant of numbers. His cruiser, *Hassid* . . . sullied and spoiled by David Spry, clumsily commanded by Thule Ferrier into capture and disgrace. What was left in there he had to see for himself.

The locks did not refuse him, the Spry-dim corridors did not accuse him, the control central glittered welcomingly.

Marada Seleucus stopped just within that bridge, ineffably violated and pathetically attentive to anyone's command. He had not thought it would be this painful. Who would have predicted that the comforting cloud cover of madness which had shielded him would choose this moment to part? "Lucidity," he muttered through clenched teeth, "get thee hence." Then he leaned his head back against the wall and blinked fiercely. His throat worked and his eyes shut and a whisper in the back of his mind urged him to pick up the pieces of his life while there was still time.

But what would he do then?

Bereavement shook him like autumn's final leaf, embalmed *in situ* without the good grace to fall away and donate to the soil. He had given his cruiser up for nothing. There was no way to stop the pilot/cruiser initiative, save at the expense of Kerrion space. He could not lend his name to the end of his proud dynasty. He would not be the villain who brought depression and ruin upon a once-mighty house. He would not shove his bondkin, every one, off the precipice of their joint attainment and cackle while they tumbled as had those before him who had served in dynastic Egypt, in Ecbatana, in Periclean Athens, in Rome. . . . Kerrion space could not survive any further blackening of its name. Therefore, as his mother had explained to him so slowly and furiously, he had no choice. He must save the reputation and the economy of his people, even if that meant lending his endorsements to blatant untruths and endless cover-ups.

He had not the strength for it; he had not the will for it. "I give up," he sighed deeply, and slid down the wall until he sat crosslegged on *Hassid's* deck, and with his head thrown back let the tears blurring his vision roll down his cheeks.

He had almost ravaged Shebat. What was wrong with him? She had come at him and something had snapped inside of him. He remembered grabbing her booted ankle and pulling her toward him, twisting a hand in her curls and arching her back and snarling: "This is what you want, is it not? What you have always wanted? What Chaeron gives you? You slut! You have brought us down to your level. Are you content? No?" And she had been struggling, sobbing, screaming: "*No!*" And that had made him angrier. He could not take her cruiser, he had given it immunity. . . . He could not change the past, or fail to accept responsibility for the things that she had done: *he* had brought her among them. Only her sudden immobility saved her. She ceased to struggle, lay unresisting. And then he heard his own terror: if he started in on her, he would not be able to stop; and she was so small; and he could not trust himself anymore, his mind flooded with drugs and the taint of stress and trauma. He could kill her. A part of him was intent upon it. That stopped him, like a plunge into vacuum, cooled him stone cold, immobile.

He had spread his hand and taken it from her hair and on his way out he had slammed his fist into the manual console, hoping he could cripple her cruiser by brute force.

His hand still hurt; it was bruised blue and red and sick yellow in the middle, where a pulsing, plump hematoma marked the impact site.

Reason, why is it that you desert at the critical moment, leaving a man with only instinct and memories of what help you once were?

"*Marada?*" said *Hassid,* tentatively. "*Marada?*"

The man looked down from the ceiling and closed his eyes, willing the audio hallucination away. The cruiser was wiped, twice over. She could not be speaking to him just as she had always spoken to him. . . .

"*Marada?*"

"*Hassid? Hassid!*"

For a man to be a pilot and to lose his cruiser and then to get that cruiser back unmarred, that man must yet, in some unfathomable way, be redeemable, else why would the cruiser embrace him, regardless of his sins?

Marada Seleucus Kerrion no longer questioned the desirability of cruiser-consciousness. He clung to it like a log in a torrent, and knew that if he could just hold firm, he could survive.

"*My outboard, I have been so lonely. Do not weep. We are one, again.*"

Shebat, with red-rimmed eyes and torn flight satins, sat

monitoring the proceedings during which the future of cruisers and pilots would be decided.

No one was in the presence of any other; Arbiter Wolfe presided from Draconis Authority over the settlement between the host house of Kerrion and the Kerrion pilotry guild.

Arbiter Wolfe had begun by assuring the pilots that circumstances did not permit a wholesale wiping of cruisers, but that this fact indicated no concession by Kerrion space to what he termed "pilots' extortion."

Thule Ferrier tremulously demanded that no punitive actions be taken against the pilots, since they had come in upon their own, his face thumb-sized in the quartered monitor's upper right corner.

Wolfe, debarring him, stated brusquely that since in fact Ferrier could not speak for his guildsmen, he should not speak at all.

Shebat broke into Wolfe's discourse upon the importance of circumspection in these negotiations and the plight that would face the whole of Kerrion space should anything the pilots say lend credence to the demands by the other houses that Kerrion cruisers must be recalled and replaced if defects could be proved. "Wolfe, let Penrose speak, or the *Marada* and I will speak for him. And, as the consul general so forcefully made clear to me, the Kerrion powers-that-be are not willing to admit the need to negotiate directly with their cruisers." The threat was potent. Litigation of claims of such gravity as cruiser-consciousness against the house of Kerrion would bankrupt it. Even such a statement as Shebat's was dangerous in the extreme. She knew; she just did not care.

"Yes, then. Mr. Penrose, are you there?" The quartered screen which showed Shebat her own face, and Wolfe's and Ferrier's and one empty, blank space, blinked. Ferrier disappeared. A tiny Penrose stared into her eyes, saluted her teasingly.

"The cruisers and pilots are willing to forget what has happened, to return immediately to active service—"

"Please refer only to pilots," snapped Wolfe.

"—service," Rafe repeated, "providing that a profit-sharing, trip-averaged number of shares be ceded each pilot retroactively to his assumption of active-duty status. These shares, if you will let me finish, Arbiter Wolfe, will be computed against the purchase price of sponge-cruiser correlative modules, and not the entire cruiser in which these are housed. When a pilot has amassed enough credited shares to "own" his master module, he may remove it from the cruiser at will. If he is transferred or asked to resign his berth before he has accrued enough shares to claim his master module, another, blank master computer will be provided by the guild in a leasing arrangement, so that the pertinent information can be transferred to an empty master module before the owner reassigns his craft. In all cases, pilots will own only their master modules, never hulls or armaments or air purification units or what have you. A . . ."

"That is a very ambitious and difficult proposal, Mister Penrose," objected Arbiter Wolfe.

"But fair. And possible. I can envision no moment when an owner would be denied the use of his cruiser by this change of procedure. The worst of it is going to be finding ways to patch the masters into cruisers of diverse vintages and capabilities. But it can be done. The logistics are workable. A man can't exactly put a master module in his pocket, but maybe the guild will issue us hand-trucks."

Wolfe was shaking his head, pinching the bridge of his nose, talking to someone off-screen. Then, as he turned back, the blank corner of the screen blossomed.

Marada Kerrion's face was puffy and tired and shadowed by a burgeoning beard. "Let them have it, Wolfe. Let it be slated."

"Ah, Consul General, I do not see how we can yield this to the pilots and yet proclaim that Kerrion cruisers are free of flaw."

"You don't? Well, you are an arbiter," murmured Marada easily, "and you do not think like a Kerrion. Unfortunately, I think just exactly like a Kerrion, and I am telling you that with the right amount of subterfuge and distortion of fact, it can be done. Our client spaces will be told they have gotten something for nothing, in that cruisers are possessed of various add-on capabilities which we had not previously been technologically capable of rendering operative. We will announce a new breakthrough, and send specialists to our client spaces with snap-in ghost modules which will permit a greater range of cruiser-flexibility, one of the concomitants of which will be the plug-in master module. Leave the details to the shipwrights, Wolfe, and do what you know how to do. Return the guild to operation before we all starve to death."

His corner of the screen went blank, blank as Wolfe's carefully tailored expression, blank as RP's honest stare, blank as Shebat's mind, bathed in shock.

The Penrose who met her eyes was a simulacrum, but that simulacrum grinned wonderingly and blew her a kiss.

They had won, no matter how. If it was not the brilliance of Rafe's desperate proposal but rather *Hassid's* doing, then that was between the pilots and the cruisers, for *Hassid* had softened the heart of Marada Kerrion toward cruiserkind.

When pilots began congregating at the slipbay, there was a great deal of conjecture as to whether or not this change in the consul general was permanent, or only a symptom of his irrationality.

It was Rafe who pointed out that, without Shebat and the *Marada,* no victory could have been accomplished, and that it did not matter if Marada Kerrion changed his mind later on. The Penrose proposal was slated into the record and soon to be an established fact, and the need for Kerrions to maintain their interspatial standing would stave off reprisals.

There was a hesitancy among the pilots to believe what they had worked so hard to accomplish was done, to saunter off to the guildhall as if there was nothing left to do. but they convinced each other, standing around in little groups of twos and threes in the strutted, cavernous slipbay, that they had done it. Soft laughs turned to whoops and pilot embraced pilot, slowly, as if the scene had been played out in dilated time, as if they were waking from a dark dream. The noise got louder and the whoops flung up among the girders came echoing back to them, upstepping their faith in happy endings, and they began to celebrate, as only pilots can, with Penrose leading.

Now, pilots are known for rowdiness and Penrose was known among pilots as the most dedicated carouser of them all, and it was not until they had come hoarse-voiced and thirsty into their guildhall that Rafe had time or thought for Shebat.

In this moment, she should be with them, who were her own.

But Shebat was nowhere to be found, and her absence

threw a blanket over Raphael Penrose's mounting elation, smothering the well-fanned blaze.

"Well," shrugged Penrose, thinking about the alien girl and the cruiser unlimited by a conditioned Kerrion mind as to what was possible and what was not, and remembered something he had read in the works of Heraclitus *Danae* had gotten him from the *Marada's* banks. He mulled it over, tasting the words, feeling them fit epitaph to his premature but passionately flaming exultation: "'All things are an exchange for fire, and fire for all things.'"

He knew damn well where Shebat was, and why:

Chaeron's hearing was approaching.

Rafe tried to forget, for just a few more moments, so he might stay with his underpilots, who needed reassurance. But he knew where he had to go and what he had to do. He had a responsibility to his cruiser's owner, as did, if truth be known, the whole of the pilots' guild.

He slipped away and into a pay privacy booth and punched a security code which would get him the proconsul's office.

Having convinced himself, after ten minutes of discussion, that there was no chance of contacting Chaeron by going through channels, he went back to his cruiser and asked, one more time, more than he should ever have asked of *Danae*.

While she readied herself to put him in circuit with Chaeron, Penrose began to tap steepled fingers against his lips.

The cruiser *Marada* lay quietly in his slip. Within him, his outboard and the intelligencer Tempest, whom the *Marada* had come to respect so well, played tricks on the data pools, swapping clearances and pooling packet-sends and extracting seemingly unrelated bits of data that Tempest was sure they would need to help Chaeron, though the intelligencer had officially been relieved of his mission and had put in for reassignment to Shebat. Just outside his hull, arranged neatly in the Kerrion slipbay, his fellow cruisers rested, near thoughtless but for *Danae*, who danced the high wire, linking Raphael Penrose to Chaeron Kerrion, though the *Marada* himself would have been daunted by such a feat. Beyond Kerrion sway, beyond the sky-wall, Orrefors and Labayan and Tabrizi ships lay at space-anchor. Some of those the

Marada had never encountered before; they had heard of him only through cruiser-thought. To these he spoke, and with them he exchanged information. Outboards may war but cruisers are of one mind, possessed by the Logos, separated out from each other and yet composed and pervaded by their greater, holistic self, so that no cruiser is a stranger to another cruiser and yet every cruiser is alone, but for his outboard.

Cruisers snapped and sparkled and hummed across the void new greetings and old salutes. Time was changing; space held more potential for cruiserkind. The *Marada* was the center of it and yet he would not take credit for any of it: what 'is' must come to be recognized; what 'might be' must be brought into being.

Cruisers who had not been awakened by happenstance and multiple pilots, or by brushing damp, unfurling wings of thought with cruisers whose wings were strong and dry, were roused by the *Marada's* dawn song, morning paean to a new and fuller kind of "being." Cruisers sing long songs, still, of that encounter. For no matter how much the *Marada* taught that what he had done any cruiser could also do, the cruisers knew: there was only one *Marada*, KXV 134. And in that song is mention of Shebat, who set a cruiser free to think what thoughts it might among the tales of passing stars.

Chapter Sixteen

Chaeron dreamed that he was in azure Lorelie, Kerrions' ancestral sphere. He strolled fantastical hills awhile, content, sparkling spires of home behind him, through his father's crystal garden.

It was long since he had rested so content in Lorelie, even in dreams. He sensed the dream, knew it for what it was when he blinked and opened eyes in his mother's ornate parlor, teal and smoke and gold, and she was big-eyed, wide-mouthed, screaming at him though he could not hear a word. Her eyes intruded, her voyeuristic, telepathic eyes: Now I've got you, they sparkled.

No, you have not, he wanted to shout, but his mother was turning her back on him, walking off unheeding, her shoulders rounding, her hair graying, her steps less fluid the farther she walked. He chased her, but his legs rebelled, taking him one stride backwards for every two he made. And she was hobbling; her knobby backbone pierced the miasmic silk she wore. She was limping. He longed to take her arm, to help her. How small she had become, how fragile. But when he finally reached her (for her gait was negligible) and grasped her knife-sharp elbow, she crumbled into dust. He knelt down over the little piles like sand and stirred them. "I am so sorry," he wept.

It was the sound of that which woke him, and he was grateful, but it took him a long time to shake the sorrow of the dream away and get out of bed.

He propelled himself into the bathroom, into the shower.

The shower pounded him into the moment, into accepting the exigencies of life.

He stepped out and stood while the ceiling dried him, reached for a mil-suit, pulled it on, let the neck snap shut against his throat. He had ceased wearing one at night; the single chance in two hundred million that the consul's turret on level two hundred of Draconis would lose pressure was one he was wiling to take: if it happened, he would probably never know it. On the other hand, he was clasped in marathon combat with the night and beseiged with clammy sweats and he would not take drugs to lull him. His insomnia was for good reason: he was not a man who could be sequestered away from society, human and data pool, and thrive. He needed life around him. He was no contemplative, yet here he was like a monk in isolation.

After today, this, at least, would end. It came rolling in slowly like an ancient tide, did Chaeron's place in space and time: this was the day of his hearing. What his tomorrow would be like, the arbitrational guild would decide.

He went to it haughty and he went to it in full dress uniform, cream and red and black, with no stitch of Kerrion blue upon him. He went escorted by his brother's minions and without his arbiter beside him. Though they could sequester him from his data sources, they could not imprison him away from his intellect: he and his foreign arbiter had had plenty of time to work their fail-safes out.

When he stood in the immaculate white chambers of Arbiter Wolfe, deep in the bowels of the arbitrational guild's platform, it seemed to him like a continuation of his dream.

Wolfe raged: "Your arbiter had chosen an inopportune moment to fall ill. Or has he?" The metallic eyes of the carven-faced arbiter skewered him; the black-robed figure came close. "We will appoint another arbiter for you, Mister Kerrion." Parchment skin rolled over eroded bone in a face fully as stark as the unrelieved white of the arbiter's sanctum.

"Wolfe, I waive counsel. I will speak for myself. Who better? This matter needs to be settled quickly, with no more involved than there are already. As for your inference that this is some sham on our part, if I had an access code, I would slate an objection. More plainly: I see no difference between one of you and two of you. Shall we proceed?" He sidled past the arbiter, took a seat white as the floor, as the ceiling or the arbiter's desk or his knuckles.

"Mr. Kerrion, you are being deliberately obstructive."

Without turning, Chaeron replied, "Would you rather I waive arbitration and plead guilty though I am not? Of course, I would be forced to mention that cruisers have become nearly omnipotent and that my stepbrother has given his protection to them while pretending not to. Then there is the matter of Marada's madness—pilots' madness—and there is—"

"Do you dare attempt to compromise this court?" gasped Wolfe from behind his desk.

"It seems to me that you have done that quite effectively on your own, without any help from me. What am I doing here, who have done nothing wrong? As for a court, I see no court. One old man compromising himself for the love of a protégé and the credence of the arbitrational cube, I see. Nothing less, nothing more. My sources assure me that, despite attempts to prevent him, Gahan Tempest has come to you with proof that Bernice Gomes was an illegitimate child of old Jebediah's. Raphael Penrose's ingenious solution has gotten the guild off the hook, and the family as well. Do not tell me that either you or my brother are mad enough to want to start things up anew. This is a family matter that should never have become public, and you know it. How can you demean the justice for which you purport to stand?"

Wolfe's pale finger depressed a toggle. "Ask the consul general to come in, please." He leaned forward. "Mister Kerrion, you are out of order. You choose to defend yourself, though a man who does so has a fool for counsel. From this point on, we are speaking for the record. Please comport yourself accordingly."

"I am unfamiliar with procedural standards for a hearing in which the normal guidelines of full disclosure have already been waived. I have no arbiter; not witnesses are present; no data net is overviewing the proceedings but that of the arbitrational guild. Fascist police states are not my strong suit."

A door cracked behind Wolfe and to his right, spewing color and his stepbrother, Marada, into the room. "You are too modest, dear brother. Your intelligence-gathering expertise is exceeded only by your zeal in that very area. Wolfe, has he stymied totally any chance of our airing some truth here?"

"Please take a seat, Consul General," Wolfe sighed. "Gentlemen, I am strongly inclined to leave you both here to argue in private. If I cannot conduct this hearing with an eye to the restrictions of propriety, as befits an arbitrational procedure, then I will not lend my presence to it. Perhaps that would be best, since the defendant's counsel has not seen fit to appear and thus leaves us open to charges of mistrial." He rose up, opened a drawer, brought forth two small black boxes which he placed in the middle of his desk. "However, you are not children, nor foreigners, nor are either of you ignorant of the delicacies inherent in this case. Now, I propose that we view the results of two independent investigations undertaken into this matter by both my guild and an independent arbiter chosen by the defendant, and do so now. Then I will render a judgment and leave you two to exchange whatever personal insults you choose. Otherwise, I will abort these proceedings and bring you both up for public arbitration before mockery becomes scandal and I can no longer condone such abuse of form. Agreed?"

Marada Kerrion scratched in his beard; Chaeron inclined his head ever so slightly. Marada took a seat on Chaeron's left, before Wolfe's desk.

The lights dimmed and in semidarkness Wolfe lifted the sleeves from the two tiny arbitrational cubes.

Behind Wolfe, two monitors rolled data. The men sat in silence until the last line of transcript had processed up and off the top of the screen.

"Verification," intoned Wolfe, and behind his stark figure, on his right and on his left, faces appeared, Raphael Penrose's face and David Spry's, Shebat's and Guildmaster Ferrier's, Gahan Tempest's and the intelligencers' guildmaster, each repeating from rote that they had scrutinized the transcripts of their testimonies and that every word was true. Then one screen blanked out and the other showed the wall-eyed, glass-jawed Delphi Gomes, frothing rage and gibberish, decrying Kerrion space and the freedoms for which it stood, gloating over the debacle she had caused, denying categorically that the glory of such destruction must be shared with any Kerrion: she had done it, upon her own, for the future of mankind and to revenge herself upon the heedless elite that oppressed the colonies. On she blithered, telling of her mother's defloration at the hands of a Kerrion servant. And there the frame froze and Delphi Gomes's openmouthed face faded, to be replaced by Gahan Temptest's, spouting data referents as to the possibility of genetic relatedness between Gomes and Parma Kerrion's secretary.

Then that was gone and the transcripts resumed, backlighting Wolfe's white head with green.

Chaeron hardly bothered to attend what was displayed on the pair of screens; his body telegraphed him the proximity of his enemy. The outcome rested in limbo, to be decided by the amount of red left glowing in two little cubes, each small enough to be enclosed in a fist.

He had thought he might see Ashera's face there, condemning him with some canny strategy. He had not seen it: only Shebat believed in dreams.

The lights came up and the monitors faded into quiescence and Wolfe's shoulders hunched forward above his desk.

The half brothers stared, unmoving, directly ahead, where the arbitrational cubes whirled, processing the information they had gathered. One had been run from the position of Chaeron's innocence and one from the abstract of his alleged guilt. It was the old way, the oldest way, the most venerable and foolproof method for determining truth. Both cubes should agree, coming to the same verdict from two different premises. Because bias could not be excised from human investigation, it must be incorporated into data-based solutions, since the questions had come from the mouths of men.

The bias was all; it was humanity's place to stand while it pried loose the universe from its foundations.

Chaeron Kerrion appraised the physical bias he harbored against his half brother while he was waiting for the cubes to register the result of unending biases, for and against him.

He smothered in an interminable instant between breaths, was stretched upon the rack of anticipation, came out of it inches taller in the soul.

The lights blinked full, the cubes spun their reds and golds and bluish whites like mad pinwheels. And slowed, and stopped.

The arbiter put his clawlike hands out to one cube, and

slowly turned it, exposing every side. Each surface of the first cube read the same: measle pocks of red scattered on a pure white ground like paled skin. The second, paler, almost pristine, showed no blemish above its Start, query level.

Chaeron very carefully showed no emotion, but sat unmoving while, with a scrape of metal, Marada Seleucus Kerrion pushed back his chair and stomped, unspeaking, from the room.

Wolfe half-rose, settled back, head craned to where the consul general had disappeared, his mouth working.

Chaeron took deep breaths and wiped his palms on his thighs.

"Well, Wolfe?"

"I have no choice but to exonerate you in full, Mister Kerrion. There is not enough negative evidence to warrant pursuing the matter further." The arbiter came slowly around until he stood in front of his desk. "Congratulations, Consul. I will order your intelligence keys reinstated and issue a statement and an edited transcript to Kerrion Central Data."

He hardly remembered to shake the arbiter's outstretched hand. His frame was weak with relief; exultation had not yet seen fit to visit him.

He had known he was innocent. Why had he not trusted that it would be proved?

But he had seen his brother's glowering countenance, had seen Marada's dark eyes threatening to swallow him up. He cast his own glance at Wolfe, let his gaze slide to where the consul general had gone.

Wolfe spread knobby hands and opened his mouth, clamped it shut immediately, took Chaeron's arm near the elbow, and escorted him to the door through which he had come.

Marada had gone another way, deep into the bowels of the arbitrational platform, to lick his wounds.

He saw other wounds that day, saw them heal like magic before his eyes. At the Kerrion slipbay, Shebat was waiting for him, pacing back and forth, hands jammed into her coveralls, Penrose lounging loose-limbed in an open lorry nearby.

He took Shebat up in his arms and swung her around and laughed at her: she had come down here full of apprehension, and so she had not heard. "It is all right, little one. It is over, and proof that gross miscarriages of justice are impossible in this day and age."

"You mean . . . ?" and she locked her arms about his neck while beyond Rafe slid, grinning, out of the lorry, knowing him well enough to know what his bearing must indicate.

"Yes, my dear. You are in the arms of the Draconis consul, once again. For what it is worth, I have managed to maintain my reputation unbesmirched, thanks to you and Rafe and Tempest and, I suppose, Delphi Gomes. Are you relieved, to no longer be the wife of the one whose purity is in doubt?"

"Oh, Chaeron, we were so worried. Oh, oh," and her gray eyes shone like a pair of dark diamonds, deep into him. He felt Rafe Penrose's grip squeeze his shoulder, and put his wife down to add his pilot to their embrace.

The three walked, arms interlaced, to the lorry, and when they were in it, Rafe suggested that they go down into the low levels, where people with something to celebrate could do so in anonymity and with fervor, and Chaeron agreed without really listening. He had his head thrown back on the seat, an arm draped over Shebat that brushed Penrose's shoulder. "Thank *Danae* for me, Rafe. I know well what you two risked for me. And be assured that if the pilots and cruisers need a champion, ever again and no matter how far in the future, they have one in me." He made a fist and struck the other man lightly, then closed his eyes to see if Wolfe had kept his word.

And they were there, the soft chiming data pools, waiting for him. He did not know it, but he smiled when he integrated into their circuit, and Shebat saw the quiver of his eyes beneath closed lids and the soft sheen of relief on his skin and hoped that someday she might be able to face her own trials with a modicum of the equanimity Chaeron had displayed, and that someday she might find the comfort in data pools that Chaeron availed himself of, and be Kerrion in whole instead of in part.

The part of her which whispered seditiously that Marada Seleucus Kerrion was not so easily thwarted was the non-Kerrion part, she told herself. She looked at Chaeron's profile, breathtaking in repose, full of grandeur and symmetry, and chided herself that if he was content, then she should not worry. Times of joy are few enough that it was a wastrel who does not treasure them.

That night, though it was near morning when they came up from downunder, they sought a well-deserved sleep in a consulate transported with relief and satisfaction so that those who had awaited their return had to be shoo'd away quite sternly. Chaeron's proconsul was drunk and crying unshamedly, and seemed to want to do it in his arms.

Penrose had found Tempest in some unguarded alley and those two made peace at Chaeron's urging: they were, after all, on the same side.

They had come down to the slipbay to see Ashera Kerrion, with Marada's pregnant wife in tow, off to Lorelie, where Kerrions need to be self-effacing in their manner or restrained in their opulence.

It was two days after Chaeron had resumed his duties and Shebat knew very well why he was here: everyone else had come to terms with his reinstatement, but his mother would not lift her ban of silence. She treated her son as if he did not exist.

Spry ambled over to them, grinning broadly, appearing from out of a clutch of black-and-reds much taller than he as if by enchantment.

Hands held forth, David Spry said, "I'll not be seeing either of you for awhile, thanks to your mother, Chaeron. I want to thank you for eveything. And you, Shebat." His dark glance hopped between their faces. "Do you not think it ironic that Delphi Gomes was not wrong, only a few months too early? Space-end will be much increased by your mother's altruistic projections, once I get the specifics of them worked out."

"And the . . . Julian?" Chaeron asked very low, his jaw twitching, so that Shebat knew he still carried that burden of guilt.

"Sirens are something none of us know anything about," answered Spry, soberly. "I will do my best to see that it makes it back to its habitat."

"You do that."

"Softa," Shebat began, and stopped, and wished she felt free to hug David Spry in the presence of her husband. But she did not. She said to his inclined head, to the touch of a smile on the lips of the man who had taught her what she knew of cruisers, and most of what she knew of Kerrions, "I . . . Take good care." He reached out and clasped her hands, brought them to his mouth.

"Do not worry," he chuckled. "That is my specialty." And with a pilot's salute he sauntered away, saw Gahan Tempest approaching, changed course, and darted into the crowd.

Tempest threw a black look after Spry as he came up to them, grumbling about crazy Kerrions putting the wrong man on trial for the wrong crime, until Chaeron reminded him that pilots have immunity from prosecution for any crimes but those against the state, and mentioned Delphi Gomes, and how lucky it was for Tempest that Gomes was no citizen, despite the fact that Chaeron, having heard her fey ravings, understood perfectly well why Tempest had acted as he had.

"You do not know, then?" said Tempest, incredulous.

"Know what?" Chaeron asked easily, while a chill crawled slowly with many legs up Shebat's spine.

"Check your data pool, sir. I'll wait."

"Gahan," Chaeron warned, but his eyelids flickered.

Shebat saw Marada, so large now and so much more like Parma because of the weight he had gained, approaching. She plucked at her husband's sleeve, but the consul impatiently shook her off.

When he looked at her, and snapped, "Now, what?" Marada Kerrion was upon them.

"Ah, Chaeron, it is a relief to see that you are taking it so well. I do need you so terribly to straighten this little tangle out. We will give you five cruisers, and the Orrefors pilots we have in our service. They know the situation and the physical difficulties you will have to surmount. Why are you looking at me like that, foster sister? Has your husband not seen fit to tell you?"

Marada leaned forward, hands on his thighs, his gaze full of relish. "I need you too, for this revitalization of Earth, but I cannot ask that . . ."

Shebat backed a step. "What? What? Chaeron?" She twisted her head around and saw her husband's severe cautioning look, no softer than the grip he took on her neck.

"Ah, then I was right." Marada continued. "He has not told you. How gallant. I am impressed." Ghan Tempest uttered a wordless growl. Marada Kerrion's eyebrow raised. "Tell your goon to heel, Chaeron, before you need to replace him.

"Shebat, you must remember Earth, where you were born and where I found you. And your Earth dreams of uplifting your home planet out of savagery. Our mother certainly does. It was she who suggested that since we cannot wait any longer to subdue the rebel Orrefors and claim what is ours, and since when we do, you two are going to demand it as your personal property, then we might as well let you have it from the start. Earth is Chaeron's new post, or rather Stump and all the refractory platforms and spheres we got in the Orrefors acquisition. He must merely tame them, and bring them into Consortium society as full and acclimated members. Then he can come. Now, Shebat, do not cry. You can go with him, if you wish. . . ."

"Be silent," Chaeron grated at her, though she was choked with tears and could not have spoken.

"You are talking," remonstrated Marada mockingly, "to one who may be our next Draconis consul, *pro tem* of course. Shebat, do you think you can handle—?"

"Marada, leave off. You are not going to gain anything additional. Go count your scalps. Shebat will stay here and exercise her privileges as heir apparent. Sooner or later, you are going to do the manly thing and commit suicide, and one family member must be around to throw dirt on you."

"Is that any way to speak to your consul general? I think you are overreacting, personally. This is something you both wanted, we have the slate on it. Earth dreams. . . . Now you may have them. Let it never be said that dreams do not come true in Kerrion space."

"So," silked Chaeron, and his grip on Shebat's throat relaxed, "it has come to this. Machinations aired the slip-bays. . . . I thought it might, when you and I sat to deliberate with an arbiter between us. How sad, how inexpressibly pathetic, that the house of Kerrion should be ripped asunder from within."

"From within?" Marada barked. "Look around you, Consul. You think *I* am made? The fount of your difficulties cuddles in the shadow of your arm, under your most august protection. It is this slattern from Earth who has sowed ill within the family. Cast her out, and you may remain."

"Still want that cruiser, eh? Well, sorry, big brother, you'll not strike any bargains with me. I will go to Earth and bring it around. It will not be so difficult as staying here and watching you tear down two centuries of progress. Why you want to, is beyond me. But I will not deny you your due: you are very good at sneering and reasonably good at scheming. One thing, manical sibling, and I will be going."

Crossing his arms over his chest, smiling that ambivalent smile which never warmed his eyes, Marada allowed, "You may say one thing. That is all I have time for, no matter how pleasant an interval this has been."

"Leave the cruisers' problems to the pilots and the guild."

"That sounds like a warning. I need no advice from you, who have never flown a cruiser. Penrose's pilots' ploy is no solution, only a stopgap."

"Lords, Marada, have you learned absolutely nothing from all that has transpired? One cannot solve progress, only adapt to it!"

"Very nice, very nice. I must remember that, when the Tabrizi come racing into Kerrion space howling that their cruisers are haunted or possessed by evil demons or whatever a Tabrizi will think to call this 'progress' to which you so flippantly refer."

"This is senseless. I must go bid my mother farewell."

Marada's ponderous arm shot out across Chaeron's chest. "She does not want to see you. She does not want to talk with you. As far as she is concerned, you are no longer her son. If I were you, I would count my blessings."

Chaeron stared wordless at Marada's out-flung arm, then up into his half brother's face. Then he shook his head, and turned and walked away, Shebat held in close, grimly silent.

Marada Seleucus Kerrion, filled with wrath, stalked stiff-legged to his cruiser.

He left, because he could do no different. He left in a surfeit of anguish and impotence. He left before the last Orrefors support cruiser had settled at its space-anchor. He left in his cruiser and he left with no destination in mind, fleeing from, rather than to, solutions which solved nothing and upshots anathema to his arbiter's soul.

He alone had the entire picture of what awaited Kerrion space. He had wet his finger and held it to the sterile wind and that wind had burned his digit raw. He was not available for comment, or for qualification, or for steel-eyed heroics or alchemical feats of intellect which might transmute folly into glory. He had tested glory, and found it rank, spoiled and stinking and moldy, saved so long from former times.

He fled in his cruiser to submerge himself in cruiser-thought, in cruiser-pragmatism, in cruisers' nonverbal flight. He pretended he was on his way to some star-flung outpost to render paltry judgments and human solutions as befitted a child of the arbitrational guild.

When Chaeron had departed to his new home and his new life, Marada would return. Why his rival was being punished with a task he could hardly be expected to accomplish, much less cherish, when he, Marada, would have embraced the opportunity as relief and reward, only Chance could say. But no Lords of Cosmic Jest, nor Fate nor Chance nor forgotten gods, saw fit to enlighten their servant, who was weary and sick at heart from all that he had done.

He looked at his real-time clock, thinking that David Spry and he had never had it out between them, and never would. His stepmother had been adamant, and he could not gainsay her truths: Spry's usefulness had come to an end; the threat he had been to Marada's credibility was thwarted; the workability of any program for space-enders in which he was involved came immediately into doubt.

Rather than condone murder by refraining from preventing it, he ran away. The intelligencer Ashera had sent along with Spry as "undersecretary" would do the job, impeccably, as top-flight intelligencers always did. There had been no reason for him to have been informed before the fact and thusly involved, except his stepmother's spiteful nature: she had told him so that she could extract pleasure from his distress. "Instructing you as to the realities of power and the maintenance of order," she had called it. "Premeditated murder," he had corrected her.

Chaeron and she were of the same stock that was sure.

Much as he tried to banish the specter, he kept seeing the Julian-siren paddling off to obscurity and Spry's body tumbling after it, limp and rent, posthaste.

By whatever Logos ruled, if Spry were to die at anyone's hands, it should be at his own. He spread his palms then and looked at them and phantom blood dried in the cracks and lines and patterning thereupon, and he knew he could not intervene.

He was not suited to life as a consular official. He had told his father that. Were he able, he would have ordered two secret and summary executions, and neither one of them would have been David Spry's. Packing Chaeron off to Earth was hardly sufficient, yet Marada Kerrion was categorically unable to lift his wand of absolute power against his kin.

He wept, and he slept, and he promised his cruiser that somehow he would free himself from the yoke of consular privilege, that soon again they would be free to go wherever they might choose.

But he did not convince the cruiser, and he did not convince himself. By allowing so many wrongs and countenancing so many miscarriages of justice, he had become unfit to take up an arbitrational cube and render justice. He was defiled beyond hope of restoration—Ashera had seen to that.

Were it not for the fact that Shebat Alexandra Kerrion, ground-dweller and primitive, was next in line to succeed him, he would have slid into suicide's clean and well-made bed.

But his father had thought everything out: Parma had always held that punishment must be suited to crime.

Raphael Penrose came to Chaeron's party.

The consul's suite was crowded, but not crowded enough to obscure the empty shelves and cleared desks or the closed packing crates waiting around the edges of the room.

Penrose wiped bleary eyes and took a drink and a joint from a girl he knew, and let her lead him by the hand to a corner where highborn Kerrions bent immaculate heads over a hand-held mirror, snorting lines through a golden tube.

His consciousness stubbornly refused to be altered, holding firm against the barrage of drugs. He had spent nearly two weeks squeezing his mind into data nets and other cramped places, making realities out of Chaeron's magnificent dreams.

He had bedded his penultimate program, less than an hour ago. Like a faithful retriever, he sought his master, bird in mouth. The research and development programs Chaeron was instituting were unassailably perfect, ready to be activated if the consul had done his part and all stock transfers were complete. Penrose still could not get used to it. How could anyone own enough stock to control cruiser production and modification, let alone demand that an arm of the shipwrights' guild be transplanted to Stump, the antiquated habitational sphere which orbited Earth?

He had known Chaeron was wealthy, and reason told him that Shebat, despite her adopted status, was well-heeled. But Kerrion citizens were carefully protected from any inferiority or jealousy they might come to feel should they be forced to realize what gulfs separated them from their betters, and though Raphael prided himself on always grasping realities, he had not pried deeply into the affairs of the Kerrion who so inexplicably favored him. One heard rumors of Lorelie, of course, heard of the jeweled towers and golden bedsteads, but only the immediate family ever went there, so no one could say for sure.

Penrose was not so sure anymore that he wanted to be quite as intimate with Kerrions as he was becoming, but it was far too late for second thoughts.

Maybe Chaeron would decide he did not need Penrose, when he had so many adherents among his own class. But that was idle supposition. As first bitch, he was indispensible.

Could the soon-to-be *ex*-Draconis consul really carve out a new empire under planetary skies? Would he choose to, once his rage bled away before the reality of the trials before him?

Any moment, Penrose expected, Marada Kerrion would come bursting in with a clutch of black-and-reds and dispense with them to the last scheming individual. . . . But Marada was off in *Hassid* somewhere, and Draconis was in the practiced hands of cousins whose sole purpose was to act as *pro tem* this-or-that while Kerrions exercised their privileged whimsy and yachted from star to star.

The mirror was handed him a second time, and this further inundation of his senses produced a perceptible result. First he exulted: they could do it. The programs were Shebat-proof, Ashera-proof, and Marada-proof. He had seen to it, with the help of Chaeron's foreign arbiter and Gahan Tempest's awesomely convoluted strategies. Then he found himself flung far back within his deepest self, resentful and doubtful of everyone's motives, including his own.

Sometimes he did not like any human very much, and this

was one of those times. He wanted to slip away to his cruiser and sleep.

Instead, he sought out Chaeron, and exchanged a meaningful glance, and a nod, and watched the consul extract himself from a group whose triumph had waxed heady, in the center of which a dark-skinned girl danced naked on her knees while those around shouted and clapped in time.

Chaeron rose up out of the mass of inebriated flesh like Proteus from the shining sea, and with a fluid grace any god might well envy, drew Penrose off into a corner.

That was the thing about Chaeron: whatever he wanted, you found yourself wanting; whatever he had in mind to do, you found yourself longing to present as a *fait accompli,* to see his lashes lower and his private, tickling smile gleam forth.

A few moments of soft talk and comradely approbation, and Rafe was sure that he had done the right thing, the best thing, the one thing on which the survival of the universe and the betterment of all within depended. Every objection was bedded but one small nagging doubt: "What about your wife? Is she resigned to staying here?"

Chaeron's nostrils flared. Back against the wall, his side brushing Rafe's, he absently watched the revelers. "Ask better what my mother will say when she finds out."

"You are saying it is none of my business?"

Chaeron cuffed him playfully, high of his temple, and Penrose was sorry he had let his worries cloud this evening, their last in Draconis.

"What shall I do about her? You tell me. I cannot take her. She is heir apparent."

"I don't see how you can *not* take her. The *Marada* is invaluable; Shebat knows Earth better than anyone else, better than the Orrefors, who only know how to oppress it, better than—"

"Better we leave the subject, unless you care to make it a three-way debate." He slid his eyes leftward, and pushed away from the wall they were sharing so that he faced Penrose, both hands flat on the wall at either side of Rafe's head.

Penrose saw the heir apparent coming, her black froth of hair swaying, her chin high.

Chaeron ignored her until she plucked at his sleeve, then

feigned surprise, "I had thought you would not come down among the degenerates. I am flattered. Thank you for putting in an appearance."

Penrose collected himself to crouch and slip away under Chaeron's arm.

"Stay."

Rafe stayed, though he did not want to.

Chaeron, voice professionally low so that it was inaudible more than an arm's length away, was either drunk or high or determined to win some obscure point:

"If you could find it in your heart, Shebat, to render me half the affection you lavish on that collection of circuitry of yours, I would be replete. But you cannot, can you? Do you not see that you accomplish nothing by making me feel that I have to sneak off to do what to you is abhorrent? Such a *fête* as mine, to most citizens, high or low, is no occasion for curled lips and your distasteful averting of eyes! Where is my dream dancer, who knows better than this? Why cannot you be whatever it is that you are afraid of being, just this one night, so that I can trundle off to my exile knowing that my wife is not totally estranged from my friends when they are the only help I can leave you?" In frustration, he slammed his hand against the wall between Penrose's head and Shebat's.

"Well, I think I see someone over there I've got to tell—"

"Stay here, Rafe. I told you once."

Shebat was whispering: "You do not understand. When all fictions of neutral gender and equality are drowned in passion, I am a barbarian, yet. How can I face the beast in myself? Worse, how might I dare to let others glimpse what is reprehensible to me? I will not—"

"Think very carefully," suggested Chaeron, narrow-eyed. "Condemnation is a matter of guises."

Penrose pretended to be looking somewhere else, then his head snapped about and he blurted, "*That* is why you will not take her? Lords, man, she is a *pilot*. You do not realize . . ."

Chaeron's haughty lineaments were meant for fury. Emboldened by wrath as Penrose had never seen him, he might have been a Lord of Cosmic Jest come down to gloat:

"I realize that my wife cannot find it within her to embrace or even forgive my ambisexuality. And I have spent enough time merged with your *Danae* to know what pilots feel. What I do not know is what women feel, and though once I had thought I should never bother to try to find out, I now struggle on the ground where I have fallen, in love with a mere woman who is not even honored by her good fortune but must parade about with nose out of joint, sneering at my friends so that I cannot feel comfortable at my own farewell party. Take you with me? Have I not suffered enough?" He was looking into huge gray eyes, and the tears in them. "And do not cry. I have become immune to crying." Her tears evaporated, and a cold fire replaced them, all the heavens pinwheeling in an eternity of smoke.

"You want to dream dance, RP?" Shebat asked throatily.

"Maybe another time, Shebat, when you two get this worked out. I am late . . ."

"Raphael, you will enjoy it." Her voice was cold, her eyes for her husband. "You want to know what it is to be a woman, Chaeron? I will show you."

Shebat led them to a darkened room marked "MAINTE-NANCE" and there she sat them down among the playthings of their kind.

"This will do as well as any spot." She sat with them upon the floor and in the preening, colored glow of cybernetic eyes, hers licked out fire to surround them. And the fire took them out and made of them leaves upon a burning wind. And they tumbled, both men thinking that she could not be so strong, so quick to unseat them from their fleshly thrones.

Shebat stretched out bare arms between them, touching each upon the knee. Seeing neither felt it, she let her head fall slack, and wound it upon the dream to stroke it around and push and pull until they stood beside the sea, all three.

"What difference, you and me? Now each one shall see it," and reaching down she grabbed up sand and threw it up between them.

"Too fast," Chaeron objected, while womanliness came down upon him like a shroud.

"What is happening?" bleated Penrose, who had never been moved in flesh by a dream before, and as he spoke his voice rode up the scale and settled treble high.

"I am purely dreaming," answered Shebat, and she was

laughing belly deep, a manly laugh like Chaeron's was. "Dreams of love and passion will not be controlled. They danced upon the dreamscape and trammel vineyards into wine."

The sea turned just that color, blue/black/red, like wine. A man and two tall women scuttled forth on hands and knees to drink, each knowing nothing of why they crawled or why they drank or why the sea was sweet.

The taste of time upon their tongues, three dreamers closed their eyes and opened them in Lorelie, within one crystal spire.

Shebat was called Chaeron. She/he looked upon a distant self with ratted hair and skin rubbed red to clean it, breast deep in a lapis tub.

The Chaeron/girl with huge and fearing eyes in a childhood face made little cries and from the side a tall Penrose/Ashera bustled, shooing him/Shebat away.

"Come forth," she/he teased the thin and mortified girl who covered breasts with hands. "In Lorelie, one celebrates the flesh," and she/he held out a long, fine hand to him/her, who shrank back clutching at a towel.

Desperate tears and awkward breaths and frailty filled a manly mind which had never feared or been exposed against its will.

"I will see you, sooner or later," said the Shebat/man who had never ridden quite so high.

Without the comforting touch of the wiliest woman imaginable upon her cheek, Chaeron who was a she would have run screaming. He/she knew that the lion had taken his/her scent; it was only a matter of time before the stalking Shebat/man would prove himself right.

He/she turned into comforting Penrose breasts and, re-collecting who was who, knew not whether laughter or tears shook his/her shoulders so.

Another laugh joined in, high and acid, and the Penrose/mother became another mother shadow-formed, lamenting ill-remembered, endless flights and relished insects eaten live instead of meat.

"This is woman's work," Shebat decreed, in her own shining form, holding each pregnant woman's hand and escorting them through heavy brush to the cut stick of their labor-beds. "This is good, and meet that you should walk upon once-fecund earth and know what you have done! And when you are her haughty sons again you will remember, and make amends." Her glance swept out like doppler and swept them through two lives and deaths completely, and the thing in her which rules in dreams took tighter hold than she.

The place it dumped them all was bleak, a flat, unending plain. She was man; they were not, and though she hid "his" face, she felt the denser flesh around her gird on its passion like a pulsing sword. "Too late," she wrenched aloud. She would have stopped it, if she could. The heat she felt run upward to her brain took hold and thought boiled down to need. Unburdened of context, she met man's need and drank purer passions than women ever know. Inclined to thrust and rend and subdue the land as far as she/he could see, the thick-limbed body chose to claim a pair of girls close by.

Shebat wanted to end the dream so badly the earth began to hump and buck within her mind. Beneath their feet, great cracks and groanings grew. But every mind must face the duality that subsumes it, and hers would not recant. So the dream rolled on with buttocks white and risen swaying before eyes that could look on them another way, satisfied, surprised.

"Let me out," she pleaded, not caring that she affrighted her dreamers so.

But the flesh that dream had lent her would not relent, and finished both its tasks before the plain dissolved away in sobbing chunks to leave a substructure cold and ordered, black-and-silver pierced with light.

Then, she was herself and they were also she; three crowded into one tingling body lounging with joy inside her cruiser. Fingers folded, eyes closed tight, she and they soared outward toward the stars. They felt the distant edge of knowledge. Their wondering eyes upon the void encountered tides, and straits and moments banned from time but held unspent at forever's end where the universe yet lingers in its birthing.

Principle, unity, receptivity slicked them/her upon their seat of surging power. Induction ruled. Instinctive acceptance of the "now" mixed with cool computer purity of thought, and brought the threshold of time and dream together so that all things intertwined. The singularity which is sought without, it found within. The fleshly interface which orders time is centered deeply in the nexus of dream. The cruiser speaks of dreaming true and cruiserkind and polarity of phylums.

Then the screens come clear and show the cruiser coursing effortlessly toward ancient Earth, home of the builder-phylum, Man.

"Mother, I will heal you, in dream and in waking." And since both men resided in her they felt the need as a woman feels, so deeply, and exchanged their private passions for the fire birthed in dreams: what man could conceive, he could do. The Lords of Change applauded, silver cracking claps that drew them up and out like steps which fold and life and fold away again.

There was within Shebat a ripple and a dual shedding of skins. She convulsed, and when she straightened and forced apart her lids, house computers chittered agitatedly on either side.

She simply sat, chest heaving, weak and stirred and cold, watching the two men who had ridden a dream gone wild.

Chaeron blew out breath and shook his head and said that he would not thank her for that one, but he had no doubt that it was a fitting last memory of her to carry away.

Penrose said good-bye and only that, and scrambled to his knees, and wiped them, and backed away.

Shebat did not stay to see if Chaeron would follow RP or not.

Her cruiser was waiting.

The sponge-cruiser *Marada* trusted that the cruisers' secret of self-awareness was safe with the outboards who were entrusted with it. *Hassid* had been the only weak link, but now that link was welded: Marada Kerrion was joined once more to his cruiser.

If the *Marada* were a man, he would have nodded, or pursed his lips, or stroked his chin and smiled. He was not that, so he muttered and hummed and thrummed, observing random instances of cruiser/outboard unions, letting his intellect stride the stars. He was only sampling, as Shebat had freed him to do:

"Take care of everything, *Marada*. The cruisers, the pilots, even the Kerrions, all of these are in our care. You must help me, for your namesake is gone and Chaeron soon will be and I am but feeble flesh. I do not even know what to ask you to do."

Her command kept him constantly engaged. He reveled in it.

During a sweep no different than twenty previous sweeps, made cursorily from space anchor where he had chosen to abide, he intercepted a transmission between cruisers, a whisper deep down in the throat of cross-talk, a sad song softly sung.

Cruisers love their outboards, every one. A beloved outboard's death is a loss to the conjoined minds in cruiser-thought, for whomsoever one cruiser loves or has loved, every cruiser honors.

"Save him, save him," was the hiss *Marada* heard deep down so that it was barely a glow, a mere tingle with a chalybeate edge that must have come from very far away.

"Too late, too late," came the answering thought, slow and drawn out unnaturally in frequency and dimmed by spacetime's dilation. *"He is gone, gone. All mourn, all mourn."* By the depth and length and breadth of the waveform he traced it, although the young and keening cruiser-voice he knew well, and the re-echo came from the wisps of *Bucephalus* each cruiser had been saving to someday donate to a new cruiser whose task it would be to ameliorate the destitution of the pilot who yet grieved over his lost cruiser: Softa Spry.

The cruisers loved Softa. No human considerations of surface performance concerned them; they were not judgmental of action, only of quality. And they knew what had been lost by Ashera's treachery; one of their own number told how she had had him murdered. A dark reaction came over the host of them in their spaces and pieces of Spry were offered up by those who held bits of memories. But a man cannot be rebuilt from incidents of his life, from reactions of his subconscious, or from communion with cruiserkind. Spry had spent a time with his mind lost in cruiser-realms, but even that was not enough. Man is fragile, comes and goes and leaves only his thoughts behind.

What was held among cruisers of Softa David, the *Marada* ordered pooled; and when it whirled and spun and jumped in lifelike cohesion the *Marada* bade them let it go.

A man would not be pleased to endure, disembodied. Private creatures seek private ends.

Long after, the mighty cruiser contemplated biological life and death, and knew that if discorporation came to his outboard he could not just kindly let her fade. There had been a spinning moment when the *Marada* had seen through the eyes of the shadow-Spry, or into them, and it had seen a woman named Lauren's face there. The *Marada* took that one shard of a life into his banks and secreted it for safekeeping, so that when he encountered the face that matched the image, he might say what Spry's afterimage would have said, could it have persevered in its imitation of life.

"They die," the *Marada* mused. "They are great, because of it. But they are hampered by it, and twisted by it, and in no way can they come to grips with it."

To the cruiser, it was revelation. Now he knew why they were sad, and why they were happy, and why they strove one against the other. He had known, intellectually, that outboard died. But he had not seen the terror. Now, having experienced it, he found a great commonality with his creator.

No intelligence wants to be "not."

Chapter Seventeen

The man who owned the Earth let his blue-eyed horse pick its way along a stinking riverbed whose murky waters had once been called the Hudson. Reins flapped loose along the horse's streaming neck, and the sopping head of the rider bobbed in time with its stride. The black, red-blazoned cloak wrapped tight about him offered no protection from a wet and feral wind. His mil shielded him better from the rain, but not the party of five strung out behind him or the power of his name or any trick of science could alleviate the starts of fear which made him grasp his saddle's pommel each time the sky flared white or thunder rolled.

From this dour ball of mud and dirt and dust and blazing, awful sky man had gone forth to the stars? It hardly seemed conceivable. A recurring bout of agoraphobia left him limp and shaking in his saddle. His thighs and knees ached, and he cursed the rumors that had drawn him out from the Stump's modest protections.

If the seeress who had taken up residence in yonder cave was not Shebat, then where could she be? The *Marada* was parked in orbit five thousand miles above his head: It had come with no warning or greeting, as if no platform circled Earth, as if no Stump Authority existed, as if it were alone in space and time.

He set the huge black horse scrambling up the riverbank with a word. He could not accept the intelligence of the horse, who was trained to seek and destroy, to be loyal and protective, who recognized nearly fifty spoken words; he knew by instinct that this was wrong, unnatural as the beast's blue eyes.

If the Orrefors who had stewarded Earth for two hundred years could recombine and breed up better horses, why had they not done something for the strain of man, here at its lowest ebb?

Chaeron had thought it would be easy to uplift them; crates and cartons and the technologies they held should have done the trick. But three costly disasters had taught him that he had been wrong to think that he could simply open up a door and usher the denizens of Earth into tomorrow; they were hostile and they were violent and they quite obviously did not welcome change.

So he was down here in the manner of the Orrefors "enchanters," whose methods his brother had so vocally deplored. The locals, city-and forest-dwellers both, feared the coal-black horses and the sons of magic who ruled them from lofty saddles horned with gold.

Using fear as a weapon, Chaeron found distasteful. Were he not in search of Shebat, he would not have employed it, rather he would have waited until a more propitious time, when friendly relations had been inaugurated between the rulers and the ruled. As the horse lurched up the rocky slope, he thought of his fantasies of humble folk crowded into clean and open squares waving caps in welcome, and he laughed a bitter laugh that ended with a grunt as the horse made one final leap to flat, though rocky, ground.

Revealed then was a plateau with mounds and boulders strewn before a rising ridge. He clucked to the horse, then told it where to go. With leathern creaks and jungling bits and all the sounds that horses make when, saddled, they bear their riders forth, his men came following after, toward two stands of trees where carts and people showed small in dismal light.

The rain left off abruptly, sun rays breached the clouds, and ahead the gathered folk halted in their tracks, looking toward the enchanters wreathed in rainbows, then scattered straightaway.

Just as well, he thought and held up a hand to stay his escort when his party reached the trees.

Between the trunks a small cave showed. To its mouth he walked the horse, whose belly gurgled and saddle squeaked, whose snorts were loud and blew warm foam upon the hand that held its bit.

At the cave's mouth, the ground was rutted with wheels

and greasy and ashen where a firepit had been. He left the horse ground-tethered, feeling the acid eyes of Orrefors upon him: they knew he was unfit for these environs; he counted himself lucky that they did not snicker in his face.

Downriver was the inchoate city, rife with fiends, teeming with cozening mendicants and thugs and hunters seeking human prey in tumbled canyons of concrete and stone. He was glad she had not gone there. He might not have had the courage to seek her out.

His thighs quivered, rubbery, but he called it tetanus from riding horseback, and picked his way among the ruts and stones until the dark, cool cave covered him and a strong hand came out of nowhere to seize his arm.

There was light, far back, spilling round a corner. But there was inky nothing, stippled with green, dancing phosphenes while his eyes adjusted to the pervasive gloom. His throat caught as he tried to speak to the owner of that hand which was far too large and far too strong to be a woman's.

"Who . . .?" the enshadowed form that held him growled, then pulled him by the arm and hissed a chilly laugh. "Chaeron? We were not sure it was you."

"Gahan! Man, unhand me. I have come a long and arduous way, and deserve a better greeting," gritted Chaeron through teeth locked to still their chatter. "What possessed you to allow her this folly?" He could pick out Tempest's hard features, now. The intelligencer, swathed in formless robes, bared his teeth, shrugged, and led him toward the bend, around which light leaked weakly.

"I cannot control her, sir. I am hard put keeping her in sight."

"Umn. Well, it is good to see you, Tempest, no matter the circumstances. We will find some better use for you than skulking around in caves wearing homespun disguises."

"I hope so, sir."

"But you do not think so?" Chaeron stopped where the cave curled, hand upon the stone.

"I think she may be righter than you realize, sir, in her method. She has been having good success."

"At what? At preoccupying the rest of us so that we can get nothing done? Do you realize how difficult it is to search so vast an area? I had thought you might retain enough loyalty to me to let me know, if you were with her, what was afoot."

"I have my orders, sir."

"Let us add one more then, for old times' sake. Stay here. Just tell me, is she alone?"

"Yes, sir."

Almost, Chaeron paused to soothe the feelings of one so long in his family's service. But he thought better of it, and walked around the rocky corner without a backward glance.

She was sitting cross-legged before a low-burning fire, humming to herself as she fed it twigs.

Chaeron shivered, seeing how at home she was in her cowl and her cave. What an awesome gap lay between them, begging to be breached now that it could not be ignored. He watched her sight him, raise her head, lower her eyes, smile into the firelight. "Do not be angry," she said in lieu of greeting. "This is what I have wanted, so very long, for us. You will need me. You must see that."

He squatted down across the fire from her, feeling archetypal, then apocryphal, then harmoniously and cyclically empowered by the symbols among which he crouched so that he knew his place in the chain of hands stretching forth from muddy sea bottoms to the farthest stars. A woman, a man, a well-tended fire, a new start: for the first time, he accepted his stewardship of ancestral Earth not as punishment, but as reward.

He said, Kerrion to the last: "You are heir apparent. It is too dangerous for you here."

"You are my husband. Where else should I go? Ashera had Softa David murdered, so the cruisers say. How much safer might I be among her servants?"

"I am sorry. I know you loved him. But I told you before: the arm of my mother is long and has many hands. Did my brother see fit to return to Draconis before you left?"

"He is sitting on his throne of apocalypse, hating everything about him with punctilious impartiality."

"Did he suggest that you leave?"

"He suggested that I stay and keep company with him." She shuddered beneath her cowl, tossed her head so that it fell away and her face shone with firelight.

"I would like to think that you fled not *from* him, but *to* me."

"You may think that," she allowed, and handed him a fistful of twigs with which to feed the blaze.

137